The Governing Crisis
Media, Money, and Marketing in American Elections

W. Lance Bennett
University of Washington

WITHDRAWN

St. Martin's Press
New York

This book is dedicated to the idea that ideas matter—particularly in politics. And to a time, not so long ago, when rhetoric was not a dirty word.

Senior editor: Don Reisman
Managing editor: Patricia Mansfield
Project editor: Cheryl Friedman
Production supervisor: Alan Fischer
Cover design: Cristina Castro
Cover art: Eldon Doty

Manufactured in the United States of America.
65432
fedcb

For information, write:
St. Martin's Press, Inc.
175 Fifth Avenue
New York, NY 10010

ISBN: 0-312-06986-3 (cloth)
       0-312-06157-9 (paper)

Library of Congress Cataloging-in-Publication Data

Bennett, W. Lance.
    The governing crisis : media, money, and marketing in American elections / W. Lance
Bennett.
        p.   cm.
    Includes bibliographical references and index.
    ISBN 0-312-06986-3 (cloth)
    ISBN 0-312-06157-9 (paper)
    1. Electioneering—United States.   2. Elections—United States.   3. Campaign funds—
United States.   4. Campaign management—United States.   I. Title.
JK1976.B46   1992
324.7'0973—dc20   91-61136
                                                                              CIP

Acknowledgments

The pleasures of writing this book have been increased by the many colleagues who offered helpful criticism and encouragement along the way. Mentioning elections and government these days is a sure way to start a conversation. Political scientists, communications scholars, rhetoricians, linguists, politicians, and journalists have stimulated my thinking on parts of the argument that touched their experiences.

The first chapter had its debut at the 1989 Alta, Utah, Conference on Argumentation. The remarks of John Nelson, Bruce Gronbeck, Michael Leff, and Michael McGee were particularly helpful. Several more chapters were added in the fall of 1989 when a Fulbright Research Fellowship and institute director Erik Åsard's invitation enabled me to visit the Swedish Institute of North American Studies at Uppsala University. I could not have asked for a better environment than an office in Uppsala Castle and an apartment in the old city. The "Americanists" in Sweden have provided valuable new perspectives on politics, culture, and communications. For all the long afternoons of good conversation and warm friendship, I owe to Erik Åsard more than these few words can express. I have also enjoyed the exchanges with Kurt Johannesson, Olle Josephson, and Rolf Lunden. One of the highlights of my stay was the lively seminar at which many of these ideas were discussed by the faculty and guest scholars of the Swedish Collegium for Advanced Study in the Social Sciences. I am also indebted to Jeannette Lindstrom of the Swedish Fulbright Foundation and to Brian Guss and Pia Hansen at the U.S. Embassy in Stockholm for making my stay comfortable and productive. Thanks also to Paul and Charlotta Levine for making Uppsala feel like home.

My return stateside coincided with a perfect forum for the emerging argument: a conference on political language and symbolism at the University of Wisconsin in honor of the retirement of Murray Edelman. His work has been an inspiration, and the encouragement for the ideas in this book is most appreciated. Thanks, too, Murray, for the tips on good mystery novels. They came in handy when I needed a break. Thanks also to Bill Haltom, David Estrin, and Irving Rockwood for special contributions along the way.

To my agent, Fran Collin, I must say how nice it was to know that you really liked this book and found the right publisher for it. Which brings me to Don Reisman, whose editorial hand has made a significant contribution to these pages. You knew when to push and when to relax. Thanks. And thanks, too, for soliciting some of the most helpful reviews I have ever had on a book project. I hope that the reviewers—Roger H. Davidson, University of Maryland; Gerry Riposa, California State University–Long Beach; Herbert Waltzer, Miami University; and Herbert Weisberg, The Ohio State University—see the fruits of their suggestions about how to combine communications and media perspectives with what we know about voting, elections, and government.

Preparing a manuscript on two continents could have been a nightmare without the help of several excellent typists. In Sweden, Liisa A. Melton learned to decode my scrawl and offered editorial assistance in the bargain. As for my secretary in Seattle, Ann Buscherfeld, I can only marvel at her ability to stay calm and error-free while doing so many things at once. Julie Morgan not only merged three separate word-processing files, but retyped most of the manuscript after I promised that the changes would be minor. And we remained friends after it was over.

The *Journal of Communication* and the *Quarterly Journal of Speech* were kind enough to grant permission to reprint portions of my previously published work in Chapters 5 and 6. And the *Wall Street Journal* gave permission to reprint parts of its editorial commentary on the election of 1990.

A final word of thanks goes to friends and colleagues who have helped my personal life and my needs as a writer fit together. To Don McCrone, David Olson, and Don Matthews at the University of Washington, thanks for the support and friendship over the years. And to Bettina Lüscher, thanks for making life fun.

W. Lance Bennett
SEATTLE AND UPPSALA

Contents

For perspective, imagine that Captain Kirk and the starship *Enterprise* trekked to the third planet of an ordinary star in an obscure arm of the Milky Way. And imagine that they discovered that the most important nation there was ruled by 535 elders, elected in their youth to life terms. Well perhaps not quite life. Elders were permitted to resign if overcome by a sense of meaninglessness, a not uncommon occurrence. And in extraordinary circumstances, say a second offense of sexual abuse, social pressure would force them to stand down.

Once anointed, of course, elders were expected to take up life at court. Their only obligation was to visit the territory from which they had been elected every two or six years, depending on their rank, to go through the formality of reanointment. While not given great wealth if they did not already have it, they were provided with everything wealth could buy: marble palaces, large staffs of retainers to do their bidding and most of all the expectation of deference by lesser humans. They could summon and bully commercial titans or certified scientific geniuses, for example. And of course, their enterprises were immune from the laws that bound common citizens.

There were intrigues and disputes among the elders, but these were resolved by subtle systems of social controls; those who defied the sacred consensus were ostracized as trouble-makers, particularly if they gave voice to plebeian objections to the provisions for or commanded by elders. This curious system called itself government of the people, by the people and for the people. Searching the anthropological tapes, Mr. Spock classified it as an elected aristocracy.

—Wall Street Journal Editorial

INTRODUCTION

Politics in the Age of Unreason

"Read My Lips: No New Ideas."

A "sound bite" from the political speech of the future? It is telling that ten-second slices—or "bites"—of speech written for airplay on the nightly news are passing for political ideas these days. While the nation's problems grow in size and number, candidates for political office seem ever more obligated to financial backers and less interested in arousing a sleeping electorate. For reasons to be explored in this book, the national marketplace of ideas has broken down. Voting and elections no longer work as demand-side forces shaping the quality of candidates and ideas. It is as though some hidden hand has restrained national debate, reducing the range of choice in one of the world's most important political forums. The search for what moves this hidden hand takes us into the netherworld of political finance, Madison Avenue–style candidate marketing, and the emerging science of media control. These facts of modern political life explain a good deal about the current national scene, from the decline of political parties, to the reasons why few politicians seem interested in drawing discouraged citizens back into the system.

Opinion polls and voting rates show that interest in politics has dropped steadily over the last twenty years. During the same time, the list of unsolved national problems has grown longer and more worrisome: debt and budgetary paralysis, foreign competition, political corruption, declining economic production, and a host of social ills—from crime, drug abuse, and homelessness, to a failing educational system. This book explores the connection between the quality of political life and society's ability to define and solve its most pressing problems.

This is not a gloom-and-doom prophecy about how America is on the brink of total collapse. Even worst-case scenarios like economic depressions can be (and have been) overcome. This said, the social and economic problems listed above have come home in ways that are nevertheless troublesome and worth thinking about. Whether we are talking about

1

the stress of holding down jobs in economically embattled workplaces, the sensory overload of city streets, the amnesia-producing atmosphere of public schools, or the risks of going out at night in crime-ridden neighborhoods, life in contemporary America is disturbingly out of sync with what one might expect in one of history's richest and most powerful societies. The trials of public life take their toll in the private realm as well. In the words of one observer, Americans have adapted to the long winter of their discontents with a "bunker mentality," zealously protecting private lives from a declining civic culture and rising social ills.[1]

When the governing center does not hold, individuals must fend for themselves. This lesson applies not just to the down-and-out, but to the up-and-coming as well, since for all of society's individuals the quality of private life depends on the quality of public life. Above all, our personal well-being rides on the strength of the political system and its leaders. This idea is hardly news. Aristotle long ago observed that the "good life" begins (and can end) with the kind of political arrangements and leadership a society accepts. Restoring public interest in government, trust in leadership, and commitment to a liveable society for all are essential steps toward real solutions for problems like crime, homelessness, drug abuse, education, economic revitalization, and other obstacles to the "good life."

The point is simply this: At a minimum, lively political debate is required to engage the creative imagination of a people. Such debate depends on leaders who are willing to articulate new ideas, take risks, and motivate public action. Tired of waiting for such leaders to appear, many people have left the political arena altogether for other, less frustrating pursuits. By the end of the last decade, for example, more New Yorkers were buying lottery tickets than voting by a ratio of 3 to 2.[2] And the current decade opened with a solid majority (60 percent) of the American public agreeing that "people like me don't have any say about what the government does."[3]

This is not to suggest that politicians are unaware of what the public wants them to be doing. Hired media consultants advise their political clients about images that can be marketed to voters who remain in the system. And so, politicians and parties do battle over who appears to care the most about the issues that most concern the voters. Case in point: Running on promises to be the environmental president, George Bush encouraged voters worried about the "greenhouse effect" to imagine the "White House effect" they could create by electing him. After the election, however, the most decisive environmental action in the first year of the Bush administration was to join forces with Japan and the Soviet Union in scuttling an international agreement that would have reduced carbon dioxide emissions blamed for most of the global warming trend.

For an encore, Mr. Bush cut funds for cleaning up Boston Harbor from his first budget—this after making the nation's most polluted harbor a cause célèbre in his campaign.

A similar avoidance of reality characterizes American leadership in international economics. After it became obvious that the nation's economy faced stiff competition from Japan and Europe, Washington's response was to bluster about how unfair these competitors were being. When the moment of truth arrived and a U.S. trade delegation visited Japan to begin official talks, their agenda of complaints must have astounded the Japanese. For openers, the delegation accused Japan of "needlessly" running a national budget surplus. Following this accusation was an attack on Japanese farm subsidy programs. And bringing up the rear was a criticism of Japanese companies for excessive loyalty—that is, for buying their own nation's products rather than those manufactured abroad.[4] The audacity of such concerns can only be appreciated against a backdrop of a chronic American budget deficit, the sacred cow of U.S. farm supports for everything from corn to tobacco, and laments about corporate and consumer disloyalty. As the "Roaring 80s" drew to a close, the chairman of Sony Corporation responded to American worries about his purchase of Columbia Pictures by saying bluntly: "I'm worrying for America seriously, seriously. I'm worrying about why America has changed, has lost industrial power, and just is making money by moving money around. Unless you produce something, you cannot have basic power in an economy."[5]

Not long after the Sony takeover of Columbia, former president Ronald Reagan visited Japan on a $7 million promotional tour sponsored by Fujisankei Communications Group, the largest media conglomerate in the country. Reagan personally pocketed $2 million for his string of cameo appearances over a nine-day period. Once among the loudest critics of "unfair" Japanese competition, the former chief executive pronounced the Japanese buyout of America a good thing, observing that, after all, the United States had been doing it to other nations around the world for years. Wasn't turnabout fair play?

This and countless similar lapses in national leadership have sent millions of Americans fleeing from public life in dismay. Failing to find leadership anywhere but on the easy moral high ground of abortion, drugs, or flag burning, a near majority have retreated from voting, which surely ranks among the least demanding forms of political participation. Meanwhile, a steady procession of candidates continues to walk softly into public office carrying the big stick of high-cost, Madison Avenue campaigning.

The Democrats these days score no higher than the Republicans on any obvious test of civic virtue. Despite opinion polls showing majorities supporting traditional Democratic positions on a whole range of issues, the party has been unable to build a governing coalition around a program for national renewal. Part of the problem is that the Democrats are not so much a party as a loose coalition of political entrepreneurs whose individual members wield more power on congressional committees and with financial backers if they continue to call themselves a party. There are signs that the party has come together more often in recent years around environmental, social welfare, and civil rights legislation. Perhaps a change is in the wind. But the pull of special interests is still on display each year during the battle over the budget and the repeated avoidance of effective reforms in campaign finance and election practices.

People who have seen these signs of Democratic disunity have reason to mistrust the sincerity of candidates who run on the issues, or to doubt the commitment of the party to stand behind candidates who really care about those issues. As a result, most of the candidates who run on "anti-establishment" issues end up losing, leading pundits to mistrust the polls themselves. Puzzling? Yes. A result of faulty opinion polls? No. Part of the trouble lies with a system that gives undue advantages to incumbents, particularly in the House of Representatives. Begin with the average representative's large campaign chest that leaves challengers unable to compete with costly and sophisticated voter marketing analyses and media campaigns. Then add the public relations points scored by incumbents who long ago realized that offering services to constituents compensates for not being able to offer many ideas. Combine these two factors and you get a Congress that is something of an upscale social service agency. The full range of services runs from delivering special favors to savings-and-loan owners who have made deposits in congressional campaign accounts, to delivering lost social security checks to senior citizens who have been loyal voters. All of which begins to explain at least one of the puzzling trends in the opinion polls: voters blaming Congress for many of the problems facing the nation, but tending to make an exception when it comes to their own representative.

There is an even deeper reason why opinion polls call for changes, but elections continue reproducing the same unsatisfying results. The link between public opinion on particular issues and votes has seldom been a strong one in American politics. What sells in America is not a collection of single issues, but the ideas or vision behind the issues. The Democrats have not had a vision since the Great Society of the 1960s. Not surprisingly, they haven't won the White House very often either. As a conservative, Ronald Reagan had the luxury of taking an old vision from the shelf, dusting it off, and, to his credit, selling it with conviction and theatrical style. Whether or not they like it, the Democrats have been cast as America's alternative to conservatism. For many Americans, when there is no compelling alternative, conservatism will just have to do. As a group of party intellectuals put it in a heated debate about what ails the Democrats, what the party needs is a "new story" about America to tell the public.[6] In the meantime, those who continue to vote continue to curb their expectations and send one party to Congress and the other to the White House— more or less putting the system on hold until a governing coalition with plausible new ideas comes along to get the national dialogue going again.

Is there a cure for the election-time blues? The answer contained in the last chapter of this book is "yes"—but not if Americans by the tens of millions sit and watch their political system break down around them. Staying on the present course of government promises little for social renewal. The latest five-year plan for getting a grip on the budget was greeted in its first year of operation by the largest deficit in American history. On the world scene, the decision to wage war against Iraq sent a clear signal that geopolitics outweighs domestic priorities on the Washington agenda. The state of this union suggests that liberating Kuwait was more important (or at least easier to imagine) than saving Newark, Detroit, South Chicago, or East L.A. This book explores one of the principal reasons why governing the nation these days is nearly impossible: the election system has shut off the flow of new governing ideas in American politics. Here's why . . .

Three behind-the-scenes factors have grown in recent years to dominate contemporary elections. The first is campaign financing. For reasons to be explained in later chapters, candidates and parties have been driven into stiff competition for the huge sums of money required to win elections in a system that has fewer restrictions on spending, advertising, and funding than any Western industrial democracy. One controversial view of the finance system has gone so far as to describe elections as investment opportunities for big business. This political investment thesis argues that Democratic candidates have been leveraged steadily to the right in order to compete with Republicans for campaign dollars from their own former backers.[7] As a result, the range of meaningful political difference between candidates has decreased steadily, moving both parties out of line with the majority of voters and leaving candidates with little to offer the dwindling numbers who remain interested in politics.

Scholars disagree about how much unity of interest exists (or ever has existed) among political backers. Our explanation does not require establishing this difficult-to-document point. Assume that there is little common interest and even less conspiracy among the diverse range of political party backers. The problem is that individual candidates at all levels, from president and Congress, down to the states, have been separated from their party loyalties by an elaborate system of individual funding from interest groups. Congress, for example, has been so carved up by the finance system that it now makes sense to talk about two levels of representation: patchwork, issue-by-issue blocs representing various national interests, and strategic district representation (service delivery and "pork barrel" projects) for the folks back home. There is precious little room left for thinking about—much less, acting on—any broader public interest. The result is a system that virtually prevents broad coalitions from taking concerted action on complex issues. There is little chance that presidents can even mobilize their own congressional parties on broad legislative agendas that might generate real public enthusiasm. What has developed instead is a veto system in which the faction of the day, either in Congress or the White House, is likely to block any sweeping initiatives contemplated by more visionary public officials. Not surprisingly, politicians as a group have declined in popularity.

The task of selling these damaged political goods brings us to the second factor: the systematic marketing of candidates. Image-making and hype have always been part of American politics, but never with the all-consuming importance they have attained in contemporary campaigning. Candidates whose inventory of ideas has been reduced by the stiff competition for campaign financing have become overwhelmingly dependent on marketing experts and image consultants to manufacture content for otherwise empty campaigns. Scientific techniques for audience analysis and product development have enabled campaigns to compensate for content deficiencies by targeting key groups of voters who respond to manufactured, test-marketed images in sufficient numbers to tilt the electoral balance.

The third pillar of the new politics is the perfection of techniques for controlling the news media. Reporters, understandably enough, resent being manipulated by image consultants. Discouraged by the often futile search for anything meaningful to write home about, journalists stalk the candidates, looking for the slightest sign of weakness or the hint of a controversial idea. Controlling the press pack thus becomes essential for the success of campaigns already mortgaged to financial backers and image-makers. Enter the technology of media management, with its Orwellian vocabulary of *spin doctors, damage control, sound bites, line of the day,* and *photo opportunities,* all orchestrated by the ever-present *handlers* whose job is to keep reporters as far removed from spontaneous contact with the candidate as possible. Welcome to the postmodern election.

Special interest money, candidate marketing, and media control have created a new electoral system. Since we are not talking about a revolution here, many reminders of the old system still remain. The names of the parties are unchanged; the rules for deciding winners and losers are the same; and there is more than enough hype, hoopla, and negativity to go around. But the heart is missing: the promise of governing is gone.

Political communication in the new American election is a private, emotional affair between individual candidates and individual voters. The aim is getting votes, not developing broad support for governing ideas. Society has become an abstraction of media audiences and voter market segments. Missing almost entirely is any sort of give-and-take exchange through which social groups, parties, and candidates might develop mutual commitments to a broad political agenda. America has arrived at a point of nearly complete separation of elections and governing.

The plan of the book is to develop the above thesis, see how it holds up under criticism, explore the consequences for democracy in America, and propose a set of simple political reforms. Chapter 1 begins by looking at the case of the 1988 election, a contest that left voters dazed by distasteful extremes of negative campaigning, not to mention a host of other puzzling features, including Michael Dukakis' abandonment of traditional Democratic constituencies while driving around in a tank like a Charles Schulz cartoon character, and George Bush's recitation of lines from Clint Eastwood movies. Beneath the tragicomic surface, we find the convergence of forces that have pushed American government into its current status as a veto system. Among other things, 1988 was that memorable year in which the House of Representatives achieved the pinnacle of a 98 percent reelection rate for incumbent candidates, while a disgusted public complained about the quality of Congress. The same public elected a president who became more popular the less he did and less popular the more that events forced him to do anything. In the end, George Bush rescued his popularity by turning away from the home front and going to war. Understanding these and other puzzles is necessary preparation for analyzing the elections of the 1990s at the end of the book.

Chapter 2 explains how traditional uses of media, money, and marketing have changed over the last several decades, resulting in a system of elections and campaigning that offers voters little promise of good government. This new electoral system is not so much a radical break with traditions of the past as a recombination of existing practices into a mass communications process that has elevated the worst tendencies of American politics to the norm in recent times. These shifts in the ways people and their leaders communicate can be traced to several historical changes in modern American politics, including the decline of voter loyalty to political parties (particularly the Democrats) beginning in the 1970s and the rise of a new campaign finance system legislated by Congress during the same period of time.

Chapter 3 explores various criticisms that might be raised against the idea that a significant change is taking place at the center of American politics. A brief review of the history of elections shows which of these criticisms have merit and which miss their mark. Chapter 4 returns to the three main elements of money, media, and marketing, showing in greater detail how each affects the quality of campaigning. So ends Part I.

The second part of the book examines the consequences for a political culture when its central ritual begins to fall apart. Beyond the command of any individual, culture is the memory bank of collective experience, the storehouse of sacred mythology, and the guidance system for defining problems and thinking about the future. The American guidance system is currently on the blink. Chapter 5 illustrates the difference between election rituals that are empty and devoid of meaning for their participants, and those that remain vital sources of social inspiration and renewal. Despite becoming increasingly emptied of social vision and spontaneous expressions of candidate character, election campaigns continue to display many familiar ritualistic trappings, including the traditional rallies, flag-waving, and negative campaigning. Candidates who continue to go through the motions of the ritual make it hard to spot, much less talk about. what has gone awry. Comparing several recent elections helps to pinpoint where the changes are occurring and why.

Chapter 6 examines the crucial importance of leadership in American politics. In many ways our elections are more about choosing the right leaders for the times than about this or that particular policy or program. Perhaps the most distressing element of the new politics is the reduced chance of seeing the candidates respond intuitively and spontaneously to each other and to the stresses of the year-long campaign ordeal. In this respect, the combined effects of high finance, candidate marketing, and media control have short-circuited the election as a basic test of character and leadership.

Instead of letting voters and candidates work out new political plots through the rough-and-tumble exchanges of an open campaign, media consultants play it safe, replaying old plot lines that worked the last time around and adding a few image twists that market researchers have tried out on "test audiences" before splicing them onto the candidate's (or the opponent's) character. The result is that American elections are becoming, in the famous words of Yogi Berra, "like déjà vu all over again." Each of our recent elections has been similarly frustrating, empty, and built on feeble incantations that serve poorly for choosing leaders, discussing pressing problems, and uniting behind sensible courses of action. Far from being the vital centerpiece or nerve center of a thriving political culture, elections have become a fig leaf for a political system in crisis. The result, as noted above, is that we are dangerously close to losing our guidance system, our collective intelligence, if you will. As Republican commentator Kevin Phillips has observed: "From the White House to Capitol Hill, the critical weakness of American politics and governance is becoming woefully apparent: a frightening inability to define and debate emerging problems. For the moment, the political culture appears to be brain-dead."[8]

The crucial question, of course, is how long will this moribund cultural condition persist? If I thought the prognosis irreversible, I would not have written this book. Part III looks at the 1990s with an eye to reforms. There are, it seems to me, a number of simple, practical remedies that would help bring the nation out of its political coma and speed the recovery of the culture. And without reforms, the electoral prospects for the future are even gloomier. Dan Quayle, anyone? Chapter 7 begins by exploring both the kind of politics and politicians we can expect if nothing is done to derail the current system of financing, marketing, and media control.

Celluloid candidates and imaginary issues are just the symptoms of deeper problems with the system. The weakening link between elections and governing is the more fundamental problem. While it has never been easy to draw straight connections between votes and eventual government policies, at least governments of the past were able to take broad actions on problems that arguably fell into some range of the public interest. In recent times, however, the centrifugal pull of special interests at every level of government has left little chance for coherent action on pressing public problems. Simply enacting a national budget each year has become a major challenge and frequent crisis of governing.

This dilemma has not been lost on the public who opened the 1990s with a whopping 77 percent agreement on the belief that the government was being run for the benefit of business and a few special interests. This belief has increased steadily with each passing decade since the rosy dawn of the 1960s when only 25 percent shared that view.[9] Not surprisingly, nearly 80 percent of the public entered the 1990s with the opinion that "America is in serious trouble,"[10] giving most Americans something in common with the chairman of Sony Corporation. Perhaps the convergence of these forces of government paralysis and public distress is reflected most strongly in three simple facts about the congressional elections of 1990: most Americans blamed Congress for a large part of the trouble with America; most Americans also made an exception in the case of their own representatives; and for the third straight election, incumbents in the House of Representatives were returned to office at a stunning rate of 96 percent or higher. How long can this pressure and these contradictions build without exploding? Which election will bring on the voter eruption? And what results, if any, will come of it? Chapter 7 closes with a set of "Scorecards" that the reader can use to follow the key political forces through the elections and governments of the 1990s.

The scenarios about politics and politicians in Chapter 7 are intended to stimulate thinking about the reform proposals outlined in the final chapter. No doubt politicians will register strenuous objections to any idea of fundamental change in the current system. After all, most incumbents have learned how to use this system successfully. Why should they want to change the rules that brought them to power? As in the past, the process of fundamental change will have to emerge from the grass roots. Just as the century opened with the attack on machine politics and political corruption launched by the Progressives, so it may close with another "progressive" crusade against political finance and distorting campaign practices. The key question, of course, is what reforms should be on the agenda. I invite the reader to be thinking about that question all along the way.

PART I

The Decline of Elections

[Postmodernism] . . . is completely indifferent to the questions of consistency and continuity. It self-consciously splices genres, attitudes, styles. It relishes the blurring or juxtaposition of forms (fiction–nonfiction), stances (straight–ironic), moods (violent–comic), cultural levels (high–low). It disdains originality and fancies copies, repetition, the recombination of hand-me-down scraps. It neither embraces nor criticizes, but beholds the world blandly, with a knowingness that dissolves feeling and commitment into irony. It pulls the rug out from under itself, displaying an acute self-consciousness about the work's constructed value. It takes pleasure in the play of surfaces, and derides the search for depth as mere nostalgia. —*Todd Gitlin*

Great speeches have always had great soundbites. The problem now is that the young technicians who put together speeches are paying attention only to the soundbite, not to the text as a whole, not realizing that all great soundbites happen by accident, which is to say, all great soundbites are yielded up inevitably, as part of the natural expression of the text. They are part of the tapestry, they aren't a little flower somebody sewed on. . . .

But that is what they've become. Young speechwriters forget the speech and write the soundbite, plop down a hunk of porridge and stick on what they think is a raisin.

. . . .

More and more the candidate was just the front man; more and more he was just the talker. Our Senate and House candidates, even some of our presidential candidates: they are becoming like anchormen. . . .

At the end of the Reagan era all the presidential candidates looked like local TV news guys.

At the end of the Reagan era they had all gone to the same TV coaches, and they all talked the same way. They talked with their voices low and cool . . . moving their hands within the frame for emphasis, moving their hands the same way with the same studied, predictable natural mannerisms. . . .

. . . candidates with prefab epiphanies, inauthentic men for an inauthentic age. —*Peggy Noonan*

CHAPTER 1

The Postmodern Election

As the title suggests, this book is about elections and the American political system, with the spotlight on presidential and congressional elections, past, present, and future. America's national political contests are moments of great opportunity for defining public problems, exploring new directions, evaluating the character of aspiring leaders, and dreaming about the future. Elections are the centerpieces of the civic culture. Yet these grand occasions for stock-taking, consensus-building, and renewal are being squandered on a regular basis. Instead of drawing people into the political arena and stimulating wide-open dialogue about the problems that threaten continued national greatness, candidates appear to be walking on eggshells. They not only hide from the press, but with the growing acceptance of image-making techniques, they even hide from themselves.

The decline of elections has been a long process, with the contests of recent years merely marking its completion. Pinpoint history, like surgical bombing, is an imprecise art. The argument here is not that before the 1980s and 1990s we were living in one political age and afterward we entered another. Rather, the last several elections cap a long process in which the very language of public life has been transformed to the point that most citizens can no longer find the sense in it. As writers like Lewis Carroll, George Orwell, Harold Lasswell, and Murray Edelman have warned, the quality of political rhetoric holds the key to the satisfactions of public life and, ultimately, to the security of private life as well. The debasing of language, and, more broadly, communications, in American elections is the mystery that this book seeks to solve. How did it happen? What can be done about it? What are the consequences for the political system as a whole if these trends continue?

Signs of electoral foolery can be traced to much earlier periods in American history. As we will see in Chapter 3, George Washington's campaign practices were anything but models of noble principle. And the likes of Thomas Jefferson, Andrew Jackson, and Abraham Lincoln were savaged by opponents in ways that make the negative campaigning of the present seem tame. William McKinley spent most of his election campaign in 1896 pandering to the media from his front porch in Canton, Ohio, mouthing such pithy sound bites as "McKinley and a Full Dinner Pail." Franklin Roosevelt's fireside chats were masterpieces of media manipulation. And few latter-day marketing feats can top the selling of the "new and improved" Richard Nixon in 1968.

The difference is that these contests of the past also contained historic choices. Perhaps they were not phrased as eloquently as intellectuals and language lovers would like, but at least there were choices. For example, there were the Jeffersonian battles over the Alien and Sedition Acts with their implications for the freedom of speech; the Jacksonian referendum on national monetary policy, and its impact on the growth of the frontier; the social and economic ordeal of the Civil War, and its legacy of industrial growth and the death of agrarian society; the birth of protective government in the New Deal; the promise of civil rights in the New Frontier; and the white conservative backlash that contributed to the Republican reformation in 1968.

Meaningful choices have been harder to find in recent years. Even the Reagan presidency could not deliver on its core promise of shrinking the federal government. Instead, it delivered a bloated national budget while handing off a long list of underfunded social and regulatory responsibilities to the states. In addition, the Reagan landslides of 1980 and 1984 were delivered by fewer than 30 percent of the eligible electorate. Perhaps most telling of all is the fact that majorities or near majorities in the opinion polls opposed virtually every major policy that made up the "Reagan revolution."

The central thesis of this book is that we have entered a political era in which electoral choices are of little consequence because an electoral system in disarray can generate neither the party unity nor the levels of public agreement necessary to forge a winning and effective political coalition. The underlying explanation is that the political and economic forces driving our national politics have created a system in which the worst tendencies of the political culture—the hype, hoopla, and negativity—have been elevated to the norm in elections, gaining a systematic dominance in campaign content as never before. Meanwhile, the best hopes for creative leadership are screened systematically out of the running by political and economic forces that are only dimly understood, when they are recognized at all.

The result is a new electoral system—one filled with paradox. As voters grow more discontented with elected officials, incumbents grow more likely to win reelection. This result is not accidental—it is systematic. Rather than brand discontented-but-seemingly-helpless-voters as fools, it makes as much sense to consider the choices they are given. Rather than dismiss declining turnouts as products of apathy, it may be that genuine anger is expressed in opinion polls, but it simply has few meaningful outlets. The disturbing possibility is that many voters have come to accept, whether angrily, cynically, or apathetically, an electoral system that grows more dysfunctional with each election. As society's problems grow in size and number, the political system generates fewer solutions and puts more issues "on hold." Society and politics move awkwardly together, as if in a dream that is all the more troubling because the citizenry cannot seem to awaken. In short, the voters are mad as hell, but they don't know how to stop taking it anymore.

At some point this political bad dream will end. A social movement could awaken the masses. A crisis of grand proportions could shake the foundations. But will people break their symbolic chains? Will the forces that have corrupted the electoral process be recognized and changed? Not if the people are led into easy analyses and patently unworkable remedies. One of the dangers of an age of cynicism is that easy explanations abound, and frustrated people often settle for them . . .

The easiest explanation for the decline of political ideas is television. Volumes have been written blaming TV for most of our social ills, from the destruction of family conversation, to the senseless violence on our streets, to dismal school test scores and widespread public ignorance of even the barest facts of history, geography, and government. Indeed, when the dim electronic glow of the TV screen illuminates the interior of the American home an average of eight hours each day, there is cause for alarm. What can politicians do but fashion their messages to this passive medium, leaving most of the challenging ideas on the cutting room floor? As New York governor Mario Cuomo put it, taking a stand on political principles these days "requires that you explain your principles, and in this age of electronic advocacy this process can often be tedious and frustrating. This is especially so when you must get your message across in twenty-eight-second celluloid morsels, when images prove often more convincing than ideas. Labels are no longer a tendency in our politics. In this electronic age, they are our politics."[1]

While Governor Cuomo may have perceived correctly the effects of our political transformation, identifying television as the cause of it all is a bit too easy. There is little doubt that television has changed the way we do politics, but it is not the sole, or even the major, source of our political decline; it is merely the most visible sign of it. Behind the television images lies a whole set of political and economic changes that limit what politicians say, how they say it, and to whom they can say it. These hidden limits make television the perfect medium for saying nothing, but doing it with eye-catching and nerve-twitching appeal.

THE POLITICS BEHIND THE IMAGES

The declining quality of the national political dialogue is subtle and, at first glance, hard to define. Neither the amount of verbiage nor the number of position papers has withered away noticeably. But there have been notable deficits in the quality of ideas—the "vision thing" that George Bush confessed to having so much trouble with. The quality of political rhetoric has vanished to the point where fewer than 10 percent of those voting in the 1988 presidential election felt the candidates adequately addressed their concerns. At the beginning of that contest, two-thirds of the voters expressed hope that the choices would be meaningful ones. By election day, two-thirds of those still planning to vote wished that two different candidates were running.[2] Despite this lack of runaway enthusiasm, a slim majority felt at least some warmth toward one or the other candidate and made the trek to the polls. For several elections in a row, similar levels of lukewarmness have registered on the "feeling thermometer" measure used by the University of Michigan National Election Studies to survey voter feelings about candidates. Perhaps the growing sense of voter distress is due partly to the frustration of going through too many lukewarm elections against the backdrop of so many hot social problems. In any event, it would be too easy to blame voter dissatisfaction on the declining quality of the individuals running for office. The pattern of citizen discomfort and candidate distance has become so familiar and pervasive that one suspects it has roots in the contemporary system of campaigning itself.

Let's begin with marketing. Since the marketplace of ideas has grown unresponsive to the demands of political consumers, many citizens have left public life to invest their human capital elsewhere. Those who continue to participate are regarded by campaign consultants as a marketing challenge. When viewed as marketing rather than a way of life, democracy takes on a different tone. For example, the political consultants who now run election campaigns will tell you in moments of candor that citizen withdrawal is a blessing in disguise. Political marketing maxim number one: the fewer people voting, the easier it is to sell a candidate.

Moving candidates off the shelves these days—even to reduced numbers of voters—is still often a "hard sell." The problem is that many political ideas that might attract voter interest have already been bought and taken off the market by political action committees (PACs) and the other political investors who finance candidates. PACs began in the 1940s as a labor union device to expand members' donations and to channel outside money into the labor movement.[3] Although they grew slowly and steadily during the next two decades, PACs experienced near exponential growth after the mid-1970s when it became clear they could be used to get around legal restrictions on direct corporate and union contributions to campaigns—restrictions imposed by the 1974 (post–Watergate) revisions in the Federal Election Campaign Act. Corporations, industry associations, interest groups, and unions created these "voluntary" action committees to channel limited ($5,000) contributions to particular campaigns, and unlimited amounts in "soft money" and "independent" support efforts for candidates and parties (about which we will have more to say later). The subsequent emergence of other PACs affiliated primarily with candidates and social causes has further accelerated the centrifugal pull of individual politicians away from parties, and single issues away from broader social visions and programs.

Of course, the corporate, labor, and special issue PACs have not gone to all this organizational trouble just to give their money away freely. The huge sums of money required to launch a credible bid for office usually come with strings attached. It is not necessary to imagine those strings pulling conspiratorially to the left or right. A more realistic image is of a mad crosswise pull, leaving the system tied effectively, if unintentionally, in knots. The financial strings can be long ones, reaching far beyond the White House and Congress to smaller state and local offices as well. An idealistic politician from California recently shared with me the hard facts of running for an assembly seat in his state. He lamented that it takes a staggering sum of money, for which the candidate must go to state party leaders with hat in hand. The leaders first size up the candidate, look at track record and marketability factors, and, finally, ask the big question: "Are you willing to get with the program on the half dozen or so major issues of interest to the investors who have put their money into the party and its candidates?" If the candidate says yes, and the leadership thinks that he or she is electable, the money flows. But, said the young candidate, if you say yes, you have already sold out on the issues that really mattered to you and your constituents in the first place. What are you supposed to go back and talk to the voters about?

In California, candidates for public office spent more than $60 million in 1988, with the legislature costing more than two-thirds of that amount. In 1990, the candidates for governor alone spent nearly $40 million. To put these statistics in perspective, a British general election costs a bit more than $10 million—this for a national contest in a country with more than twice the population of California. By contrast, the total cost of running for public office in the United States in a presidential year is pushing $2 billion. The average winner in a U.S. Senate campaign spends close to $4 million, and the typical cost of a House seat is nearly $400,000.[4] Unless serious reforms limit campaign spending, restrict television advertising, and change financing procedures, these staggering figures will continue to drive out any serious, grass-roots competition in the American democracy.

If the problem of what is left to tell the voters is daunting for a candidate from a small district in California, imagine the dilemma at the presidential level. Candidates who raise the huge sums necessary to launch credible national campaigns (until the federal funding begins to flow) are left with very little to say. To make matters worse, each year more disgruntled citizens stop checking the box on their tax returns authorizing $1 or $2 of their income tax to be spent on public financing of presidential elections. When combined with the rising costs of campaigns, this spells insolvency for the Presidential Election Campaign Fund. In a move that sent the Federal Election Commission and Congress scrambling for alternatives, the Treasury Department proposed cuts in federal funding for the 1992 presidential primaries. Any decline of public funding only increases the power of private money in elections. Even with substantial public funding, the candidates' scramble for private money translates into a simple equation: The more viable the candidates wish to become, the more money they must raise, and the more money they raise, the more they end up sounding like their opponents, who are competing for much the same financing with the same strings attached.

Making this political "hard sell" to voters becomes easier when there are fewer voters who need to be convinced. The electorate these days is sized up in much the same way that a market is tested and analyzed prior to the release of a new breakfast cereal or an underarm deodorant. With any luck, a small segment of that market can be identified as the key group whose votes could swing the outcome of the contest. And so, a whole campaign may be pitched in subliminal images that play in Peoria, or wherever that target audience is found.

In this upside-down world where Madisonian ideals have been traded for Madison Avenue methods, the political challenge is not to inspire and mobilize the great and diverse masses of people, as a romantic notion of democracy might lead us to hope. Rather, the challenge of contemporary politics is to isolate key groups (the smaller and more homogeneous, the better) who can be persuaded to go out and pull their levers in response to test-marketed images like wimpiness, competence, liberalism, prayerless schools, burning flags, tax-paid abortions, and weekend rapists on prison release programs. The nervous systems of target audiences seem to twitch more violently if the weekend rapist is black, and all these symbolic effects are enhanced when distracting "noise" is screened out of the communications between candidates and their chosen publics. "Noise" in this age of political unreason consists of things like serious proposals, programs, and spontaneous moments in which candidates act on their own instincts. Thus, our electoral process revolves around small but scientifically chosen segments of the public who are bombarded with images of candidates standing squarely behind flags, fetuses, bibles, and other market-tested and, therefore, politically unassailable symbols of the day.

Add to this mix of money and marketing the growing repertoire of techniques for keeping a growling press pack at bay, and voilà, a system emerges in which we witness celluloid candidates pronouncing suspect lines to listless voters while the managed media try to point out the absurdity with mixed success. The origins and workings of this electoral system will be explored in detail in the next several chapters of the book. But first, let's drop in on a memorable case in point.

WELCOME TO THE POSTMODERN ELECTION

"Read my lips."

"Senator, you're no Jack Kennedy."

"Make my twenty-four-hour time period."

Just a few of the high—or low—points of Campaign '88, depending on one's view of political language and its proper uses.

For most scholars, commentators, and the majority of the American public, the presidential election of 1988 was the worst in memory. It was no easy last-place finish, considering the stiff competition in recent years. Evidence from polls, editorials, and academic studies suggests that, even by minimal standards, the most expensive contest in history failed to accomplish what an election campaign should do: introduce intelligent, well-reasoned, and occasionally inspiring debate into the voter choice process. Yet—and here's the rub—these superficial one-liners and telegenic sound bites seem to be what speech writers, consultants, and willing candidates aspired to achieve in their communications with the electorate.

Welcome to the first postmodern election: all text and no context; all rhyme and no reason. And meet the candidates: George Bush, Blade Runner; Mike Dukakis, Max Headroom; Dan Quayle, the Happy Camper; and Lloyd Bentsen, the first candidate who couldn't lose.

If the rosy electronic theme fashioned for the election of 1984 was

"Morning in America," then 1988 was, in the characterization of a noted political scientist, "Brunchtime."[5]

Begin with the TV image. Looking at television gives us a rough picture of how political messages have been transformed over the last few decades but not much of an idea about what transformed them. Though tantalizing, it is ultimately unsatisfying to leave our understanding at Marshall McLuhan's household phrase, "The Medium Is the Message." It is useful, however, to begin with this glassy surface of elections—the transparent screen through which most people experience their political reality.

For several elections, television has been the decisive factor in the reports of voters about how they make up their minds on a candidate. For reasons that will soon become clear, political advertising is often the most influential part of the TV picture. Yet the election of 1988 struck many observers as something of a capstone in the TV age—not so much for voters, who have already adapted to televised information, but for campaigns and candidates. After decades of experimentation and flirting with TV as a strategic weapon in election battles, Election '88 suggested that campaign managers had fully and unashamedly accepted the use of TV technology to reconstruct candidates. The subordination of communication between candidates and public to the dictates of "tele-campaigning" was revealed, among other places, in Democratic candidate Michael Dukakis' transformation during the campaign from traditional campaigner to a creature of television (albeit an unsuccessful one).

Many observers agree that something happened in 1988.[6] "Some invisible line has been crossed," said Marvin Kalb, a former network correspondent and, more recently, director of Harvard's Barone Center on the Press, Politics, and Public Policy.[7] That line, according to John Buckley, a media consultant who has worked for both the Republican party and CBS News, is between print and video, the word and the image: "This is the first election of a newly mature style of politics wherein it is accepted as absolute gospel by both sides that what you need to do is create . . . a message . . . that communicates itself on television. . . . There is no longer a value judgment on the need to tailor a message to television. It's now a matter of survival, not a matter of ethics or intellectual honesty."[8]

Like most historical changes, this realignment of our political discourse to fit the medium of television did not occur overnight. The first step over the electronic line probably occurred in 1960, the year Richard Nixon arguably won the presidential debate in print and on the radio but lost it, along with the election, on television. Goodbye *logos,* hello *logo.*

logos: reason as constituting the controlling principle of the universe, as manifested by speech

logo: short for logogram: the word replaced by the sign, or the visual image

Crossing the line from intellectual to anti-intellectual discourse has altered the ways in which we (are forced to) understand and participate in politics. The most fundamental change, as noted above, is the decline of the traditional political argument itself. A case in point is the now legendary incident in the 1984 campaign involving CBS correspondent Leslie Stahl's attempt to point out the logical inconsistencies between candidate Ronald Reagan's campaign appeals and the contradictory positions and policies Mr. Reagan advocated on the same issues as president. To her amazement Stahl received a thank-you call from the White House after the lengthy piece was aired. The reason for the thank-you was that the visual images of Reagan speaking, no matter what the contradictions in his speech, were more powerful than the argument that Stahl fashioned to go along with those images. The moral we can derive from this incident is that political ideas are no longer anchored in reason, logic, or history; political ideas as we may have known them once upon a time don't exist.

A number of shock waves flow from this fundamental transformation in our national political communications. Witness, for example, the eclipse of the newspaper as a significant factor for the mass public in the electoral process. It is too easy to blame the decline of the print media on creeping illiteracy or lack of time for reading. To the contrary, we are beginning to learn that printed information is highly valued when it is available in useful form. The key words here are "available" and "useful." Consider the possibility that crossing over to the television side of the communications line has created a political content so disjointed and diminished that it isn't fit to print. Newspapers have become the odd medium out in elections because they are literally starved for content.

This judgment on the demise of the newspaper was handed down in the spare postmodern vernacular by ABC correspondent Brit Hume when he referred to the newspaper reporters following the candidates as "printheads" (translation: logocentric throwbacks to the age of reason, the modern era, if you will; people of little consequence for the outcome of the postmodern election). Yet Hume later lamented to colleagues in a postelection seminar, "I'd like to tell you anecdotes about what it's like to cover George Bush up close, but I never got close to George Bush."[9] Nobody ever said that being significant in the postmodern age would be meaningful.

Crossing the rhetorical line to the bullier pulpit of television embold-ened ABC News president Roone Arledge (president of ABC Sports at the end of the modern age) to pronounce the Democratic National Con-vention boring. He found it so boring, in fact, that he threatened to cut back coverage of the Republicans the following month.[10] Something must be going on when a threat like that is issued on the heels of a convention that offered its audience no fewer than four or five excellent speeches by prominent members of the party—speeches recalling a bygone era of rousing, thought-provoking, morally challenging rhetoric.

No matter. Speech of any caliber or length greater than a sound bite seems to be the problem. ABC's executive producer for the conventions dismissed the television coverage of these speech fests as a "dinosaur."[11] So, we witness the demise of what has been the most important rhetorical form at least since the time of Aristotle: The Speech. Welcome to the postmodern election.

Basking far too long in the fleeting electronic glow of his convention speech, Michael Dukakis finally woke up to the fact that he was losing the election, and was losing it badly. His midsummer dream lead of seventeen points dwindled to a dead heat following the Republican National Conven-tion and then plummeted to a fifteen-point deficit in October.

Responding to the cries of state and local campaigns and the encour-agement of liberal editorialists, the Democrats finally lifted a page from the Republican play book: think short, talk negative, get mediated. In the closing weeks, the Duke's handlers withdrew their candidate from infor-mal contact (especially question–answer sessions) with the press corps and replaced his basic stump speech emphasizing competence and economic recovery with a positive–negative format emphasizing the profound mes-sage "I'm on your side. He's on theirs."

Meanwhile, the campaign went after Bush's "negatives" (another key word in the postmodern political vocabulary) with a vengeance. So negative was the closing Democratic campaign that its newly appointed advertising director estimated an even higher negative-to-positive ad content (60–40) than the Bush campaign's more "balanced" target ratio of 50–50.[12]

Although Dukakis still lost the election, and lost it convincingly, his rhetorical rebirth near the end of the campaign is significant. It suggests that what I propose to call "tele-rhetoric" has become the absolute gospel that media consultants proclaim it to be. One suspects that Dukakis did not bow easily to the new rhetorical doctrine. Much of his punishment at the polls and on the editorial pages may well have resulted from his stubborn resistance to the dogma of the electronic age. Yet, convert he did, even if too late.

Once the decision was made, and a new ad man was in place, the candidate went before the cameras with exhausting, if not shameless, determination. A *New York Times* "Campaign Trail" piece on his TV blitz began "H-e-e-e-e-r-e's . . . Michael." A splashy front page article the same week aptly summed up the tone now unifying the two campaigns: "TV's Role in '88: The Medium Is the Election." The author, Michael Oreskes, described the last weeks of the Dukakis campaign as an electronic whistle stop: "This is the electronic age's equivalent of the final whistle stop tour, seeking Nielsen ratings, not crowds at the tracks."[13]

Once all the candidates were on board, that rhetorical train moved rapidly down its electronic track. The average length of a TV sound bite plummeted to 9.2 seconds in 1988, down from a robust 14 seconds in 1984.[14]

As the very concept of sound bite indicates, the postmodern election comes complete with euphemistic and ambiguous jargon to help bridge the uneasy gap with more familiar and, one might add, meaningful, electoral realities past. It is hard to discuss the meaning of any 9.2 second slice of a text, particularly when such slices are constructed to stand alone, rendering the rest of the text something like a serving utensil. But in the new age, it is unnecessary to fret over meaning; meaning, as it were, is a pre-postmodern phenomenon.

The new language of postmodern politics is preverbal; it is anything but proverbial. It transcends easy distinctions between issues and candidate images, reason and feeling. May the Greeks forgive us, it throws out the classical categories of *logos, pathos,* and *ethos.* Indeed, it was when the Bush message, for all its rhetorical hubris, was universally declared effective, and the Dukakis message, for all its traditional tenacity, was pronounced a blur that Dukakis entered the new age.

What he found on the other side of the line was something the Republicans had known ever since they began winning the presidency on a regular basis. Mike Dukakis, meet Roger Ailes, the electronic guru who brought us Spiro Agnew, the "new" Richard Nixon, Dan Quayle, and the George Bush who parlayed his "wimp factor" into a "kinder, gentler" guy who "goes ballistic" only when he really has to. As Ailes put it, "There are three things that get covered: visuals, attacks and mistakes."[15] As a challenge, try to fit this typology into any of the traditional ways of thinking about argument, debate, or public speech.

The new political language is slippery by design. It is as if baseball legalized the spitball as a concession to pitchers and paid no mind to the inevitable declines in batting averages and fan interest in the game. And so, to pursue the analogy, the new political rhetoric comes as a welcome change only to the political pitchmen and the winning candidates. Despite the disapproval of spectators and journalists alike, the place of minimalist, ambiguous language seems secure in the postmodern campaign.

Assuring the marginality and ambiguity of language has become so important that campaigns these days employ people known in the new vernacular as spin doctors. These specialists come into play when a political pitch is released and heads too straight for the plate. The spin doctors rush out ahead of it, trying to influence or deflect the way reporters pass it along to the mass audience.

In 1988, the Democratic National Convention boasted a Spin Control Coordination Unit. In October of that year, when Bush's campaign chairman, the late Lee Atwater, made a rare appearance on the press plane, he was surprised with a chorus of boos and a chant for a "Spin Moratorium." Undaunted, he solemnly explained how Dan Quayle had done a splendid job in the debate. Initially pleased that everyone seemed to be taking him seriously, Atwater looked up to discover a sign being held above his head. It read: "The Joe Isuzu of Spin—He's Lying."[16]

Perhaps cartoonist Lynda Barry said more with a picture than these words can convey. Her cartoon version of Election '88 was titled "The Election from Hell." The devil was a journalist.[17]

Given the decline of traditional concerns about meaning, reason, debate, and evidence in postmodern rhetoric, it becomes challenging just to talk about, let alone evaluate, it. For the sake of American democracy, one can only hope, as Mark Twain is rumored to have said about the music of Richard Wagner, that "It is really much better than it sounds."

Unfortunately, the best evidence from the consumers suggests that the new tele-rhetoric is really no better than it sounds. As with other products of postmodernism, from slam dancing to gourmet microwave meals, people consume tele-rhetoric despite (one hopes it is not because of) being actively offended by it.

True, the 1988 voter turnout—the lowest since 1924—indicates that many people chose to preserve their sensibilities at the expense of giving up the franchise. But the more remarkable figure is the 50 percent who made a voting choice despite the self-confessed moral and intellectual pain involved.

What this tells me is that we cannot understand the new rhetoric on the traditional grounds that it reflects some sort of positive, responsive communication, however "deep," worked out between candidates and their audiences. There is little that is sympathetic about tele-rhetoric. Even as they made their decisions, voters told pollsters that they disliked their choices and regarded them as negative, uninteresting, and insubstantial.[18] Nevertheless, these same polls, along with other market research studies, showed that the offending political messages "worked."[19]

This perverse dynamic of disaffected voters who tuned in but did not drop out of the election built to a crescendo of sorts on election eve. The NBC/*Wall Street Journal* poll followed levels of voter dissatisfaction throughout the contest. At the time of the conventions—the last memorable moments of traditional speechifying—two-thirds of the voting public were satisfied with their choices. By the last week of the campaign, when Dukakis had made his conversion, two-thirds wished that two different candidates were running.[20]

Perhaps the most telling set of statistics on the disjuncture between the popularity and effectiveness of the new rhetoric came from a *New York Times*/CBS News poll reported on October 30, 1988. Fully 63 percent of the voters said that issues were the most important factor in choosing a president. Next, the respondents cited their most important issue. Health, homelessness, education, the economy, the deficit, and defense accounted for 64 percent of the responses. Then, a majority (54 percent) revealed that neither candidate was talking enough about their issue. Even more telling, only 5 percent for Bush and 4 percent for Dukakis felt that either candidate addressed their issue adequately.[21]

Trying to make sense of why people were planning to vote at all in light of the above information, the *Times'* analyst argued that there really must have been issues out there somewhere but that they just didn't look the way voters expected them to. The *Times* can be credited for publishing one of the few pieces anywhere claiming that meaningful issue differences had been located in the campaign. However, the analysis quickly dissolved into the suggestion that many deeper, seemingly personality-related appeals were really issues in disguise. This was precisely how the Bush campaign introduced its personal attacks on Dukakis (e.g., that he was "naive" and "weak" on foreign policy)—namely, as issues.[22]

No wonder voters were fed up. To their credit, many journalists in postcampaign laments recognized this mass disillusionment. At first, the press appeared as caught up in the negative thrall of the campaign as the public. Yet, as events unfolded, there came a faint signal from the press. Actually, there may have been two faint signals from the media—a sort of one-blink, two-blink communication between a paralyzed press and its bedside public.

The first sign of media dis-ease is revealed in a study by Marjorie Hershey. She found that, on average, print media (largely wire service) coverage from September to election day dealt with issues only one-third of the time, while devoting two-thirds of the content space to campaign strategy. Even though the prestigious *New York Times* tried to hold to issue coverage 50 percent of the time in September, it was filling less than 20 percent of its campaign "news hole" with issues by November when it actually topped the wires in percentage of campaign strategy reports.[23] In short, the campaign became its own news. The media reflected on their own role as never before, resulting in redundancy, self-referential logics, and loss of context, which are the hallmarks of postmodern symbolics. The media couldn't get out of their own loop.

The second signal that the media seemed to send to the political audience was an unprecedented number of stories on voter disaffection itself. In the past, reporters generally have been happy to buy the political science dicta that nonvoters would have voted the way voters vote and that voters find their acts meaningful. This time around, however, the press interviewed thousands of disgruntled citizens who challenged both assumptions.

Typical of these stories is one of a series by *New York Times* senior correspondent R. W. Apple, Jr., titled "From Jersey to Missouri, Voters Are Fed Up."[24] In another "fed up" article by another reporter, the wife of a former (read: unemployed or underemployed) steelworker lamented that current voting choices made no sense to people like her who grew up in normal, modern households "with mothers like June Cleaver that stayed home with the children. . . . And now we are in our thirties and forties and, bam! Everything falls apart on you."[25]

When things fall apart (as manifested in industrial decline, an emerging underclass, homelessness, health care costs, the disappearing dream of home ownership, etc.), people expect the election rhetoric to sharpen the issues, define the problems, and point to the solutions. Yet just the opposite occurred in 1988. An early warning for voters to disabuse themselves of their normal expectations came in June when two publications no less diverse than *The Nation* and *Time* agreed on what the coming contest held in store. In what may well have been a first, a *Nation* editorial cited *Time* as its source: "As *Time* aptly put it last week, 'The contest . . . will be less about ideas and ideologies than about clashing temperaments and styles.' "[26]

Perhaps it requires greater distance to appreciate the irony here. As Lynda Barry's cartoon cuts to the quick of it, so, too, did French television's response to the first debate (arguably the more "exciting" of the two). After no more than a few words had been exchanged, French viewers were whisked back to the newsroom where a deadpan newscaster pronounced judgment: "This debate is not too exciting. Let's go to the Olympics."[27]

EXPLAINING THE NEW RHETORIC:
THE VIEW FROM THE ACADEMY

It would be surprising if crossing this thin rhetorical line had been lost on the academy. It is the job of academics, after all, to keep track of the various thin lines within which our realities are contained. To be sure, the importance of television has been a favorite subject of communications scholars since its advent. However, recognition of the transforming effects of television on political rhetoric is a more recent phenomenon.[28] A number of high-quality analyses came along within the year leading up to the 1988 election. Even more notable is the fact that the media latched onto these books and gave them wide play, both in reviews and in interviews with their authors. Such media attention to fine-hewn, often esoteric, scholarly labors is rare. Perhaps it constitutes a third signal from media to audience that something is happening here, and what it is was painfully clear.

Approaching the "rhetorical presidency" from different angles, Jeffrey Tulis,[29] Roderick Hart,[30] and Kathleen Jamieson[31] all concluded that the contemporary presidency has become essentially a rhetorical office increasingly bent to the medium of television. Not only were their books all favorably reviewed by more than one national publication, but similar popular treatment was accorded an even more technical book by Shanto Iyengar and Donald Kinder that demonstrated through a series of laboratory experiments that television may not be able to tell us what to think, but it is amazingly successful at telling us what to think about.[32]

Of all these analyses, Jamieson's explores most fully the transforming effects of television on political (mainly presidential) communications. Drawing on the traditions of classical rhetoric and modern mass communication research, she concludes that the electronic medium rewards a "feminine" style. (I prefer the concept of an "intimate" political style suggested to me by Swedish professor of rhetoric Kurt Johannesson.) This style is warm and personal, and it emphasizes narrative over reason and logical argument. The intimate style accounts for the "great communicator" in Ronald Reagan, and, I think, it helps explain why the unpopular, offending rhetoric of Campaign '88 still had a powerful effect on its audience. Since tele-rhetoric works at a preverbal, prelogical, affective level, it permits voters to reject its content on logical, rational terms while still being moved at deeper levels that determine attention, commitment, and behavior.

The intimate style thus transcends positive and negative. Ronald Reagan was positive. The "kinder, gentler" George Bush had a negative streak that came out on cue 50 percent of the time. Both moved large audiences who disavowed much of what both men said at the level of truth, logic, and reason. For example, polls repeatedly showed that majorities of Americans disagreed with nearly all of Ronald Reagan's specific policy initiatives both as candidate and president.[33] And, as noted above, George Bush's specific issue appeals played to the full satisfaction of a tiny 5 percent of the voters prior to election day. Yet both men captured the presidency.

Jamieson's view of tele-rhetoric contains the seeds of an even more important insight into the contemporary electoral and political scene. During her tour of duty as one of the most cited academic experts on the 1988 election, she told a *New York Times* reporter that there was, in effect, nothing about television itself that determined the vacuity of the new rhetoric. There was, she said, a glimmer of hope that television might lead the way back to an age of reasonable rhetoric. To put it simply, there is no reason why television couldn't extricate itself from the candidate's loop and create an independent context for viewer evaluation of everything said during a campaign. With the achievable technology of a computerized tape retrieval system, TV could play for its viewers everything a candidate has ever said and done about any given subject, and let the audience judge whether the rhetoric of the moment has any historical or other contextual significance. When the networks made brief use of this potential in Campaign '88, Jamieson seized on it as a ray of hope, saying that "what you're seeing is the very beginning of an attempt to hold candidates accountable for inconsistency without placing the reporter as an intruder."[34]

One can hope that the contextualization of attacks, visuals, and sound bites becomes the wave of the future, but I am not so sanguine. To begin with, as the Leslie Stahl incident suggests, it may not be possible to create sensible contexts that unify the disparate images and free-floating messages of video collages, or clusters as they are known in the trade. Even if it is possible to contain tele-rhetoric within some larger logical context, these efforts will surely be condemned loud and long by all candidates as editorializing, for all candidates subscribing to the new gospel will appear heretical by the standards of the old. And, as we know, television does not stand up long in its own defense against a chorus of authoritative condemnation—particularly when it is a chorus that it is compelled to televise. More importantly, however, the media, and especially the electronic media, have no compelling reason and surely no corporate interest in rocking the political boat. No matter how shoddily built, that boat continues to float the phenomenal profitability of the mass media. More will be said on this point later. For now, suffice it to say that the full extent of media response to the perverse politics of postmodernism may well be what we have already seen in 1988: self-flagellation and grumbling from reporters, knowing winks and blinks to the suffering voter, and endless media coverage of media coverage of media coverage . . .

There is, however, a less conjectural line of argument in Jamieson's observation: perhaps television isn't inherently to blame for the degradation of contemporary rhetoric. Taking off from Jamieson's insight just might help us reach a new understanding of the problem. Unfortunately, where I propose to take this line of thought doesn't lead to a very optimistic forecast, but it may offer a better explanation for the current state of affairs than pointing the finger of blame (or in social science, the causal arrow) at television alone.

TOWARD AN EXPLANATION OF ELECTIONS WITHOUT CHOICES

Consider the possibility that tele-rhetoric is something known in academic circles as an epiphenomenon, or, in everyday parlance, as a symptom of something deeper. Television, after all, is a passive medium, having the capacity to show us everything from talking heads, the public affairs people, to Talking Heads, the rock band—everything from commentators trying to make sense of it all, to a rock concert video called "Stop Making Sense."

What this means for elections is that television could bring us an entirely different political reality. Debates could become true forensic exchanges. Conventions could be conferred special status rather than threatened with cancellation. Candidates could be grilled one at a time by journalists for extended periods under the television lights as they are in Sweden, for example.[35] Again as in Sweden and many other countries, networks could be required to provide free air time to candidates, and restrictions could be imposed on the length and format of political commercials (encouraged, of course, by appropriate legislation).

The list of "coulds" and "what ifs" is too long to continue. The point is that TV isn't an explanation; it is merely a medium. Who uses TV? Why do they use it? How do they employ its mediating potentialities? These are the underlying elements of an explanation of tele-rhetoric. As for television itself, it may be a worthy object of blame and a useful window on an important problem, but it is not a valid cause in an explanation.

Stepping back, we can view postmodernism in general as the product of deeper social forces. The whole syndrome: multiple realities, strange loopiness, power lunching, slam dancing, microwave meals, nostalgia for "Leave It to Beaver" reruns, the generalized loss of meaning, diminished concern for truth, the spinoff academic disciplines of deconstructionism and Foucault studies, and the pervasive social schizophrenia and collective amnesia that artists and writers have been trying to call to mind. All these things, including the emergence of the idea-less, choice-impaired election, may be traced to identifiable and quite palpable social, political, and economic forces.

As a first step toward identifying these forces in the electoral arena, consider the curious role of the political audience. Murray Edelman has argued that this is the age of the political spectator.[36] Citizen-spectators confronted with mass media spectacles may be entertained, dazzled, confused, or bored—the normal range of audience emotions. There is even a role for the audience to play: voting. Elsewhere, Edelman has argued that voting and elections are important mainly for legitimizing the governments that are installed in Washington.[37] By giving voters a meaningful part to play in the process, they are more likely to support what governments do to them or don't do for them. However, Edelman argues that meaning for voters tends to be a shallow affair produced by symbol-waving and flimflamming by candidates. These would-be leaders create enemies, announce crises, and generally push symbolic buttons in ways that make political audiences see red, or red-white-and-blue. The most substantial result of voting is that people get meaningfully involved in the battle of symbols and the seal of public approval is stamped on the government that goes into office. At the very least, then, elections legitimize governments. Or do they?

The decline of voter interest and satisfaction suggests that even the symbolic meanings of electoral choices have become undermined in recent elections, raising questions about this legitimation function of elections and the stability of public support for any elected governments put in office. The main reason for the loss of voter involvement and the declining legitimacy of elected government is an interesting one. Unlike audiences of other spectator media—even television—the political audience is a captive of a political system with no competition. Political marketers have finally figured out the beauty of the captive political audience: voters are unable to command new programming when their lack of interest sends the ratings plummeting. To explore this point a bit further, there are, it seems to me, two important differences between political spectators and the audiences who respond to theatrical performances and other entertainment in various ways from buying tickets to laughing at the funny lines. First, spectator displeasure with the quality of the electoral performance, even to the extent of the spectator not voting, does not shut down or otherwise "condition" the spectacle itself—as lack of patronage conditions the content of both the fine arts and popular culture media. Second, the converse also holds true: those who choose to participate in the political audience do not do so because they necessarily enjoy or find meaning in the experience—as one expects audiences for music, theater, or film to connect with their chosen medium. Recall here that full satisfaction with electoral choices in 1988 was expressed by a tiny 9 percent of those planning to vote for the two candidates.

In most other spectator arenas, decline of patronage and rise of antipathy would be more consequential. Whereas other cultural forums are responsive to the marketplace of popular taste, elections seem relatively immune from the most important market forces of consumer dissatisfaction and outright withdrawal from the marketplace. This curious feature of elections helps us recast traditional thinking about candidate–audience communication. The easy assumption is that the effectiveness of electoral rhetoric turns on some sort of meaningful, positive, responsive exchange between communicator and audience. Throwing out this assumption raises the question of what does shape the content of electoral language these days.

Begin with Money . . .

Consider this possibility. Instead of competing with each other for audience approval, candidates increasingly compete for the support of a much more select and seldom recognized group: political campaign contributors. Presidential candidates spent more than $300 million in 1988. Although federal funding covers part of a candidate's immediate costs, campaigns must raise more than half these amounts from private backers. Competition for these staggering sums of money is stiff, and the nature of this offstage maneuvering does not reward those who expand the domain of issues and policy proposals. To simplify the point, a restricted range of political ideas makes backing a candidate a safer bet for big money interests. In fact, restricting the range of ideas enables backers to hedge their bets and support both candidates. This is, of course, a bad thing for the health of democracy but a very good thing for those who invest their money in elections.

The most controversial version of this investment theory of elections has been developed by Thomas Ferguson and Joel Rogers who argue that the Republican party has won over many of the Democrats' big backers.[38] This core of multinational (read: free trade) business and financial interests initially put their money behind the Democrats at the time of the Great Depression to counter the protectionist economic policies of the Republicans. Since the Nixon years, however, the Republicans have recognized the financial and political advantages of adopting the free trade rhetoric. Now, so the theory goes, the two parties compete head on for much the same core of financial support, with the result that the Democrats have been leveraged to the right on a whole list of major issues like defense and foreign policy, unemployment, domestic industrial decline, and the structure of the national budget. This "right turn," as Ferguson and Rogers call it, has put the Democratic party at odds with sizable numbers of traditional voters who support more liberal policies in areas ranging from defense to social programs.

It is not clear, however, that the Democrats "can go home again" to their old liberalism. And, for reasons discussed further in Chapter 4, there may be less convergence of interest among financial backers than Ferguson and Rogers claim. It may be more accurate to say that the pull of interests this way and that simply erodes the abilities of most candidates (at presidential and congressional levels) to express broad policy programs or to join in stable political coalitions. After deducting the silent commitments made to the numbers of financial backers required for successful campaigning, candidates are left with little in the way of credible governing ideas to offer voters.

Next, Add Marketing . . .

This brings us to the second major constraint on campaign discourse: the wholesale use of marketing techniques and strategies to generate campaign content. Enter marketing experts into elections in a big way. Their task is to transform a product of diminished or dubious market value into one that wins the largest market share. The result is an emphasis on communication that short-circuits logic, reason, and linguistic richness in favor of image-making techniques. This means that candidates are not sold to a broad general public but to narrow slices or "market segments" of that public. These market segments need not understand the candidates; they need only vote for them. Thus, people are induced to vote for Candidate A over Candidate B much as soap buyers may favor Brand X over Brand Y without feeling they have established a meaningful relationship with their laundry detergent in the process. This further diminishes the importance of language, logic, and reason in the articulation of campaign issues.

Since at least 1980, the Democrats have encountered a difficult problem that once paralyzed the early Goldwater Republicans until the party solved it with the successful marketing of the "new" Richard Nixon and the even newer Ronald Reagan. The problem is simple: a narrow, unpalatable issue agenda that is hard to sell to the general public. The Republican secret was to turn the liability of voter avoidance into an asset by targeting key segments of the shrinking audience that continued to vote. Since votes aren't dollars, profitability isn't an issue. Only victory counts, no matter how many voters boycott the electoral process altogether.

In a classic commentary on the new political age, a Republican strategist ushered in the election of 1980 with these words: "I don't want everyone to vote. Our leverage in the election quite candidly goes up as the voting population goes down."[39] Borrowing this page from the Republican play book, the Democrats in the 1980s went after the narrow market segment of blue collar Republicans with a vengeance. Perhaps the most blatant example involved the Dukakis campaign's avoidance of anything resembling an overt appeal to Jesse Jackson's constituency. This market analysis, even though flawed, was followed to the end: the liberal Jackson wing of the party was not viewed as essential to victory, while the Reagan Democrats were. The constraints on campaign rhetoric and issue definition were equally clear: it was feared that anything said to liberal segments of the fragile voter market would send more conservative segments into the Republican camp. As it turned out, this feared pattern of conservative defection occurred anyway, owing in part to Dukakis' withering at the charge of being a "liberal" (the dreaded L-word), and in larger part to the inability of strategically hamstrung Democrats to compete rhetorically on remaining issues like prayer, patriotism, civil rights, and abortion. Such is political life without a credible rhetorical vision.

Now, Try to Control the News Media . . .

In the three-factor model proposed here, the above two constraints necessarily engage a third limiting condition operating on electoral communication: the highly controlled use of the news media. The press, like the voters, generally regards issues and ideas as the most important grounds for electoral choice. Idea-less elections antagonize reporters searching for meaningful differences between the candidates to write home about. An aroused press can be expected to assume an adversarial role, leaping on inconsistencies, making much of candidate slips and blunders, seizing on anything inflammatory in the absence of much to say about policy positions. As a result, campaigns tend to isolate their candidates from the press corps, and stick to a tightly controlled and carefully scripted daily schedule. This means, in Roger Ailes' words, that reporters are handed a lot of visuals and attacks, while mistakes (and ideas) are held to a minimum.

It is by now well accepted that good media strategy entails three requirements: keeping the candidate away from the press; feeding the press a simple, telegenic political line of the day; and making sure the daily news line echoes ("magnify" may be the better word) the images from campaign ads, thus blurring the distinction between commercials and "reality."[40] Candidates and their "handlers" vary in the ability to keep the press at bay, but when they succeed, reporters are left with little but an impoverished set of campaign slogans to report. As ABC reporter Sam Donaldson said on an election-week news analysis program in a tone that resembled that of the coroner disclosing an autopsy result: "When we cover the candidates, we cover their campaigns as they outline them."[41] Thus, a willing, if unhappy, press becomes a channel for much the same meaningless tele-rhetoric that emerges from the interplay of advertising strategy and the concessions made to campaign contributors.

In recent years the media have shown signs of becoming more critical of campaigns. Encouraged by a public that is angry at candidates and politicians, the news contains increased coverage of the celluloid world of marketed candidates and media manipulation. This increase in media coverage of media campaigns, however, has not brought candidates out of hiding or appreciably affected the way campaigns are run. The ironic result of media attempts to "deconstruct" candidate images and expose the techniques of news control may be to reinforce public cynicism about the whole process. Taking the public behind the political illusions has not succeeded in bringing the candidates out of hiding behind those illusions. The net result is still an election system dominated by mass-marketed, Madison Avenue messages that deliver quick emotional punches instead of lasting visions and governing ideas to voters. In other words, the way in which news organizations have exercised their critical skills may result less in changing the system than in reinforcing (albeit inadvertently) the public cynicism that helps keep it going.

One might think the press would do something bold to elevate election news content above the intellectual level of political commercials. For example, the various news organizations could separate themselves from the pack mentality and develop a thoughtful agenda of important issues (based, if need be, on opinion polls) and score the candidates on how well they address these issues. But that is not very likely. A news executive vetoed out of hand a very modest version of this suggestion. When asked why the media did not make more of George Bush's well-documented connections to the Iran–Contra arms scandal and the CIA hiring of Panamanian dictator Manuel Noriega, the producer of one of the three network evening newscasts explained simply, "We don't want to look like we're going after George Bush."[42]

Despite this reluctance to tackle candidates on the issues, it is apparently appropriate to go after them on grounds of health (Thomas Eagleton in 1972), character (Edmund Muskie, 1972), gaffes and malapropisms

(Gerald Ford, 1976), family finances (Geraldine Ferraro, 1984), extramarital sex (Gary Hart, 1988), or hypocrisy and gall (Dan Quayle, 1988). However, the press draws the line when it comes to pursuing issues beyond where the candidates are willing to take them.

Never mind the resulting decline in the quality of campaign discourse and citizen interest in politics (not to mention public faith in the press), the media seem determined to steer a safe course of "objectivity." Elaborating the doctrine behind Sam Donaldson's earlier words, the ABC vice president in charge of campaign coverage in 1984 and 1988 said: "It's my job to take the news as they choose to give it to us and then, in the amount of time that's available, put it into the context of the day or that particular story. . . . The evening newscast is not supposed to be the watchdog on the Government."[43]

This self-styled impression of what the media are "supposed to be" has changed about 180 degrees from the hallowed role of the press defined by the likes of Peter Zenger and Thomas Jefferson. The new norm of press passivity enables increasingly profitable and decreasingly critical mass media to chase political candidates in dizzying circles like cats after their own tails. To wit, two-thirds of the coverage in 1988 was coverage of coverage: articles on the role of television, news about campaign strategy, and updates on voter fatigue in response to meaningless media fare. As the irrepressible French social critic Jacques Ellul said about the contemporary mass communications industry: "The media refer only to themselves."[44]

Each of these related constraints on political communication imposes a substantial limit on what candidates say to voters, creating, in turn, important limits on the quality of our most important democratic experience. Taken together, these limiting conditions go a long way toward explaining the alarming absence of meaningful choices and satisfied voters in recent elections. These restrictions on political speech also explain the mysterious elevation of tele-rhetoric to gospel standing in contemporary campaigns. With ideas safely out of the way and the press neutralized, television has little use other than as a medium for turning a seemingly endless election process into the world's longest running political commercial without programmatic interruption.

Other puzzles about the contemporary election scene also become less baffling. Take the rise of negative campaigning, for example. Because of the severe content restrictions imposed by the three limits outlined above, candidates suffer the marketing problem of appearing unattractive (i.e., negative). In this strange world, victory goes to the candidate who manages to appear the least unattractive or negative. The easiest strategy is to play up the opponent's negatives, in an effort to look less negative by comparison. (One can hardly hope to look positive in this context.) Hence, the obsession with the opponent's negatives, as emphasized in commercials and played up in news sound bites spoon-fed to the press.

All of the above—the rhetoric without vision, the telegenic sound bites, and commercialized advertising and news production—happen to play best (or, in keeping with the new spirit, less offensively) on television. In the words of a leading campaign consultant commenting on a race in California, "A political rally in California consists of three people around a television set."[45]

Considering the magnitude of these forces working against the traditional forms and contents of political communication, it is not surprising that candidates say so little these days. One marvels that they are able to say anything at all.

ARE THE VOTERS BLAMELESS?

Where do citizens fit into this picture? On the one hand, the long list of public complaints makes it understandable why many have dropped out of the political process. Yet, without some sort of effective public input, little is likely to change. Even when signs of citizen life emerge, it is not always clear that people are tracking on the big picture. Led by Oklahoma, California, and Colorado, for example, a national stirring to limit the terms of state legislators has begun. In an action that raised constitutional questions, Colorado voters even approved limits on the length of time their national representatives can serve. There is little doubt that elected officials at all levels hear these signals from voters. The question is whether term limits will accomplish anything beyond signalling voter displeasure to lawmakers. (For more details, see Chapter 8.) The larger issue here is whether most citizens understand enough about what displeases them to do anything effective about it. The irony of the electoral breakdown I am about to describe in the next chapters is that it may not be possible for people simply to vote their way out of it. And, if stronger measures are required, who will think of them?

Displays of voter anger may be healthier than withdrawal, but anger does little good if it is not motivated by some understanding of the underlying problem and its solution. There are signs that most Americans grasp at least some parts of the money, media, and marketing puzzle, but few seem to put it together in a useful way. For starters, it is clear that most of those who continue to vote do not see their own roles in the system very clearly. For example, as mentioned earlier, polls taken on the eve of the 1990 election showed a substantial majority blaming the incumbent Congress for much of the national mess, but solid majorities also said they approved of their own incumbent representatives.[46] This approval translated into votes, making 1990 the third consecutive election that returned incumbents to Washington at a 96 percent or better rate. It doesn't take a Ph.D. in statistics to know that 96 percent of Congress could not be performing above the median while the other 4 percent was causing all the trouble.

These and other voting paradoxes will be taken up later, but for now, our questions are broader ones: What are we to make of the whole collection of strange American voting habits, ranging from one of the lowest turnout rates among Western industrial democracies, to reelecting incumbents after blaming professional politicians as a group for the mess in Washington? Are these and other curious features of voter mentality signs of gross negligence and ignorance, or are they the results of people trying (unsuccessfully) to respond sensibly to a system that offers them few meaningful choices? This last question, it turns out, is one of the oldest and still unresolved debates about the American voter. There is evidence for both sides, suggesting that we are not dealing with an "either–or" type of choice, but a more complex relationship between individual voters and the political system in which they operate.

On the "voters are fools" side of the argument, there is considerable evidence that Americans possess little knowledge about the "who, what, when, where, and how" of government.[47] Moreover, voters do not tend to think in big-picture, ideological terms; instead they rely on party and group identifications, along with an occasional big issue to guide their choices.[48] Given this portrait of the voter, it is tempting to conclude that candidates have little incentive to elevate the level of national debate. Even if they did, there is little chance that such ignorant voters would approve of sophisticated political debates. Two leading students of American elections have described voters in the following terms:

> Most of them are not interested in most public issues most of the time. In a society like ours, it apparently is quite possible to live comfortably without being politically concerned. Political activity is costly and eats up time and energy at an astounding rate. . . . One must attend meetings, listen to or participate in discussions, write letters, attempt to persuade or be persuaded by others, and engage in other time-consuming labor. This means foregoing other activities, like devoting extra time to the job, playing with the children, and watching TV.[49]

"Wait a minute!" say proponents of the opposing "voters are *not* fools" school. If voters sometimes act like fools, it is because politicians treat them that way, offering few meaningful choices and seldom inviting the public inside the decision-making process. Supporting this claim is a long research tradition that attributes the failings inside voters' heads to the choices they are offered in the election taking place outside.[50] Viewed this way, voters make the best sense out of what little candidates may offer them. When few issues are solid enough to use for thinking about the future, voters look back and vote "retrospectively," based on their judgments about who did the best overall job in the past.[51] When there are no issues or ideas (whether forward- or backward-looking), voters tend to screen candidate personalities for information about leadership and emotional qualities.[52] When reliable information of any sort becomes scarce, voters continue to do the best they can, trying to decode political advertisements and well-staged public appearances for clues about what the candidates represent.[53] All of this explains why many voters say they are increasingly unhappy with their choices these days, but remain willing and able to make them (and why other voters, finding nothing in the way of useful information, have simply given up).

Are voters a cause or a casualty in an electoral system that offers few meaningful choices? Probably both. The dual dangers of unsophisticated voters and shallow candidates have been with us for some time. In recent years, the problem has been that these weaknesses in the electoral process have increasingly been moved to the center, institutionalized, if you will. As a result, candidates with ideas and voters who might want to think about them are less and less likely to find each other in the numbers required to create governing coalitions. In order to understand how the worst tendencies of American politics have become elevated or institutionalized in the electoral process, it is important to expand the eternal debate about "ignorant voters versus shallow elections" to include several other aspects of citizen behavior that affect the emerging changes in American politics:

- First of all, consider the decline in party loyalty, particularly the drop in voter identification with the Democrats, and the rise of the "independent" voter over the past two decades. Among other things, this change has reinforced the importance of candidate marketing strategies aimed at these elusive swing voters.
- Now, include the gradual decline in voter turnout over the same period, which has reinforced the temptation of campaigns to pour more marketing dollars into the chase for fewer voters.
- Finally, to this portrait of fewer and more independent voters, add the fact that most Americans draw the "political participation line" at voting and, in some cases, giving money to interest groups. If neither voting nor ordinary lobbying activities are likely to produce adequate reforms

in the current system, what will motivate people to take the grass-roots actions required to organize an effective political reform movement?

Each of these features of individual political behavior will be addressed at an appropriate juncture in the argument, beginning with the rise of the independent voter. It is ironic that a potentially positive "market force" like greater voter independence may have contributed to the decline of candidate and party interest in trying to market new ideas. How so? The answer is contained in the next chapter.

CHAPTER 2

Origins of the
New American Politics

Money, media, and marketing have been factors in American politics for some time. The corruption of big money goes back at least to the Gilded Age of Robber Barons and the rise of the industrial giants following the Civil War. Precise measures of power are elusive, but a reliable observer of that era credited the captains of industry with so much financial clout that they "declared war, negotiated peace, reduced courts, legislatures, and sovereign states to an unqualified obedience to their will, disturbed trade, agitated the currency, imposed taxes and boldly setting both law and public opinion at defiance, have freely exercised many other attributes of sovereignty."[1] No less an authority than President Grover Cleveland warned in his 1888 State of the Union Message to Congress: "We discover the existence of trusts, combinations, and monopolies, while the citizen is struggling far in the rear or is trampled to death beneath an iron heel. Corporations, which should be carefully restrained creatures of law and servants of the people, are fast becoming the people's masters."[2]

The Robber Barons purchased much of their political protection by financing electoral politics, an arrangement that culminated in the Republican party funding system under the direction of Mark Hanna. The election of William McKinley in 1896, for example, was funded by something akin to a tax on big business, whereby corporations and "fat cat" entrepreneurs were "assessed" contributions according to their wealth and prominence.[3]

The infancy of modern media manipulation can also be traced back to at least 1896 when Hanna staged McKinley's campaign largely from the front porch of the candidate's house in Canton, Ohio. Complete with marching bands, parades, and pilgrimages by loyal supporters, the campaign from beginning to end was what we would today call a media event.[4] It even had a sound bite. "McKinley and a Full Dinner Pail" was the slogan aimed at tens of thousands of urban workers who had been uprooted from the farms and were suffering the hunger produced by the nation's first major industrial-era depression in the cities.

The differences between then and now, however, are considerable. Swirling around McKinley's gilded campaign and its fledgling attempts at media manipulation were fierce national debates. McKinley's opponent William Jennings Bryan toured the country in 1896 calling for nothing less than a national referendum on the American future: small-town agrarian society versus urban industrial wasteland. In the process, Bryan delivered some 600 speeches to crowds that totaled 5 million people (almost the number who voted for him that year). Meanwhile, the Populist party which allied with the Democrats in support of Bryan's candidacy was divided intellectually over populism's failure to mount an effective national appeal to the workingman to counter McKinley's tempting "full dinner pail" imagery. In the end, enough voters rallied around the idea that both labor and business shared a common interest in industrial development to forge a governing Republican coalition.[5]

The moral of this story involves "governing ideas." Ideas that guide the process of governing are the central concern of this book. The genius of a political system lies in its capacity to innovate and articulate broad visions and ideas for citizens and politicians to follow. A governing idea or a governing vision, put simply, is a broad set of national goals supported by enough citizens and powerholders within institutions to sustain new courses of action aimed at changing basic social and economic conditions. Throughout this argument, the concern is not so much with whether governing ideas are good or bad, right or wrong, but whether they are likely to develop and be sustained given the limits of the contemporary political system.

Not only did a governing vision emerge from the money-tainted contest of 1896, but also in the decades before and after, society was alive with grand political debates and galvanizing conflicts. Voting turnouts in the late 1800s rose above 80 percent of the eligible electorate. Even if inflated by some degree of corruption, as in the infamous "voting graveyards" of Chicago, political participation was not dampened by the uses of money as it is today. Nor was corruption left solely to government to correct. After the turn of the century, the Progressive Movement actively pushed for reforms in corrupt party politics at state and local levels. The fight even broke out within the Republican party itself, when Theodore Roosevelt became president after McKinley's death and moved against a few of the worst industrial offenders, quarreling with his own party over corporate campaign contributions.

In the decades between 1900 and 1930, alternative political visions were presented and debated in a muckraking press, in novels, especially those of John Dos Passos, Theodore Dreiser, and Sinclair Lewis, and in a militant labor movement. All contributed to the intellectual ferment of the times. After the economic bubble finally burst in 1929, a new governing coalition came to power and drew from that legacy of political debate. Under Franklin Roosevelt, the Democrats promoted a new governing vision (the New Deal) and built a forty-year foundation of voters and party government in support of that vision.

Today, we may ask, where is the national leadership, the principled opposition, or the legacy of competing ideas swirling around government? On what basis would a new governing coalition govern, even if given a chance at power? Why would voters bring such a coalition to power— much less, sustain it—in the absence of an intellectual foundation or a political vision? In short, money, media, and marketing have been around for many years, but not in the same way they operate today. The rest of this chapter explains the differences between the new election system and the old.

HOW THE NEW POLITICAL WORLD TURNS

As noted, campaign finance problems go back over a century, but the effects of money are different today, acting more as a centrifugal force pulling political coalitions and governing visions apart, rather than as a centripetal force pushing them together.[6] A similar case can be made for the media component of the system. If media management was born in the front porch campaign of William McKinley, it was schooled in the fireside radio artistry of Franklin Roosevelt and graduated in the advanced press-handling techniques of the Reagan White House.[7] It is this latest incarnation of media management in conjunction with the workings of money that is most worrisome to a democratic society. Even the seemingly broad political vision offered by Ronald Reagan turns out to have been built on unstable foundations of promises made to competing interests and on public support delivered through fragile marketing strategies. This argument will be developed later in this volume, but for now the general point is that even the best example of a contemporary political vision (whatever one may think about Reagan's goals or ideology) turned out to be an unsuitable basis for governing in the long run. In the short run, however, effective application of media management techniques can screen fragile ideas and their political advocates from press criticism.

In the Reagan White House, the repertoire of press handling included putting out a line of the day for the media, orchestrating corroborating statements throughout the government, controlling leaks fairly well, conducting extensive opinion polling and market analysis to come up with new script material, employing a brain trust of press managers, and, not incidentally, having a politician who was a good actor and charismatic, to boot. As a result, opponents' criticisms did not stick in the media. The real secret of Reagan's so-called Teflon presidency, however, may have been his obedience to the iron law of media management: don't engage with press criticism on its own terms. Consider the comparison case of George Bush. For reasons to be explained in Chapter 7, the press has been more critical of Bush, particularly on the domestic front, and on numerous occasions has succeeded in pointing out the emptiness of his agenda. Whether Bush's domestic program was truly more illusory than Reagan's, or merely less well handled with the media (or both), is not the issue here—at least for the moment. What matters is that for all the White House breakdowns in the fine points of press handling, and Bush's propensity for winging it at the wrong time, he has managed fairly well to stick to the iron law: don't engage in debates with the press. That is, don't respond to the substance of criticism. Thus, the irony is that, even when the press exposes ideas as empty, ill conceived, or contrived, the refusal to address the substance of the criticism effectively blunts that criticism.

When the press corps is well managed, resulting in the notorious no-stick criticisms of the early Reagan years, persistent attempts at criticism may make the press look foolish. When the press corps is not as skillfully handled, as has sometimes happened during the Bush presidency, the politician may look foolish. In either case, as long as the politician refuses to engage with opponents, the result is that ideas are left poorly explored, debated, and evaluated. In the case of Teflon politicians, the result may be to foster false hopes among the people that principled governing is going on. In the case of politicians exposed as having no ideas, policies, or visions, the result may be to reinforce public cynicism about the unresponsiveness of elected officials to reasonable standards of accountability. The main results of media management within this system tend to run from sowing false hopes to feeding public cynicism. Indeed, the profile of opinion polls from the early 1980s to the early 1990s appears as one long cycle of hope turning into cynicism.

These observations bring us to the indispensability of marketing in this system. These days political ideas are sustained less by the heat of debate or the light of policy success than by the suasions of marketing. As with money and media management, political advertising has a long history. Television commercials for candidates date virtually to the dawn of the medium with Dwight Eisenhower's "Man from Abilene" spots in 1952.[8] The selling of the "new" Richard Nixon stands as one of the great marketing triumphs of modern times.[9] What is different about marketing in the current election system is that it affects every stage in the life of political ideas. When politicians introduce what appears to be a broad vision to the electorate as Reagan did in 1980, marketing disguises the extent to which that vision sits uneasily atop unstable, money-driven coalitions. When candidates or parties manage to agree on an issue or two, marketing puffs them up into grander visions. Most often, however, marketing is called in to fill the void when all-too-substantial commitments to political backers leave candidates with little of substance to offer voters. Marketing also turns up new issues and image ideas when the press exposes politicians as intellectually barren. In other words, marketing provides an ongoing, stopgap repair process for politicians and ideas caught up in the pull of money and the resulting inability to communicate openly with the public through the media.

Thus, the vicious cycle goes round and round, and one can cut in at any point, finding a dynamic that keeps the process spinning. Consider, for example, just a few aspects of the marketing dynamics that operate in this system. Begin with the marketing of fragile ideas that require constant protection from public debate, only to fall apart later in the policy process. This pattern, in turn, fuels public cynicism, which requires even greater reliance on marketing, which costs more money, thus bringing us to a point of entry into a similarly vicious money cycle. As is typical of all dysfunctional social systems from families to organizations to, in this case, governments, the points of greatest weakness or dysfunction eventually become central to the perpetuation of the whole process. Of relevance here is the apparent problem of the growing number of citizens who are leaving the political marketplace in disgust. But with the number one marketing maxim operative—fewer voters are a marketing plus, not a minus—this is no problem at all. Reduced numbers of active citizens allow marketing resources to be concentrated more effectively. Thus, we witness greater fortunes spent each election cycle on capturing the short-term attention and support of ever smaller numbers of voters. In a similar fashion, each element of this emerging system contains a fundamental weakness or contradiction that requires shoring up from the other two components to keep the system going. Money begets media management and marketing; marketing requires money and media management; media management fuels the need for new marketing strategies which require more money. And so on. . . .

Each piece of this system is explored separately in Chapter 4. In this chapter, the goal is simply to persuade the reader that the system sketched out above not only exists, but also has consequences far greater than are ordinarily attributed to any of its individual parts. The first step, then, is to explain how the system came into being over the last twenty years. Following, in Chapter 3, is a discussion of criticisms that might be raised against the thesis that this system has fundamentally altered the ways in which we as a people communicate, select leaders, and govern.

THE WINDS OF CHANGE IN AMERICAN POLITICS

As with most broad historical changes, the merging of money, media, and marketing into a new system of electoral politics was not due to the force of a single event, a sinister conspiracy, or a dominant individual. Rather, a convergence of historical forces during the 1960s, 1970s, and 1980s created the conditions for forming this system. In what will necessarily be a brief review of this history, the main developments discussed in this chapter are these:

- The decline of the old Democratic vision and the rise of the independent voter (late 1960s–1970s).
- Campaign finance reform and the power of PACs (1970s–1980s).
- The rise of a national veto system and the decline of the new Republican vision (1980s–1990s).

The Decline of the Democrats and the Rise of the Independent Voter

The Democratic heyday of the 1960s came to a screeching halt in 1968 and went into reverse in 1972. After refashioning the New Deal of the 1930s into the New Frontier and the Great Society visions of the 1960s, things fell apart. The Vietnam War began to appear both corrupt and unwinnable, creating huge divisions at home. At the same time, southern voters started to express anger at the Democrats' imposition of civil rights on their communities. "Middle America" joined the reaction against the civil rights movement as urban riots and protests created turmoil across the land. The rebirth of religious fundamentalism took on a political dimension in reaction to the loose morals of the "liberals." And the welfare system created by the Democratic War on Poverty came under fire from all sides for creating dependency, being overly bureaucratic, and generally not producing the desired results.

The Democratic party itself was split into three factions: traditional New Deal liberals; the rising radical flank from the antiwar and civil rights movements; and the conservative southern ranks who threatened to bolt the party altogether at the national level if the radicals became more dominant. The election of 1968 was the turning point. After a season of violence, protest, and the assassinations of civil rights leader Martin Luther King, Jr., and Democratic antiwar candidate Robert Kennedy, an embattled Democratic party convention nominated Hubert Humphrey, a candidate who was offensive to two of the party's three wings. An old New Dealer, Humphrey angered the antiwar movement by his association as vice president with government policies in Vietnam; at the same time, he alienated conservative southern Democrats with his support for civil rights. Meanwhile, what was to become the most successful third party candidacy in history (not counting the Populist–Democratic coalition of 1896) had been launched by the conservative Alabama Democrat, George Wallace. When the chaos finally settled on election day, Richard Nixon eked out a narrow Republican victory, but pointed to a growing block of southern support, despite Wallace's candidacy, as the basis for a grand Republican renaissance.

Meanwhile, the Democrats went back to the drawing boards and began reforming the party structure itself. Blaming the old party's backroom politics for nominating an outdated candidate in Humphrey, the radical wing of the party (grass-roots organizers, civil rights leaders, antiwar factions, and women's groups) reformed the nomination process drastically to open more seats at nominating conventions to delegates who were directly elected by voters in state primaries. Unfortunately, the party reached little consensus about a new unifying vision or program. As a result, in 1972, the nation watched a Democratic convention that appeared to be out of control, with groups of all sorts fighting to get their issues into the party platform. In the end, antiwar candidate George McGovern discovered how little sympathy middle America had for his grass-roots Democratic agenda, and suffered one of the most decisive electoral defeats in history. This time, Richard Nixon's claims about a new Republican majority and a solid Republican South appeared to be convincing.

Political scientists have debated the wisdom of opening up the Democratic party to more direct democracy in the nominating process—perhaps more than any major party in the world. Some argue that the party now suffers a lack of organization and leadership through the ranks.[10] Others retort that the Democrats were in trouble before the reforms and that the decentralization of a dying organization is actually a sign of vitality and life.[11] For our purposes, this debate misses the rush of later events. To appreciate the larger implications of the decline of the Democrats and the resurgence of the Republicans in the 1970s, we must also look at changes in the voter market and the campaign finance system before we can put the whole picture together.

As the Democrats' old vision failed them and it seemed difficult for them to focus on a new one, the first signs of a major voter change in several decades began to emerge: the rise of the independent voter. Increasing numbers of citizens declared no allegiance (or only weak allegiance) to either party. This trend continues to the present day. In the earliest voter studies conducted by the University of Michigan in the 1950s, slightly over 20 percent of the electorate declared themselves independents. Today, over one-third make that claim. In the current era in which massive marketing efforts will be launched to win the votes of just 10 or 15 percent of the voters in the middle, this change becomes significant. The political plot thickens when we add the fact that most of the shift has been away from the Democratic party. The plot gets downright interesting with the discovery that, although the Republicans picked up some of these shifting voters, most have remained in the independent ranks, showing a continuing willingness to split their tickets, often voting Republican for president and Democratic for Congress.

Today, this electorate presents a continuing marketing challenge for candidates. Candidates who have little ideological affiliation with parties are rejecting old party trademarks. This is particularly true of the Democrats who still have not come up with a party program to replace the New Deal/New Frontier/Great Society era programs from 1932 to 1968. Moreover, individual candidates (again, this has been more true for Democrats than Republicans) have less to gain by advertising themselves with a party label to voters who are more inclined to resist such traditional appeals. In short, the decline of the Democrats resulted not so much in a migration to the Republicans as a halt in the middle of the road. This created a new electoral dynamic that could have taken the system in any number of directions, some of them very positive. However, the ensuing political developments turned independent voters into the objects of what might be called the *great marketing chase*. In recent years the Republicans have discovered the limits of the marketing chase, but in the beginning it was the Democrats who appeared to be caught in a futile chase to sell themselves to their own former voters. In the beginning (the mid-1970s to mid-1980s) the great marketing chase looked something like this:

- A collapsing Democratic vision led to defections among party loyalists and increased the ranks of independent voters who were more easily persuaded by candidates without strong party (particularly old-style Democratic) identifications.
- This made building new party (particularly Democratic) visions all the more difficult and the marketing of "individualist" candidates all the more compelling.
- Since there was little to be gained from appealing to those still loyal to the Democratic and Republican parties (because they will vote for party candidates anyway), the marketing competition increasingly played for the votes of those elusive independents in the middle.

Concentrating candidate competition on the voters in the middle of the former party spectrum further weakened the abilities of both parties (but particularly the Democrats in the early years) to develop distinctive party visions. Even if they had one, it would discourage them from advertising it. Thus, the first major change was in the voter market itself. Today's voter alignment is roughly as follows.[12]

Democratic voters (who vote less often than their Republican counterparts): 35 percent

Independent voters (including those with weak "leanings" toward one party or the other): 35 percent

Republican voters (who vote more often than their Democratic counterparts): 30 percent

At this point it is irresistible to ask whether the Republicans fully capitalized on the Democrats' marketing dilemma. Although the Reagan landslides of the 1980s would urge us to give an easy answer of "yes," caution is advised. Many pundits (most notably the conservatives) who declared the Republicans triumphant in the 1980s ushered in the 1990s with gloomy prospects—including more than a few urgings for the GOP to "declare bankruptcy." (For more on this subject, see Chapter 7.) Hindsight always being easier than prediction, it is possible to see that the Republicans did not succeed in swinging many independent voters to their side of the party loyalty line—and to explain why.

Unlike the declining Democrats, the resurgent Republicans did offer a governing vision. Ironically, it was a vision that eventually fell prey to marketing and money forces that at first seemed to favor the Republican cause. Beginning with Richard Nixon and continuing with the presidencies of Ronald Reagan and George Bush, Americans were invited to join the Republicans for a trip back to "Morning in America" (Reagan's view of it). This society was hyped as one held together by traditional morality, in which citizens would not be burdened with a big-spending government taxing them to death, because the dawning of the New Federalism (Nixon and Reagan each attempted different versions of this "program") would restore power to states and localities and hold big government in check.

Although for a time it appeared that this vision would sweep the Republicans into a new governing coalition backed by enduring voter support, the emerging political scenario for the 1990s suggests a different picture. The stubborn independent voter bloc is holding. A nonvoting majority (or near majority in presidential years) makes it hard to talk about governing "mandates." The Democratic lock on Congress appears more secure than ever, and a conservative Supreme Court may continue to dismantle the old liberal vision while playing havoc with any attempts to forge a new one. As for the New Federalism, significant responsibilities were shifted back to states and localities, but promises to discipline the national government were clouded by a number of factors, including an increase in federal regulations on how states were to manage their reduced allocations; an unprecedented spending spree and national budget crisis; unpopular efforts to cut entitlement programs like social security and medicare while defense spending soared; tax cuts and reforms that did little for the middle classes while favoring the rich; and a growing collection of local problems including health care, education, homelessness, and various tax, budget, and service crises. One result of the New Federalism was to turn many states into lobbying organizations with branch offices in Washington. (At last count California had more than seventy Washington "offices.") The more important result, however, was the impact of rhetoric versus reality on the public. A look back from the 1990s reveals a steady erosion of support in the opinion polls for the policies and programs that actually flowed from the new Republican vision.[13]

It would be misguided to say that the Republican vision was simply wrong or inherently unworkable, for either verdict generally reflects some combination of ideological bias and circular reasoning. This is the same kind of reasoning that claims that successful political visions were inherently logical and workable, while failed visions were not. Rather, it is more interesting to consider the possibility that the same system of forces that blocked the emergence of a Democratic vision ultimately blew the Republican political dream apart. Understanding the reasons why requires adding the next element of the system. To the marketing chase we now add the *money game*. Let's pick up the story again, going back to the promising-looking Republican landslide of 1972.

A simple "snapshot" of that grand but ultimately lost Republican opportunity might show the Democrats busily shooting themselves in the left foot, while the Republicans under Richard Nixon were shooting themselves in the right. Although Nixon survived four more years of the Vietnam War to win handily in 1972, he did not survive his own venom against his political critics. Using a system of campaign finance (and here we get to the next chapter of our story) that resembled the old tithing or assessment scheme from the Mark Hanna days, the Republicans amassed a political fortune that it socked away in foreign bank accounts and often delivered to party "bag men" in cash. In what has been described as a shakedown racket, both wealthy individuals and corporations were pressured to give 1 percent of their net worth in the case of private parties and 1 percent of annual sales in the case of corporations.[14] Much of this money was used to fund illegal activities that included spying on the Democrats and a host of other political opponents. By the time the ensuing scandal was over, dozens of companies, top executives, White House officials, party employees, and Nixon campaign workers were found guilty of illegal activities. As for the commander-in-chief, Mr. Nixon resigned and rode out of town ahead of an impeachment posse. But the legacy left behind still haunts the Republicans.

To an extent we will never know precisely, the spectacle of power and corruption seen on television daily during the Watergate hearings halted independent voters in their tracks, at least temporarily heading off any grand migration to the Republican side. Even a temporary halt in a possible Republican conversion was important for the formation of a new election system. Millions who had just voted for Nixon learned the seamy details of how the Committee to Re-Elect the President—or CREEP as it not so affectionately became known—channeled millions of dollars in unmarked bills into White House spying efforts against the president's political enemies. Those activities involved break-ins, burglaries, buggings, and political sabotage against people whom White House officials believed to oppose their political goals. One of those presumed enemies turned out to be the Democratic party and its candidate, George McGovern.

When a team of burglars was caught at Democratic party headquarters in the Watergate office and condominium complex in Washington, in 1972, the whole scheme began to unravel, and the nation was transfixed by what came to be known as the "Watergate scandal." For nearly two years the public followed the media spectacle of spying, wiretapping, political extortion, laundering of campaign funds, and flagrant disregard for (if not intentional subversion of) the principles of democratic politics. In the wake of Vietnam and the demise of the Democrats, a weary public now watched what looked like the self-destruction of the Republicans. Again, it is impossible to know how many independents were halted in the middle of the road by those distressing events, but rising levels of general distrust of parties and politicians following Watergate suggest that many probably were. What is clear, however, is that after Watergate a fundamental change in the structure of American politics occurred: campaign finance reform. Under Ronald Reagan, the Republicans would rebound from the Watergate scandal, but despite some early heady success they would discover the difficulties of cornering the voter market in a new era of campaign finance reform.

Campaign Finance Reform and the Power of PACs

First, a brief history of political finance reform. (Don't worry, this is one of the shortest histories around.) Seeking to distance himself from the scandals of the Mark Hanna era, Teddy Roosevelt made a show of giving some corporate donations back in 1904 and promised to reform the system. The Tillman Act finally appeared in 1907, setting limits on corporate contributions but merely winking at enforcement. Companies blithely gave "raises" to their executives, who passed them along as personal contributions to politicians. The scandals returned with a vengeance in the 1920s when the Harding administration made it a practice of selling government posts and favors to the highest bidder. The Federal Corrupt Practices Act of 1925 made vague gestures at establishing spending limits and recordkeeping, but contained little in the way of serious reporting, accounting, or enforcement procedures. As a result, not much changed in the hazy world of political high finance. However, the 1929 shakeup in the economy itself brought a serious round of political reforms aimed at curbing the worst abuses of big business through direct government regulation. In the process, considerable amounts of political money were redistributed between the two parties.[15]

After the Second World War and continuing into the 1960s, a growing list of problems plagued the political system as a result of a haphazard campaign funding process. Among the troubles that finally moved Congress to take another stab at reform were the huge personal fortunes spent by wealthy individuals and families (e.g., the Kennedys and Rockefellers) to establish political dynasties; the misfortunes of candidates who had neither personal wealth nor the backing of party fat cats (several presidential campaigns of this era lived hand-to-mouth, incurring large debts for candidates like Harry Truman in 1948 and Barry Goldwater in 1964); and last but not least, the shakedown tactics of the Nixon regime which struck many Democrats in Congress as scandalous, not to mention politically threatening. Over the objections of Nixon and many other Republicans, work began in the late 1960s on the Federal Election Campaign Act. After securing agreements not to put its provisions into effect until 1976 (when his allowable time in public office would be over), Richard Nixon signed the bill into law in 1971.

In the meantime, the CREEP abuses of 1972 made the 1971 legislation calling for modest federal election subsidies and better reporting procedures look like another cosmetics job. With an election scandal too large for cosmetic treatment and the Democrats smarting under the double blast of the Nixon attack and the voter retreat, Congress settled down to more serious reform business and passed a series of amendments to the 1971 law. The Federal Election Campaign Act of 1974 (FECA) created the basic campaign finance structure that we know today: (1) detailed public reporting of contributions, (2) limits on individual contributions, (3) federal matching funds for presidential candidates, (4) limits on how much personal money candidates can spend (amended in 1976), and (5) creation of a Federal Election Commission to watch over the system, along with criminal and civil penalties for violations. This system was adjusted several more times, beginning in 1976, after the Supreme Court ruled in the case of (U.S. Senator James) *Buckley* v. *Valeo* that it was unconstitutional on First Amendment/free speech grounds to limit the total amount of personal candidate spending in a campaign.[16] As a result, Congress passed a 1976 amendment to FECA that established the principle of voluntary spending limits. This means that presidential candidates who voluntarily accept federal funding for their campaigns must also accept the campaign spending limits attached to that funding. A second major amendment came in 1979 when the parties realized that all the emphasis on giving money to individual candidates further threatened the viability of parties. The 1979 amendments to FECA permitted broader roles for state and local party branches in national elections, and authorized unlimited PAC and individual donations to party activities "unrelated" to specific candidate races.

On paper, these reforms looked pretty tough. Indeed, compared to the freewheeling money madness of the past, they were very strict. In addition, the FECA reforms spared weak national presidential candidates the occasional indignity of begging for money to keep campaigns going. The combination of finance reforms and the party nomination reforms that preceded them even enabled relative outsiders like Jimmy Carter to have a shot at the highest national office. Debates have arisen about whether this sort of opening up of the top political office without a disciplining party structure around the lucky winner is desirable.[17] Nonetheless, the larger point is that underneath all the positive aspects of the reforms was a loophole big enough to push a Trojan horse through. This loophole—PACs—interacted with other political conditions of the times to create a new electoral system.

The Federal Election Campaign Act of 1974 permitted business, labor, and other groups to form political action committees for the express purpose of channeling money to candidates, parties, and campaigns. On the face of it, the PAC provisions looked innocent enough. For example, no PAC could contribute more than $5,000 to a single candidate, and in practice most PACs do not give even that much to many candidates. Many saw it as only a drop in the bucket at the presidential level, and not much more than that at the congressional level, but American politics is still reeling from the millions of drops that turned into a downpour of political pressure.

As we will see, even the $5,000 PAC contribution has its effect, but it is important to realize that these limited contributions to individual candidates are just one part of the larger system. As politicians, interest organizations, corporations, and lawyers began to understand the possibilities contained in the fine print, several creative developments occurred with PACs. The first creative innovation was the discovery that individual candidates could allow PACs to be created for them, thus amassing huge personal war chests, collecting political favors by giving large sums to other candidates, and, in many cases, saving the balances as fat retirement funds when the days in public office were over. But that is another story. The model of the candidate PAC in our story was Ronald Reagan's Citizens for the Republic. Years in advance this committee raised millions to launch Reagan's 1980 candidacy. In addition, the Reagan PAC gave millions to other Republican candidates, personalizing the Republican party financially and, it seemed, ideologically. It was a model that nearly all major national politicians were soon to emulate. The list of personalities in both parties who have since formed their own so-called "leadership" PACs to promote their political fortunes reads like a "Who's Who" of American politics.[18]

The second creative innovation was the discovery that it was legal for independent PACs to form and to pour unlimited amounts of money into campaigning for (or against) candidates as long as the PAC was not directly or legally connected with the candidate's campaign committee. ("Direct" links are, of course, easy enough to avoid.) The model for independent PACs was the National Conservative Political Action Committee (NCPAC) which spent millions for and against candidates in pursuit of its agenda of moral issues. Following the success of NCPAC, other "independents" popped up around agendas as diverse as guns, medicine, conservation, and abortion.

The third creative innovation was the 1979 amendment to the law that opened the door for state and national parties to raise (and PACs to give) unlimited amounts of what has become known as soft money to the political parties for help with voter registration and organization-building activities. Again, the donations cannot be earmarked for a particular campaign or candidate, but, such fine lines are often hard to draw in practice. The model for soft support by PACs was pioneered years ahead of the 1970s reforms with labor union support for the Democrats through the AFL–CIO Committee on Political Education (COPE). COPE also mounted independent efforts for the Democratic cause in the form of voter registration and get-out-the-vote drives. However, FECA opened the door to a flood of soft support from newly formed PACs to state and national party organizations.

The ultimate irony is that these laws, though aimed at curbing personal and corporate (direct) contributions to campaigns, in the end created a "money engine" capable of pumping previously unimagined amounts of money into the political system. But the final plot twist in our story is the way all that money has undermined any broad political consensus in the system. Special interest money is indispensable to political success, yet any base of special interest support for a broad political vision is inherently unstable, requiring the use of media management techniques to disguise, and marketing methods to repair, continual fissures and defections in such support.

Consider just one of the many ways in which PAC pressures undermine institutional support for governing ideas: In Congress, even small contributions add up. A few thousand dollars may not seem like much, but the average incumbent's political career depends on his or her ability to keep hundreds of PACs making their small contribution each year. Suppose, for example, that Senator Truegood needs to raise $6 million for the next election. That translates into $1 million a year over the six-year term, or around $3,000 that must be raised every day of each of those six years, weekends and holidays included. Suddenly those small PAC donations start to make sense. Just as suddenly, it becomes clear that even if U.S. representatives cannot promise their votes in advance, neither can they afford to turn PAC representatives away from their office doors very often.

Next, factor in the power of big PACs that have the resources to shower funds on dozens or even hundreds of representatives each year. Just to cite one example, the American Telephone and Telegraph PAC gave over $1 million to virtually every member of both parties in Congress in 1988.[19] With all the key votes "wired," so to speak, it becomes easier to secure passage of legislation and, more importantly, regulations affecting an industry. Now, consider that not only can a large industry or a group of related industries create PACs representing different companies (and subsidiaries), but also that these "overlapping" PACs can concentrate their collective contributions. In the defense industry, for example, individual companies may be competitive when bidding on specific contracts, but there is no better way to ease the pain of competition than an increased overall budget for defense spending. During the heyday of military spending in the 1980s, Congress and the president turned on the afterburners on defense spending, and the defense PACs generously subsidized both political parties. One study showed that 82 percent of all military contracts in 1987 went to one-third of the states with the 11 percent of key legislators who served on the Senate and House Armed Services and Defense Appropriations committees. Those lucky legislators received millions in defense–PAC campaign contributions for the billions they awarded in defense contracts.[20]

Any direct exchange of campaign dollars for national priorities is, of course, scandalous, not to mention illegal. But many members of Congress are coming to precisely such conclusions.[21]

> "The only reason it isn't considered bribery is that Congress gets to define bribery."
>
> "If you give a dog a bone, he'll be loyal forever. And if you give a congressman some money, he may not fetch your slippers for you, but he'll always be there when you need him."
>
> "I fear we could become a coin-operated Congress. Instead of two-bits, you put in $2,500 and pull out a vote."
>
> "I take money from labor, and I have to think twice in voting against their interest. I shouldn't have to do that."
>
> "More and more on the floor I hear people say, 'I can't help you. I've gotten $5,000 from this group.' "

The point of this discussion is not to debate whether defense spending is a boondoggle, or tobacco subsidies are silly, or junk food legislation is junk. The question, rather, is whether any semblance of governing is possible when the governors are being pulled from so many sides at once, by so many narrowly defined and often utterly unrelated interests. Perhaps Senator Robert Dole (R-Kansas) has made the point best: "When these political action committees give money, they expect something in return other than good government. It is making it difficult to legislate. We may reach a point where everybody is buying something with PAC money. We cannot get anything done."[22] And yet Senator Dole has been one of the most successful of all in playing the PAC game.[23] Therein lies the essence of the system.

Now, consider another PAC dynamic that makes it difficult to maintain institutional support for governing visions: In Congress and the White House, they're all leaders, not followers. Add to the divisive forces outlined above, a system of personal PACs in which individual politicians allow funds to be gathered for their own campaign efforts. In Congress, this means that dozens of powerful leaders accumulate huge financial bases independent of the political parties. Those with presidential aspirations may even rival (or try to capture) party organizations so they can control the financial rewards given to supportive colleagues as well as the punishments meted out to competitors. If we factor in the capacity of independent PACs to work alongside politicians who support their pet issues, we see the rise of feuding political fiefdoms within Congress, the executive, and the parties themselves. No wonder that anyone or any party that emerges from this system claiming to have broad political ideas ends up sustaining those claims with illusions created by marketing and media management techniques.

The best illusion of all was sustained for nearly a decade by Ronald Reagan who promoted the new Republican vision of a return to traditional morality, a small and fiscally responsible national government, and the restoration of local powers through the Reagan brand of New Federalism. This is not to deny that Reagan left his mark on the government; in fact, he shook things up considerably. The question we should ask is whether he left behind a continuing policy agenda guided by that early vision—an agenda that had the party support, the institutional power base (particularly in Congress), and the voter loyalty to keep it going. From the perspective of the 1990s, the answer is "no" on all three counts. Let's examine why.

In the early years of the so-called Reagan revolution, the Republicans came close to capturing all three institutions of government; if they had done so, they might have implemented their vision more fully. The problem is that, even if they *had* captured the institutions, the methods required under the newly emerging system of politics would have left them implementing a governing vision of rather dubious legitimacy. Anything resembling a stable political realignment or a political sea change under the new electoral system would have required the Republicans to win decisively both the money game and the marketing chase over the Democrats in the 1980s. Even if they had done so, the results would have been strange in at least two respects: the effective elimination of any semblance of party competition from national politics, and the subsequent implementation of a policy agenda voted in by less than 30 percent of the eligible electorate. Capturing the government through success at the money game and the marketing chase rather than through the traditional methods of attracting broad voter support and party loyalty would have required considerable *media management* skills to suppress questions about the legitimacy of the resulting governing vision.

As it turned out, this scenario did not emerge. Although the Democrats initially appeared baffled by the changing rules of the electoral game, they eventually proved smart enough to produce a stalemate, if not a victory, for their side. What happened to the Republican governing vision of the 1980s, to put it simply, is that the Democrats finally learned how to play the money game, and then they figured out how to play the marketing chase well enough at least to capture Congress. The result was the institutionalization of a national veto system grinding away at what was left of the Republican vision. Not that the Democrats had a vision to offer in its place. But never mind, this veto system would have dismantled any emerging vision simply by protecting all the special interests whose money keeps the Democrats in power.

As a result, Reagan relied increasingly on media management to sustain the illusion of a viable political vision, even as its substance was wearing thin. Eventually, the media management wore thin, too, as scandals and policy failures took their toll on the administration. Scholars and pundits may long debate whether the Republican vision failed because it was cynical and flawed by too many false promises and insider deals, or whether it fell prey to an inherently unmanageable political system. What seems more clear, however, is that, as the last political vision on the national horizon fades from government, the veto system that rose in its place will continue. And so begins the final historical change that brought about a new electoral system.

The Rise of a National Veto System
and the Decline of the New Republican Vision

Not surprisingly, many people were quick to declare the institutionalization of a new Republican regime, when in fact all that the Reagan Republicans and their PAC allies had done was to get a big jump on the Democrats in figuring out the new system. Indeed, many of the Republican warning signs in the early stages of the new system were hard to read and thus easily ignored. Meanwhile, many other signs clearly pointed to trouble for the Democrats. The Republicans had a vision, and the Democrats did not. The Reagan victories in 1980 and 1984 were big ones. Democrats in Congress were on the run, even losing control of the Senate for a time. The Republican party in alliance with independent PACs like the National Conservative Political Action Committee launched sophisticated and initially successful campaigns against Democratic incumbents on a broad moral agenda of prayer in school, abortion, school integration, civil rights, law and order, sex, drugs and, yes, even rock 'n' roll.

Disorganized and clearly outmaneuvered electorally, in the early years the opposition party offered little legislative resistance to the Reagan agenda. It appeared that the combination of New Federalism and old morality was on an unstoppable political roll. Indeed, when Reagan later made appointments that tilted the Supreme Court in his ideological direction, many experts on American politics began to lean toward a declaration that a political realignment was taking place. In edging toward this declaration, Walter Dean Burnham, for example, reasoned that:

What happens in these realignments is often not success in disposing of the crisis source that gave birth to them [referring to the earlier Democratic New Deal failure to "solve" the depression and the Republican abolitionist failure to peacefully solve the slavery crisis] *but success in capturing the intellectual high ground, in authoritatively defining the agenda of politics, and in organizationally building a revolution by institutionalizing it.* To a very striking extent, this is just what Reagan and a now thoroughly Reaganized Republican party have been able to do at decisively important levels of presidential and, increasingly, judicial politics.[24] [Emphasis added]

Yet as we will see in the next chapter, Burnham was uneasy about pushing his own analysis too far. And for good reason. His and other interpretations of the Republican realignment were based largely (and understandably so) on assumptions that the old American political system—the one with voters, parties, and institutions capable of becoming committed to visions—still existed. All along the way from 1980 to date, however, coexisting with the familiar signs pointing to Republican realignment was another set of rather confusing and unfamiliar signs that did not point that way. The trouble was that in order to make sense of those trouble signs in the Republican vision, it was necessary to see that the political system itself was changing in fundamental ways. Indeed, even the Republicans appeared to be unable to figure out the warning signs until it was too late. The Reagan crusade marched ahead as though the new system of money, media, and marketing could be played for the same results as the old system of at least somewhat disciplined parties, loyal voters, and ideologically organizable institutions.

Ferguson and Rogers were among the first analysts to recognize the existence of unsettling signs all along.[25] However, they also tended to interpret those signs in the context of the old system, claiming that the Democrats paved the way for the Republican renaissance by moving to the right in pursuit of campaign money, and thereby abandoning many liberal constituents who continued to share the old Democratic vision. This conclusion overlooks the first big step toward the new system, namely, the many voters who had long since abandoned the old Democratic vision to declare their independence of political parties. Moreover, the idea of a Democratic right turn fails to explain how the party began turning back to its old liberal agenda by the beginning of the 1990s, despite even deeper commitments to the same money sources. What probably did happen is that the Democratic entry into the money chase turned the party into a veto bloc, a loose-knit organization that came to wield electoral power without vision.

What is important first of all is to see that very early on cracks and fissures appeared in the Republican vision, and, second, to understand how they grew into major faults. To their credit, Ferguson and Rogers provide a good analysis on the first score, showing that from the beginning public opinion ran moderately to strongly against almost every item on the Reagan legislative agenda in those early years. Moreover, during those same years of greatest legislative success, Reagan's personal popularity was strikingly low—certainly not high enough to justify the heroic labels that vocal supporters pinned on him, and that a well-managed press passed along.[26] In addition, the Reagan landslides of 1980 and 1984, along with the victories of party candidates in campaigns centering on the moral agenda of prayer, patriotism, and abortion, were tempered by exceedingly low and declining voter turnouts. Similarly, claims of a Republican mandate were contradicted by small gains (around 5 percent) in voter declarations of Republican loyalty during the 1980s, while the solid independent middle held firm.[27]

To this already impressive set of mixed signals, we may add yet another confusing sign: some key items on the Reagan political agenda were defeated by opposition from groups that were otherwise supportive of Reagan and his visionary rhetoric. For example, senior citizens successfully resisted administration efforts to cut social security and medical benefits. Although many conservative seniors might have been counted among an emerging governing coalition, they resented attacks on programs they regarded as sacred entitlements. As poll results introduced in Chapter 7 show, otherwise supportive members of the middle class would become less enthusiastic about tax cuts that gave them a few hundred dollars when it became clear that corporations were being given hundreds of millions. By the end of the Reagan era, not even an out-and-out media campaign could drum up middle-class support for a tax reform that to many seemed to bear more similarities to the delivery of silent promises made by both parties to corporate America than to the much heralded middle-class economic vision. Indeed, the wholesale delivery of silent promises is precisely what ate away at the Republican vision both from within the party and, more importantly, from the Democratic opposition.

A correct reading of these signs as they began to emerge was difficult, in part, because the new election system that would give them meaning was being born at the same time. Sign-reading was all the more difficult because what emerged in the mass media over the same period was a picture of an invincible leader striding ahead of a national political reformation. To some extent, the prevailing media image surely resulted from the now legendary White House management efforts to put a favorable administration "spin" on the daily news. But this was far from the whole story. In addition, members of the administration simply ignored or avoided early press efforts to question the administration policy agenda, leaving the media looking like a pack of howling but ineffectual wolves. Perhaps most important of all, however, the Democrats were on the run ·and were unable to mount much of a vocal (much less legislative) opposition to the administration agenda.

For better or worse, most of the critical content of the news in the American press system is introduced when there is a strong vocal opposition (i.e., elite opinion is divided) within the government itself.[28] In the Reagan years, not only were the Democrats unfocused and unable to provide the media with a sustained critical voice, but also the Republicans and their independent PAC allies quickly realized the public relations advantages of silencing the opposition. Throughout the Reagan presidency, a team made up of the White House, the Republican party, and their independent PAC allies ran local campaigns in home districts against members of Congress who opposed the Reagan policy agenda. In summary, the early weaknesses in the Republican vision were disguised by one of the most sophisticated media management campaigns in history that included a three-tiered strategy: (1) almost daily White House orchestration and coordination of news events, (2) a disciplined refusal of the president and other administration officers to engage with press criticism when it emerged, and (3) the electoral intimidation of political opponents of the administration, effectively silencing the most common channel for opposing views to enter the news.[29]

The illusion of Republican invincibility continued to grow, following the economic recovery that boosted Reagan's personal popularity after 1983. A tax cut that same year put money in middle-class pockets, offering short-lived but timely tangible evidence that the Reagan revolution was at last beginning to pay economic dividends. Ironically, at this point between 1983 and 1984 when things looked unstoppable for the Republican vision, the fissures that had been there all along turned into deep cracks in the political foundation itself.

The turning point came when the Democrats learned to play the money game and then turned their newfound fortunes into successful marketing efforts for congressional candidates. This turnaround surely would not have been possible if large numbers of independent voters had sided with the Republican vision, declared party loyalty, and begun voting against Democrats as a matter of principle. As it happened, the Republican "landslide" victories of the 1980s occurred within the rather confined limits of a declining, independent-minded electorate. As a result, all these sophisticated marketing efforts produced about as many Republican votes as possible within those limits. The bottom line is that some combination of Reaganomics, the New Federalism, and the conservative moral agenda gained popularity among a minority of the eligible electorate, but never achieved enough popularity to boost turnouts or convert large numbers of independent voters into Republicans. As a result, the Republican vision was vulnerable in precisely the same terms on which it was built: money and marketing.

At this juncture the Democratic money game came into play. After losing its grip in the Senate, the party realized that only one institution— the House of Representatives—stood in the way of Reagan achieving an institutional monopoly to secure passage of his agenda. (The Supreme Court was already going Reagan's way.) Beginning in 1982, the Democrats under the leadership of since-disgraced Tony Coelho began approaching the PACs and suggesting that an organized Democratic resistance in the House could create a lot of trouble for PACs who did not support party candidates. The PACs responded much like a business community buying into a protection racket—which, in a sense, is just what it was. By 1984 the Democrats were in a financial position to regroup. Although they still lost the congressional election game that year, they won the PAC game, with a healthy advantage of 57 to 43 percent of PAC contributions going to Democratic candidates. Even corporate America was coming around, with 38 percent of its donations going to Democrats by 1984, despite the more obvious ideological alliance between the corporate sector and the Reagan economic agenda. By 1988, the trend was crystal clear: for the first time in the history of the new PAC system, a majority of corporate PAC money and an even heftier majority of nonbusiness PAC financing were going to the Democrats.[30]

As a result of this sudden balancing of financial power in the new system, the Democrats were for the first time able to enter the marketing chase on an equal footing with the Republicans, and they did it successfully enough to win back their majority in the Senate. In the process, Congress was effectively turned into a veto institution, capable of blocking not just the rest of the Republican vision (culminating with George Bush finally being forced to move his lips on taxes in the budget battle of 1990), but virtually any broad vision for any party or group that threatened the hundreds of special interest commitments on which the Democratic power base depended.

With the financial foundations of their own political agenda thus exposed, it would not take long for the Republicans in Congress to begin going back on their commitments to different aspects of the party vision. George Bush was even deserted by his own party whip in the House after the president changed his stand on taxes. Talk quickly surfaced about challenges in 1992 from within the party against the president who had looked so invincible after his victory in 1988. With the addition of the veto system to the existing configuration of PACs and independent voters, the George Bush Story, like all stories in the new political era, has three morals: Live by the money game, die by the money game; Live by the marketing chase, die by the marketing chase; Live. . . . Well, you get the idea. Only his victory in the war against Iraq restored Mr. Bush's illusory and elusive political fortunes.

With the money advantage moving to the Democrats in Congress, the Republicans were in confusion and experiencing related trouble forging any kind of domestic political agenda. This turn of events seemed to surprise even some party insiders. Meanwhile, Bush seemed content to cast his personal political fortunes as world leader: after invading Panama, sending the largest post–World War II military deployment to Saudi Arabia, and personally dropping in on much of the rest of the world, the president ultimately sent those deployed troops into war against Iraq. It is debatable whether Bush would have been so eager to go to war against Iraq if his domestic political situation had not started to deteriorate so dangerously.

After the president went off on his own foreign policy course, those still loyal to the dying Republican vision remained behind, shaking their heads and sometimes their fists at the party's misfortunes. Perhaps some sincerely misread the warning signs all along, thinking wishfully that the new combination of money, media, and marketing could sustain a governing vision as well as the old combination of voters, parties, and principled leaders. Republican dismay was summed up most bluntly by one of the House conservatives who helped create the original corporate PAC base for the Republicans. Representative Guy Vander Jagt of Michigan once traveled the country persuading corporations to form PACs with the provocative claim that a company without a PAC was un-American. Now that he began to read the political signs more clearly, Vander Jagt declared that "The PACs are whores."[31]

Why should this discovery have come as a surprise? With very few exceptions, PACs are formed not in pursuit of principle, but out of concern to protect the narrowest of special interests. Why should PACs give money if they do not get results? Thus, after it really got up and running, the PAC system created a veto system capable of blocking the implementation of most principled visions that conflict with the narrowly defined interests that keep the system going.

Although the effectiveness of this veto system did not become fully apparent until the budget crisis of 1990 when Bush did his famed flip-flop on taxes (see Chapter 7), the first clear signs that the system was operative came much earlier, in 1986 with the Reagan push for tax reform. Seeking to deliver on a 1984 campaign promise of a fair tax system, while offering something tangible to preserve the loyalty of the middle-class/business coalition to the Republican cause, the Great Communicator launched a media campaign as grand as any he would initiate during his eight-year presidency. Yet his rhetorical promise of a tax system that would be fair to average Americans contrasted almost daily in news accounts to the special interests lining up at the doors of both parties in Congress.

With a revitalized Democratic opposition (even if it was only a veto bloc), the news could now sustain another story to counter the president's rhetoric. It soon became clear that Reagan was having as much trouble getting the cooperation of his own party leadership as that of the Democrats. After a season of bargaining and interest-protecting that exposed the fragile political reality behind Reagan's rhetorical vision, a tax plan was finally passed (largely because neither party could face the next election being labeled as the one opposed to tax reform). Many pundits and more than a few scholars initially expressed pleasant surprise at the outcome; they were less discouraged by the specter of congressional feudalism than encouraged by the idea that Congress was still able to act at all.[32]

Yet the public quickly realized that there was little substance behind the rhetorical claims by either party that each was defending the middle class against the special interest vultures on the other side of the aisle. Throughout the year-long reform process, the public was moved neither by Reagan's language of fairness nor by either party's claim to being the true defender of the people against the PACs. Within a few years, when actual tax bills hit millions of American homes, people concluded that they had not been skeptical enough about all that rhetoric. After the tax reality was experienced, opinion polls showed people increasingly disillusioned with the reforms. They regarded the new system as, at best, no better than the old and, at worst, less fair.[33]

What are we to make of all this? First, we see that the electorate, too, has become part of the veto system, deeply suspicious of candidate promises during elections and of government policies in between. A prickly, disloyal, hard-to-convince electorate means that the politics of the 1990s (barring reform or system-changing upheaval) will rely increasingly on marketing—both for candidates and for policies. This means that the system will require more money—and so the cycle continues.

In addition to Congress and the voters, there is a third veto bloc in the new system: the Supreme Court. With its Reagan–Bush appointees the Court may go on dismantling the old liberal (civil rights, abortion, economic regulation) agenda while blocking new ones. The presidency, too, may become just another veto in this system, blocking any visions emerging from Congress and concentrating on foreign policy as the only career-building option for incumbents disconnected from a party base on the domestic policy front in Congress.

In brief, we have the multisided, crosswise pull we talked about at the opening of the book. "But," said a skeptical colleague who heard a version of this argument, "that is just good old Madisonian democracy carried to its logical extreme." The original system, after all, was designed to hold factions in check. Perhaps at this ripe old age as a Republic, the United States has simply succeeded in completing the Madisonian vision to the point of near governmental paralysis. Perhaps. But while Madison's Constitution was designed to hold warring social groups at bay, a principled national leadership was envisioned forging economic and foreign policy, while strong state governments were busy managing the domestic life of a much simpler society. Today, half the states are facing financial receivership, and we are living in a society more complex than even the visionary Madison could have imagined. Instead of a principled national leadership with the power to govern by keeping the factions at bay, the leadership has been captured by the factions themselves. Therefore, instead of leading and governing, elected officials cannot do much beyond getting themselves reelected, and in order to do that, they must fashion the most delicate kind of political promises: the kind they cannot possibly hope to keep.

MADISONIAN DEMOCRACY MEETS MADISON AVENUE

It is not surprising that people still try to interpret a transformed present as a natural extension of an old Madisonian past. Consider one view of the origins of the old system. Madison and most of the other Federalists really used the term *faction* as a euphemism for that most threatening single group in society: the masses of people with no property who might use democratic power to take over the wealth of society. In designing a system to limit this possibility, thanks to the twists and turns of history, the Founders ended up creating a system that checked all the other factions as well. Advocates of this interpretation of Madisonian democracy might argue that even a paralyzed system could be regarded as protecting the interests of the rich over the poor, not only because the status quo favors the rich, but also because in a veto system the most highly organized special interests are the wealthy propertied and commercial factions who can promote their interests better than the poorly organized, poor factions. Indeed, the income distribution figures over the last decade offer some crude support for this thesis. According to Congressional Budget Office analyses of the 1980s, the top 10 percent of American families gained more than 25 percent in real income (adjusted for inflation), while the bottom 10 percent lost more than 10 percent of their real income over the same period.[34]

For the sake of argument, suppose that the new system accomplishes at least this one goal of Madisonian democracy: protecting private property and the related economic prerogatives of the state from the vicissitudes of faction. Yet the new system also undermines the possibility of legitimate national leadership and governing visions in ways that Madison surely would have feared. Madison, though clever enough to design a system that kept factions in check, was not so cynical as to design one that cast its own leadership in doubt among its own people.

And so the paradoxes of the new system sit uneasily with the understandings we carry forward about the old. In one interesting analysis, Benjamin Ginsberg and Martin Shefter puzzle over the decline of parties and the disappearance of voters, and offer the hopeful possibility that government may be going on "by other means."[35] For example, people who leave the electoral system may be entering the interest group/PAC system. By spending money or working for organizations, people may have decided that if they can't beat the system, they'll join it. Indeed, there is evidence that support for interest organizations and PACs (including citizens' groups like Common Cause) stands at an all-time high.

Yet there is something distressing about a system in which citizens have become just another interest and must lobby in competition with thousands of others to promote something called the "public interest." In such a system, neither governing nor the public interest is likely to be served very well or very often. Instead, the more likely picture of government is that of a mad political scramble for short-term voter support. There remains just enough party organization to deliver the legislative vetoes (interest protection) needed to raise the money needed to keep marketing the votes. Those politicians who play the media, money, and marketing games skillfully will survive, while those who don't will disappear. Meanwhile, the tendency of the system requires that more energy be devoted to the communication strategies necessary, as Jarol Manheim put it in the title of his recent book, to fool *All of the People, All the Time*.[36]

This, in a sense, is the key. Whereas in the past, grand campaign promises were often broken, they were often kept, too. Some elaborate rhetorical visions fizzled when put to the test of public policy, but others succeeded in governing the nation. While American politics and elections seldom offered more than simple rhetoric, those simple ideas often turned out to mean a great deal (and in one case, a New Deal) to people. In the political system emerging in today's America, the common quality in most political communication is an eerie emptiness.

Yet the emerging system of American politics contains within it so many ghosts of the old that critics can still be heard saying that elections like 1988 or 1990 (see Chapter 7) do not represent a qualitative departure from the past. Promises are always broken, they say; rhetoric is always simplistic, voters are always lazy and apathetic. However, surrounding the ghostly reminders of elections and politics from the past is a new system that effectively makes the worst of the old about the best we can expect from the new. In the next chapter we respond to those critics who say that nothing important has changed.

CHAPTER 3

Wait! Hasn't It Always Been Like This?

Complaining about the quality of elections is as American as apple pie and as old as colonial times. No less a figure than George Washington was condemned for sleazy campaign practices in his prerevolutionary races for the House of Burgesses in Virginia. James Madison bemoaned the ways in which Washington and the other candidates "recommend themselves to the voters . . . by personal solicitation."[1] Among the most popular endorsements was that of John Barleycorn. On the use of alcohol to separate the voter from his vote, Madison observed: "On election day the flow of liquor reached high tide. . . . [D]uring a July election day in Frederick County in the year 1758, George Washington's agent supplied 160 gallons to 391 voters and 'unnumbered' hangers on. This amounted to more than a quart and a half a voter."[2] Madison's verdict on that political scene has been echoed through the ages, even as the nature of offending practices has changed from one era to the next: "[T]he corrupting influence of spiritous liquors and other treats [is] inconsistent with the purity of moral and republican principles."[3] The same might be said today about the corrupting influence of slick political advertising that appeals to unthinking passions, and about "other treats" like the promise of no new taxes when government is bending under the weight of huge budget deficits.

If questionable campaign practices can be traced all the way back to the father of the country, it is reasonable to ask what all the fuss is about. A critic might argue that our elections, if no better, are at least no worse than they ever were. By the end of this book, of course, I plan to demonstrate the errors of such thinking. However, much is to be gained from seeing how the decline of elections argument holds up against the strongest objections that might be lodged against it. In the process, we will take a look at some of America's fascinating electoral history and see if the complaints about recent elections truly stand the test of time.

At least three objections could be raised against characterizing present-day campaign content as nasty, brutish, and short. In ascending order of importance, these criticisms can be stated as follows:

Objection No. 1: The Good Times Theory. The elections of the last decade are just what we would expect them to be during a period of peace and prosperity. Far from culminating a trend of impoverished political ideas and unresponsiveness to public problems, the elections of the late 1980s (and at least up through 1990) were mere blips on the TV screen. They were perfectly predictable responses to a period of domestic prosperity and superpower harmony. The cold war was over, and the economy was relatively sound. What was there, after all, for the candidates to talk about?

Objection No. 2: The Hidden Issue Theory. There were really plenty of ideas, issues, and signs of candidate character to be found if only one bothered to look. As in every election year, sizable tracts of national forest land were sacrificed to print voluminous position papers and issue statements. The real problem is that the people just don't pay attention to them.

Objection No. 3: The "What You See Is All You Get" Thesis. American elections have always been shallow and issueless affairs, which means that the hype, the hoopla, and the horserace are what an election is all about. Eloquence and vision would be lost on the American voter.

RESPONDING TO THE OBJECTIONS

Elections are bad when the times are good. It is tempting to believe that the quality of American elections rises to the occasion of social crisis, so that we tend to get great leaders just when we need them. In this view, decisive contests, clear issues, and big voter turnouts emerge only in response to big national problems. This version of history is too neat and far too complacent. It makes little sense, in any event, to think of the recent era as one of untroubled complacency. To the contrary, we get a different picture of the times by looking beyond the optimism of a few national cheerleaders and taking the worries of the public seriously. As noted earlier, opinion polls at the turn of the 1990s showed majorities seriously concerned about a long list of national problems, not the least of which was a government captured by special interests. On the world front, lurking beneath the surface of reduced cold war tensions were worries about a perpetually oversized defense budget draining hopes for social programs. (These worries became even more realistic with the huge military involvement in the Middle East.) If we add to all these concerns the economic jitters of a badly leveraged economy and the specter of the last great political hope, the Reagan revolution, being ground down slowly by special interest veto politics, no one can conclude that the late 1980s and early 1990s were a trouble-free age. A better assessment is that the times were as troubled as many in the past and more strained than a number of earlier eras. The difference is that this time around, there was remarkably little national dialogue or organized grass-roots pressure for change.

Certainly, the social scene of the early 1990s was a far cry from the era a century and a half earlier when the French observer Alexis de Tocqueville described American political life with these words:

> The political activity that pervades the United States must be seen in order to be understood. No sooner do you set foot upon American ground than you are stunned by a kind of tumult. . . . To take a hand in the regulation of society, and to discuss it, is his biggest concern, and, so to speak, the only pleasure an American knows.[4]

Until recently, conflicting social visions have dominated nearly every era of American politics, beginning with the first struggles of the Federalists and Jeffersonians over political rights and the limits of government power in the early years of the Republic. In fact, a sweeping look at American electoral history by a distinguished group of historians and social scientists suggests that struggles over governing visions have characterized most periods in our history, including many with arguably greater claims to social harmony than our own times.[5] Consider just a few of the major governing debates of years past.

With the exception of the brief Era of Good Feelings, the first three decades of the Republic witnessed the rise of the first political parties; struggles over various institutional powers; the nullification crisis and states rights controversies; conflicts over a national banking and currency system; the rapid settlement of the frontier; struggles against property requirements for voting; and the strains of armed conflicts both abroad and at home. All these crises reverberated through political institutions in the form of great electoral debates and party alignments.

In the next era, a society ready to burst under the pressures of an expanding agrarian frontier and chafing under the dictates of a rapacious Eastern banking establishment elected Andrew Jackson in 1828. That contest marked the rise of the Democratic party, along with the emergence of grass-roots power in a fledgling American democracy. Jackson's reelection in 1832 became a national referendum on his veto of a congressional charter for banking czar Nicholas Biddle's Bank of the United States. The resulting (temporary) setback for paper or "rag" money favored the growth of frontier society with a hard currency or specie economy. These elections addressed some of the most important issues to confront the young Republic in its first half century.

The decades before the Civil War saw the importance of governing ideas grow to the point that parties began holding conventions and hammering out platforms. In 1840, for example, the Democrats forged the first recognizable platform around southern demands for limiting federal government powers. Platforms advocating the ideas that would eventually result in the Civil War were proposed in 1844, 1848, and 1852. The Whigs began responding with formal answers to the Democrats in 1844 and 1852.[6] Meanwhile, national debates on issues as fundamental as slavery, territorial expansion, and economic values drew the attention of the nation. Great rhetorical matches like the Lincoln–Douglas exchanges in the Illinois Senate race of 1858 drew national interest. Voting turnouts were high and the electoral struggles were intense.

Next came the critical election of 1860, which served as a tortured forum on the problem of slavery. The North–South conflict proved too big for an election to contain, as indicated by the fact that four candidates ran for president in that contest. In effect, there was one race between Lincoln and Douglas in the North and another between Bell and Breckinridge in the South. Lincoln was roundly vilified by the others and by much of the national press as well, being called a scoundrel, hatchet-faced, a "horse swapper," a "nutmeg dealer," and a man fit for petty treason who would spoil the great office for all decent white men to follow.[7] Although he carried the electoral college easily, Lincoln won only 40 percent of the popular vote and had little legitimacy anywhere in the South. Shortly after the electoral college results were announced, South Carolina seceded from the Union, and other states soon followed, whereupon Lincoln made his fateful decision to lead the nation into war. Thus, a new direction was charted for the course of history.

During years of painful reconstruction, the North–South conflict became inscribed in the party system. To complicate matters further, the East–West struggle, long simmering since the Jackson years, came to a head again in 1896. A nation suffering under its first great industrial depression agonized over the nature of complex and wrenching new problems. Was it to be workers against capitalists? Or an agrarian society with a free money economy versus the Eastern establishment led by J. P. Morgan and his cozy banking deals guaranteeing the gold standard? Or was it tariffs against free trade? The Republicans readily settled on tariffs as a quick pitch to industrialists and workers alike. As mentioned in Chapter 2, the slogan "McKinley and a Full Dinner Pail" drew many workers into the Republican camp, particularly in response to the agonizing of the Democrats. After a long and divided convention that failed to agree on the problem that needed to be solved in order to pull the country from the pit of economic stagnation, the words of a young orator from Nebraska captured the moment.

William Jennings Bryan galvanized the Democratic convention with his impassioned speech favoring the free coinage of silver money. He proposed free silver as a platform plank aimed at protecting local economies from the tentacles of big banks. His stirring Cross of Gold speech, as it came to be called, sent the convention into pandemonium. His final words produced a thunderous roaring outburst: "You shall not press down upon the brow of labor this crown of thorns, you shall not crucify mankind upon a cross of gold." Bryan was hoisted on the shoulders of the crowd and paraded around the hall, creating a spectacle that led one Eastern delegate to remark, "For the first time, I can understand the scenes of the French revolution."[8]

Bryan was nominated by the Democrats and endorsed by the Populists, even though they feared (correctly, as it turned out) that his nostalgic vision of a rural farm society would drive many rootless urban workers into the arms of the Republicans. At thirty-six, Bryan became the youngest candidate ever to run for president. As tireless as he was eloquent, he whistle-stopped around the country delivering more than 600 campaign speeches (as noted in Chapter 2), but to little avail. His defeat left both the Democrats and the Populists in disorder, paving the way for a Republican-led era of unprecedented industrial expansion.

Like the two *critical elections*[9] that came before it, 1896 created the new political conditions necessary to change the course of history and to address growing social strains. These conditions usually include some combination of *strong new leadership* (Jackson in 1828, Lincoln in 1860), *a single party rising to dominate national institutions* (the Republicans in 1860 and 1896), and *voter loyalties* lining up behind the leading party for a generation or more. This combination of political forces creates the potential for a system easily paralyzed by its own checks and balances to take decisive actions to resolve intolerable social and economic tensions.

These solutions are not always heaven-sent, as the Civil War and the later excesses of laissez-faire capitalism suggest, but the point is that they move an unwieldly and conflicted political system beyond a sticking point. A new set of problems often emerges from the solutions to the old. Witness, for example, the legacy of civil rights problems since the Civil War, or the frightening loss of control over big business in the 1920s that ultimately resulted in the Great Depression beginning in 1929. It was in response to that last great social crisis that the holy trinity of political forces (leadership, single-party dominance of government, and realignment of voter loyalties) shifted again, shuffled the political cards, as it were, and issued a "New Deal." These political conditions necessary to move the nation in new directions emerged in the election of 1932. That contest produced the proper mix of leadership (Roosevelt), party dominance (Democrats), and lasting voter loyalties required to forge new policies (the New Deal) and take decisive actions to relieve terrific social strains. As a result, the country managed to emerge from the economic darkness, by way of entry into a second great war, and, at the time of Roosevelt's death, stepped into the dawn of its preeminence as a world power.

As noted in the last chapter, the shock waves of civil rights and white backlash, the loss in Vietnam, corruption in Washington, and prolonged economic recession all set the stage for Ronald Reagan's vision of social renewal. However, for all the reasons pointed out earlier, the vision faltered and ultimately fell apart. Although the first condition of governing was satisfied in the presence of strong leadership (Reagan), the other two conditions failed to materialize. First, the required party and ideological dominance of national institutions (particularly Congress) failed to happen. Second, and perhaps more importantly, the shift of voter loyalty and enthusiasm to the Republican camp also failed to take place. The result was that a society with tremendous social strains witnessed the defeat of one governing vision and then suffered a string of elections (1986, 1988, 1990) in which no visions or potential governing ideas emerged to arouse—much less, capture—the popular imagination. An awkward silence fell upon the land in place of a much needed exchange of ideas.

When we look back from this vantage, it appears that instead of a governing vision 1980 brought us a great communicator. This scenario therefore makes it difficult to point to 1980 as a critical election that set in motion a decisive political realignment. Rather than realignment, we witnessed the rise of the first truly postmodern president and the consolidation of a new system of campaigning that is likely to haunt us until either reform or disaster destroys it. For all the cracks in the political foundation beneath him, Ronald Reagan remains a fascinating figure with undeniable skills as a master of symbolism. Historians may conclude that he rode as tall in the symbolic saddle as Roosevelt did. That was no easy accomplishment considering the lack of a broadly supported social program to go along with the rhetoric. Perhaps it was the movie actor's instincts that made it all possible, while at the same time making his act so difficult for others to follow. Reagan lived a political career true to his own maxim:

"Politics is just like show business. You have a hell of an opening, you coast for a while, you have a hell of a closing."[10] In keeping with this inspiration, Reagan "communicated" his way to continuing popularity despite opposition to most of his specific policies, despite the growing social dislocation that resulted from those policies, and, perhaps even more impressively, despite the scandals that rocked his administration. While giving the nation a good show and managing to rescue his own popularity from the fires that burned all around him, Reagan did not leave behind much of a course-changing political legacy. Certainly it is not the sort of political legacy that would permit us to view 1984, 1988, or 1992 as mere political holding actions—holding to the bold new course charted in 1980.

A number of anomalies surround the post–1980 period. As noted in Chapter 2, the veto system wore down any forward-looking, strain-relieving programs or courses of action that might have emerged—unless, of course, one considers indebtedness, militarization, and the gutting of social programs to be stress-reducing measures. Next, far from realigning and solidifying voter loyalties, the legacy of the 1980s seems to be the large numbers of voters with divided loyalties: voting Republican for president and Democratic for Congress. Consequently, neither party amassed a concentration of power within the legislative branch to move the country decisively out of its social and economic ruts. This state of affairs would probably not have resulted if either party had presented a political vision grand or bold enough to capture the popular imagination. Failing to see such a vision, many voters simply left the political arena altogether. Here we have the last sign that 1980, for all its symbolic portent, was not a source of governing ideas leading to political realignment. The Reagan mandate of 1980 was delivered by less than 30 percent of those eligible to vote. The Bush victory of 1988 came on the wings of the smallest electoral turnout in sixty years—a figure that jumps to 164 years, as Burnham notes, when we look at voting patterns in the non-southern states where the majority of the people live. All these factors led Burnham to withhold 1980 from the pantheon of great American elections like 1832, 1860, 1896, and 1932.[11] So, the elections that came after can hardly be regarded as mere holding actions.

There is a second, much more vulgar good times argument that over-looks the broad political failure of the new Republican vision in favor of a narrower concern with the economic boom of the Reagan years. It is a scaled-down thesis that ignores the decaying social scene, the dark clouds of debt, and the overburdening military commitments. This narrow view is backed by an undeniably popular myth. All that voters really care about, according to this myth, is the short-term state of the economy, so there's no point in candidates sticking their necks out about anything else. This is a fascinating proposition because, if true, it means that the money, media, and marketing forces described in Chapter 2 are not so much the causes of our political disarray as the side effects of a sort of political dementia that rests almost entirely with the people themselves.

This blunt version of the good times thesis states that all the public wants is a regular paycheck and a stable dollar. Devil take the hindmost. If so, the money, media, and marketing ploys are not designed so much to shrink our universe of political choice as to pander to the already shrunken heads of the American people. It is admittedly tempting to think ill of the intellectual and moral reach of a people who watch eight hours of television a day, prefer the *National Enquirer* to the *New York Times,* and tune into "Wheel of Fortune" in greater numbers on a daily basis than to presidential debates that occur only once every four years. Still, the real question here is which came first—the shrunken heads or the head-shrinking political apparatus that currently cranks out electoral content by the numbers? Granted, such chicken-and-egg questions seldom resolve themselves into simple either–or answers. However, if even a small part of the national political decline can be attributed to an electoral system gone astray, then we have a place to begin pushing for reform. Without such reforms, there is little point in calling for the reformation of individual political souls by the millions. What would all those renewed spirits do when they contemplated the political wasteland before them?

A typical economic good times analysis of 1988, for example, was delivered in August of that year by a political analyst who looked at short-term economic indicators like unemployment (at 5.3 percent, it was the lowest in fourteen years) and inflation (a respectable 4 percent rise over the preceding year) and pronounced Bush unbeatable on those grounds alone: "If you cranked all this into a computer, it would tell you the Republicans can't lose."[12] While it is true that incumbent parties seldom lose the White House when the short-term indicators are up, and often lose when they are down, the unanswered question is "why?" Is it because that's all the voters care about? Or is it because voters are held hostage by politicians who threaten and promise them with little else than talk of economic well-being?

Actually, economic indicators like employment and inflation rates are among the few issues that are hard to disguise. People tend to notice the presence or absence of a paycheck, along with its purchasing power. As for promises of balancing the budget or winning the war on crime, these things are, after all, only promises. Why should people put any store in them, particularly when it is widely known that politicians are only saying these things to win votes in the first place? The idea here is that people vote on crude measures of personal well-being because they aren't given anything better. Period. Consider this evidence from an interesting article about the 1988 election written by political scientist and public opinion analyst Everett Carl Ladd. He asked, Why do elections reduce themselves so quickly to referendums on how well we're doing—especially economically? According to Ladd, people are aware of the long list of problems facing the country. In fact, polls show the public to be both aware and concerned about a host of national problems. The trouble is that *problems* do not automatically translate into *issues* on which people can make voting decisions. As Ladd puts it, "But problems aren't necessarily issues. A problem becomes an issue only when voters see the parties differing in their approach to it or their capacity to solve it."[13]

There it is. Since candidates and parties seldom address problems in ways that convince voters they really can or even want to do something to solve them, elections become vague referendums on "How well are we doing?" Or as Reagan put it, "Ask yourself 'Are you better or worse off than you were four years ago?' " This, as noted in Chapter 1, is one voting principle on which Ronald Reagan and most political scientists can agree: lacking other information, people tend to vote retrospectively, that is, by asking whether or not the incumbent president or party has left them better or worse off than they were when they last voted.[14] The important qualification here is that people vote retrospectively not because they prefer it, but because they have no other choice. Thus, we have become a nation of 240 million souls backing cautiously ahead with our eyes fixed squarely behind us.

A poll released about a month before election day, 1988, adds more evidence to this electoral law that voters make the best of what little substance they are given. The number of voters dissatisfied with "the way things are going" dropped to 45 percent from a May high of 55 percent. Meanwhile, the number satisfied with "the way things are going" soared from a May low of 39 percent to an October high of 50 percent.[15] These results were bad tidings for Dukakis and good news for Bush. But what would account for such a dramatic turn of the national mood? None of the key economic indicators had changed, and no major world events had intervened. The Yankees were not headed for the World Series. What was it? My guess is that voters had been holding their breath waiting for the candidates to propose any kind of credible response to the well-known list of national problems. By October, people were ready to turn blue, and the national breath eventually expired. Then the populace took a collective sigh, turned around, and prepared to back into another election. The view from behind was, after all, satisfying in the eyes of enough people to elect Bush.

What will come next, particularly when people abandon hope that the electoral arena will provide viable political solutions? This dangerous scenario left political scientist Burnham unable to offer anything more optimistic than an intellectual shrug: "Perhaps time *never* runs out for the United States."[16] Then, again, perhaps time is running out.

There were really plenty of issues. People just weren't paying attention to them. In the light of this objection, consider the case of George Bush, environmentalist. Bush's environmental positions entailed more than just posing in front of polluted Boston Harbor in an anti-Dukakis commercial or standing in waders hip-deep in a Wyoming trout stream. Were these his only gestures to environmentalism, we might accuse him of being . . . well, rather bush about the whole issue. To his credit, Bush the candidate proposed no fewer than a dozen specific measures to save the environment.

Bush cheerleader Martin Anderson (former domestic policy adviser to Ronald Reagan and later a senior fellow at the Hoover Institution) collected these policy positions into a single article that likened Bush's promised environmental impact, if elected, to that of Teddy Roosevelt. Anderson encouraged us to believe the candidate's oft-repeated line "I am an environmentalist; always have been and always will be." "Whenever he said that," said Anderson, "he wasn't kidding." As evidence for the sincerity of Bush's environmentalism, Anderson recalled Bush's twelve well-defined campaign policy statements on the subject. These included the following promises in the candidate's own words:[17]

> "I'm for a complete ban on the ocean dumping of sewage sludge after 1991 . . . I favor bringing in the FBI to track down those who dump medical waste illegally."
>
> "A Bush administration will enforce environmental laws aggressively, putting the responsibility for clean-up where it belongs—on those who caused the problem in the first place."
>
> "We must speed up the clean-up of toxic waste dumps . . ."
>
> "We must give a high priority to groundwater protection . . ."
>
> "If I am sworn in as your president, one of my first priorities will be to win passage of clean air legislation."
>
> "I would make the US the world leader in tackling environmental problems. . . . In my first year in office, I will convene a global conference on the environment at the White House."

Needless to say, that year came and went without a conference. A small conference held subsequently left participants grumbling about no agenda and no signs of commitment. Further tainting this environmental record was the U.S. performance at an international conference on the greenhouse effect in the Netherlands. Since America alone is contributing nearly 25 percent of the carbon dioxide emissions responsible for global warming, Bush had a golden leadership opportunity to do something to inspire other nations. Instead, U.S. representatives teamed up with Japan and the Soviet Union to block all initiatives. As a result of this holdout from the big three emitters of carbon dioxide (with over two-thirds of world levels among them), the conference was a failure. The final agreement merely acknowledged the need to stabilize emissions "in the future." What did the environmental president promise on this issue? Here were his words from the campaign: "Those who think we're powerless to do anything about the greenhouse effect are forgetting about the White House effect. As president, I intend to do something about it."

With the exception of the Clean Air Act of 1990 and some modest movement on groundwater pollution, nothing appreciable happened on the majority of the points, leading eleven environmental groups to issue a critical judgment on the president's performance in office. In the words of a Sierra Club spokesman, "We have great rhetoric but no leadership."[18] Still, it is tempting to regard the production of such elaborate campaign promises, along with Dukakis' equally sincere expressions of concern, as serious issues. The only trouble is that for all the candidate bloviating (as Warren Harding referred to political promising and speechifying) on the environment, it appears that the voters were unmoved. The important question here is why were the voters so dispassionate on a subject that so many considered to be important?

We already know what the good times crowd would say: All voters care about in peacetime is whether inflation is down and employment is up. To this the "issues are abundant" school would simply add: Besides, people are busy, and the issues are complex and confusing. Who has time to keep track of them all?

Like the good times thesis, the issues are abundant view of elections has its advocates all along the political spectrum, finding support from left, right, and center alike. An entertaining version was put forward by no less a liberal than Nicholas von Hoffman, in no less a liberal publication than the *New York Times*. In response to the loud chorus of complaints about Election '88, von Hoffman dismissed the call for good (or at least better) elections as nothing more than the tired hymn of good government idealists, or goo-goos as they have been labeled disdainfully:

Goo-gooism is Calvinism in politics. The operative word is duty as in civic duty. And duty, to win Brownie points in the great Electoral College in the sky, must be onerous, there being no easy road to salvation. The rubrics of goo-gooism prescribe that no man or woman may vote without having given over many hours of thoughtful study to the issues. In a culture like that of ancient Athens, where politics was a central preoccupation of the minority entitled to vote, this hard standard made sense.

So what happens in a mass culture like ours? Von Hoffman goes on to say that

> For the majority, it is red, white and blue balloons and the 30 second sound bites so deprecated by goo-gooists the nation over. The majority must be the generalists, the ones who give a few of the issues a quick study before they check their intuitions, consult their prejudices, cross their fingers and vote.[19]

Yet there just might be another explanation. Perhaps few people bothered to keep track of what George Bush said about the environment or what Michael Dukakis promised to do about defense, because they know it really didn't matter what the candidates said about these things. As Ladd put it earlier, these subjects may be widely recognized as problems, but problems don't turn magically into issues just because candidates open their mouths and begin spouting off about them. To reiterate Ladd's argument, "A problem becomes an issue only when voters see the parties differing in their approach to it or their capacity to solve it."

Nevertheless, there remains an undying hope that somehow all the bloviating on the issues will amount to something. Thus, for example, we saw respectable papers like the *Christian Science Monitor* devoting election-eve overleaf spreads to blow-by-blow candidate comparisons on the issues. In this impressive bit of journalism, identifiable candidate differences were spelled out on no fewer than nineteen issues, and few of the positions were shallow enough to be stated in twenty-five words or less.[20] During the primaries, the *New York Times* ran a similar issues scorecard, comparing thirteen candidates on seven key issues, totaling more than ninety issue positions.[21]

If there was any reason to think something would come of these preelection pledges, people might have bothered to keep track of them. Indeed, the human mind is capable of following much more detailed things. Witness the baseball fan's ability to commit to memory hundreds of players, along with highly detailed information about each one; the chef's capacity to remember the most complex combinations of ingredients and know their culinary effects; or the musician's recall of thousands of notes and entire compositions at the touch of a finger without exerting the least struggle to bring them to consciousness. When things matter—

that is, when they make a noticeable difference in our lives—we tend to pay attention to them and retain them in mind. The more vivid, credible, useful, novel, or important the experience, the richer and more detailed our memory of it. The reverse holds true as well, as in the case of empty campaign promises and fanciful issue positions that voters quickly learn to forget. In the campaign, we had Bush, the champion of child care.[22] Do we really need to read the fine print? Or Dukakis, the expert on the deployment of land-based nuclear missiles in Europe?[23] Why bother to remember his lengthy defense positions?

If voters can't take them seriously, then what are all these issues about? To put it bluntly, candidates need something to talk about every day, something that makes them sound serious and sensible. So it is that they serve up a daily issue menu, a sort of "conviction du jour," as cartoonist David Wiley Miller characterized it. "Speaking out on the issues" enables candidates to strike leaderly postures, to pontificate, to parade their styles before the voters, and, not least of all, to fill an otherwise embarrassing amount of dead space during our year-long campaigns. Knowing all this at some fundamental, ritualistic level, most people don't have to take the issue posturing seriously just because the candidates are saying all those things with a straight face. Behind the glazed eyes, the voters are not necessarily stupid; they're just dazed.

The result is that voters become turned off, and candidates begin to fall behind in the horserace, which makes them desperate enough to resort to name-calling, sloganeering, wild symbol-waving, and negative campaigning. They seemingly do anything to regain the distracted attention of the glazed masses. A case in point is the Bush campaign's decision to pursue the Willie Horton (prison furlough) attack on Dukakis. This decision emerged from the darkest early hours of the campaign when most experts, backed up by Bush's dismal showing in the opinion polls, were saying that he couldn't win the election. Another illustration of how issues become submerged by name-calling and symbol-waving involves the candidate debates which in the last twenty years have become the centerpieces of presidential elections.

A fascinating study by Marjorie Hershey compared Bush and Dukakis in terms of how much time they spent addressing subjects plausibly construed as policy issues (e.g., health care, education, drugs, defense) and how much attention they devoted to more abstract, moralistic concerns like prisoner furloughs, leadership, competence, and the L-word. Several interesting patterns emerged. In the first debate, both Bush and Dukakis maintained a fairly even balance between issues and symbols. In fact, Bush had a perfect balance with sixty-eight mentions in each category. But Dukakis outblustered Bush by a whopping margin of 225 total mentions of subjects (both issue and symbol) to Bush's more restrained 136. Eyes Glaze Over. Both camps, of course, claimed victory, and a host of independent judges were divided fairly evenly on the outcome. However, that first "word wrestling match," as one paper headlined it,[24] was so boring in the opinion of scholar Stephen Hess that "great gobs of people had tuned into something else by the time it was half over."[25]

Attentive to such criticisms, both camps adjusted their strategies for the second debate. Hershey's research shows that Dukakis cut his verbiage by nearly half, outmentioning topics by a much more merciful 135 to 111 margin over Bush.[26] Beginning to read the signs more astutely, the Dukakis camp also began to soft-pedal the issues and to engage in more symbol-waving. But he was clearly outdone by Bush, who reduced the number of issues mentioned in the second debate by well over half, enabling him to launch more symbolic salvos (at better than a 2 to 1 ratio of symbols over issues) on the ACLU, the flag salute, prison furloughs, and the L-word.[27] At last, Bush got the desired rise out of Dukakis. In a rare moment of what appeared to be anger, the Duke looked into the camera and said, "Of course the vice-president is questioning my patriotism. And I resent that."[28] Deciding that he could no longer ignore Bush's symbol-bashing, Dukakis even worked an angry-sounding response into his campaign speech: "My friends, this is garbage."[29] However, Dukakis' campaign began to take on its own dirty character after the candidate descended from the high road of issue-posturing and entered into the lower reaches of symbol-slinging. As noted in Chapter 2, in the final weeks of the campaign Dukakis actually became more negative than Bush.

The Dukakis strategy shift came too little, too late in the opinion of many state and local Democratic party leaders who felt shut out of the Boston-based national campaign. Bob Slagle, chairman of the Texas Democratic party, accused the national campaign of being "slow to take the advice they've been given on things like gun control, and the ACLU." The chair of the Alabama party, Al LaPierre, winced at the lawyerly answers Dukakis gave for too long in response to Bush's Pledge of Allegiance attack, while prohibiting local campaigns from responding in kind. LaPierre lamented, "We know how to run and do what the Republicans are doing—a down and dirty campaign. We're used to it." The whole fiasco was summed up by one Democratic strategist who preferred to remain unnamed: "I felt it showed . . . that they did not understand the extent to which symbols like that can be used to devastating effect."[30] Indeed, when voters cannot take the issues seriously, there is little more for candidates to do but engage in name-calling, finger-pointing, and general symbol-waving. Not that the voters like it, mind you. It's just that there isn't anything else for the candidates to do after their commitments to big backers have removed the chances of saying anything meaningful (or even different) about the larger issues like defense or economic policy.

A classic anthropological fable tells of an anthropologist asking a local informant to explain about the earth and the cosmos. Well, says the informant, the earth sits atop a large bird. And the bird?, the anthropologist asks. Ah, the bird stands atop a huge lizard. And the lizard? You see, the lizard rests on the back of an elephant. But the elephant, what does it stand on? A turtle, of course—a large and sturdy turtle. But the turtle? On what does it rest? Ah, my good anthropologist, it's turtles all the way down from there! So, too, with elections these days. Had Dukakis bothered to ask a local informant from, say, a state campaign organization, he might have heard that an election rests first on a pledge to keep the economy strong. And on what does that rest? On a promise to keep our defenses strong. And that issue, what does it stand on? On the appearance of being a good leader, of course. And that appearance, on what does it depend? Ah, there we have a big symbol showing moral superiority over the opponent. And beneath that symbol? Another symbol showing we can take the opponent's symbolic attacks better than he takes ours. And beneath that one? My good candidate! From there, it's symbols all the way. As noted in Chapter 1, Dukakis finally succumbed to this wisdom late in the campaign, but by then he looked desperate and anything but a master of the symbolic universe.

But that's the way it's always been, and there never was anything more to American elections than that. This is in many ways the most stubborn knee-jerk response to the decline of elections thesis. As this and the last chapter make clear, the elections of the 1980s and 1990s depart in many ways from more typical patterns of the past. Still, it is often said that, historically, elections in America have amounted to little more than symbol-waving and flimflammery. Out of a deep cultural mix of political festival and farce comes the selection of a leader who has withstood the rough-and-tumble of a campaign to emerge victorious as the best of the competition. In this view, the campaign is an elaborate character test, and negative campaigning is simply the custom by which candidates subject each other to withering fire to see who is left standing when the smoke lifts on election day. Central to this perspective is the proposition that eloquence and political vision are a rarity in an election campaign.

As indicated at the beginning of Chapter 2, the difference in years past is that in addition to the festivities and familiar posturing, competing social visions have been central to many elections in American history in ways that make today's politics disappointingly empty. It is probably true that eloquence, detailed issues, and inventive rhetoric may be the exceptions rather than the rule in American political campaigns. However, this does not mean that simple words and deeds cannot represent a clear vision or a decisive policy course for the nation to take. A couple of extreme examples will illustrate what I mean here. Neither Andrew Jackson nor Abraham Lincoln uttered a single word in public during their respective elections, yet the voters had little doubt about what these candidates stood for or that the nation would embark on a decisively different course if they were chosen over their opponents. Neither Lincoln nor Jackson said *anything* in public during their respective election campaigns because for almost the first hundred years of the Republic, it was regarded as unseemly to campaign for oneself. The practice of candidates touring the country and speaking in their own behalf did not begin until Lincoln's opponent Stephen Douglas did it in 1860—and he was soundly criticized for doing so. This is how an editorial in an Illinois newspaper characterized the outlandish idea: "Douglas is going about peddling his opinions as a tin man peddles his wares. The only excuse for him is that since he is a small man, he has a right to be engaged in small business, and small business it is for a candidate for the Presidency to be strolling around the country begging for votes like a town constable." An Iowa paper chimed in, saying that Douglas "demeans himself as no other candidate ever yet has, who goes about begging, imploring, and beseeching the people to grant him his wish."[31]

As for Lincoln, he stayed at home in Springfield, Illinois, during the convention and during most of the election, vowing not to "write or speak anything upon doctrinal points."[32] The campaigning was left to his seconds who secured the nomination and arranged for local celebrities to make the speeches. A stickler for detail, Lincoln went so far as to cut his own name from his ballot before voting a straight Republican ticket. The point is that Lincoln didn't need to say a word in order for voters to know what his election meant. He was among the most outspoken opponents of slavery in the years before his nomination. Among the nation's most popular speakers, he drew the healthy sum of $200 per appearance. Morever, he had already publicized his views by debating Douglas in an earlier Illinois Senate race. By campaign time, Lincoln saw no reason not to honor the customary dignified silence of the aspiring candidate. As for Douglas, he faced competition from three sides and decided to risk campaigning for his own election. The point is that there was little doubt about what Lincoln stood for; ideas need not be finely detailed during a campaign in order to be clear and consequential.

In 1832, Andrew Jackson also spoke no words in his political behalf, but he took a political action that spoke louder than words about where the country would go with him as president. He opened the presidential campaign in July with a veto of the congressional bill rechartering the Bank of the United States. Mindful of the symbolism, he then retired to his home in Tennessee, the Hermitage, making a show of paying for all his expenses along the way in gold. Ever a popular symbol, the precious metal became known in the campaign as "Jackson money."[33] As for the seconds his managers sent out to speak for him, Jackson doubted the need for them, remarking to a friend that the campaign "will be a walk. If our fellows didn't raise a finger from now on the thing would be just as well done. In fact . . . it's done now."[34]

These examples show that complex rhetoric and expansive articulation of issues are not required to make an election significant. Neither, of course, is there a taboo on eloquence as the cases of Woodrow Wilson and Franklin Roosevelt illustrate. What matters is that candidates offer, *by whatever means,* clear alternatives to the voters. This is what makes for meaningful elections: clear alternatives that would send the national destiny in one direction or another, offering voters reasonable hopes of alleviating the strains that plague society. When such an election comes along, people vote in great numbers because they see the alternatives as clear and the consequences as great. The irony of the 1980s was that for all his rhetorical skills, Reagan did not win large and enduring majorities to his side. Meanwhile, the Democrats proved even less successful at mobilizing popular support for any competing rhetorical vision. Yet both parties succeeded in using the new electoral system to capture one of the branches of government, giving each party an appreciable power base from which to draw wealth and prestige for its supporters. At the same time, the electoral methods used to secure power have left both parties lacking the capacity to generate the ideas (and the organizational commitment to them) necessary to govern.

The important point is that the history of elections is filled with a wide range of rhetorical styles, some of them eloquent and perhaps most of them not. What matters is whether voters find a political vision credible enough to support. Credibility depends not only on capturing the political imagination in words, but also on getting institutions to turn those words into actions. Neither party vision of the 1980s was successful in either endeavor. The result is that America has entered what may turn out to be one of its most challenging decades without governing ideas at its disposal. Running out of ideas is neither a failure of creativity nor a sign that today's problems are unsolvable. Rather, the historical forces described in Chapter 2 have eroded the communication process between leaders and followers, leaving candidates these days with little to say and with few people who want to listen.

CHAPTER 4

The Big Buydown:
Media, Money, and Marketing

The prospects for governing ideas and the chances for spontaneous glimpses of candidate character have been reduced by campaign contributors, and have been kept down through a combination of Madison Avenue–style marketing and media control strategies. Perhaps it sounds harsh to make this statement so bluntly, but if there is even a grain of truth in the idea—and this chapter intends to demonstrate more than that—then the shock value of saying it straightaway may motivate the kind of public debate needed to begin the process of reform. First, we will look at the big picture.

CLOSING THE MARKETPLACE OF IDEAS

In recent years there has been growing concern that the all-important marketplace of ideas in American society is becoming monopolized and closed to many viewpoints worthy of public consideration. Ben Bagdikian, former dean of the Journalism School at the University of California at Berkeley, has demonstrated the frightening rate at which the national news media have been monopolized as a result of the merger mania and leveraged buyout craze of the 1980s. As of this writing, twenty or so large holding companies own the lion's share of the mass communications industry. Many of these companies are oil and defense industry giants with economic interests and image concerns that may not always be conducive to the free flow of ideas.[1]

The link between the ownership of mass communication companies and the content of the news and entertainment they produce is not direct or, at least, not easily documentable. It is not enough, however, just to point to the media monopoly as a disturbing sign and leave it at that. It is more helpful to suggest a few general ways of thinking about a national political communications process in which both the ownership of the media and the financing and resulting public relations aspects of elections play important parts (along with a number of other forces, of course). Since we are talking about a complex system of national communications, it makes sense to think of the various component parts working loosely together: pushing and pulling, giving and taking, buying and selling, much as a marketplace (of ideas, in this case) is affected by pressures from a large number of only loosely related market forces. The notion of elections as part of a broad marketplace of ideas helps avoid the temptation to home in too closely on cause-and-effect relations between isolated parts of the larger system. Rather, the goal is to begin placing elections and the new election process outlined in Chapter 2 in the larger context of a national communication system—the marketplace of ideas, if you will.

Toward this end, let's consider election financing and media ownership as loose links in a long chain of influences that affect both the production and the communication of governing ideas in the national marketplace. We could begin linking up the pieces of this pressure system with elections, and work toward news coverage patterns and media ownership issues. However, we will gain more perspective by looking at it the other way around and seeing (if only briefly) the place of elections as a small part of a much larger political communications process. Beginning, then, with the business end of the media, we can sketch the following top-down chain of loose relationships in the marketplace of ideas, ending up with the business end of elections:

• Although the public image interests of parent companies may occasionally lead them to interfere in the editorial content of the news companies they own (see Bagdikian for examples), the more important influence may come from the accounting department. With nonjournalistic owners, the pressure is on news divisions to operate like any other business. News divisions are expected to maximize profits and efficiency, boost advertising and other sales revenues, and market their product (in this case, news) according to consumer tastes. The ramifications of these business trends in the news industry are numerous enough to be the subject of a separate book and have filled the pages of national journalism reviews in recent years. One way in which business considerations in the media contribute to the chain of pressures slowly closing down the marketplace of political ideas is this one:

• More profit-conscious and efficiency-minded news organizations are less likely to spend resources on high-risk, high-cost news products like investigative reporting. Rather, they are more likely to fall back on routine news gathering. What this means is that reporters are even more likely to stick to the standard beats, travel in packs, gravitate toward the obvious stories, and, above all, rely on government officials as the cheapest, most efficient, safest (from criticism), and most reliable means of filling up the daily news hole and meeting deadlines. Not surprisingly, research suggests that news organizations rely on government officials to generate the lion's share of news content.[2] This may not be a bad idea when the government is alive with conflict between elected factions. After all, if democracy is thriving, why should the press go outside the center of public debate and controversy for its news? However, if government is stagnant, devoid of idea conflict, and lacking in public support, all the media attention focused on Washington ends up playing back to the people a rather narrow and empty set of ideas. Yet the pressures on news organizations reinforce the dependence of journalists on officials for most of the content in the daily news.[3] All of which has led to a newly emerging norm in the news business:

• Disappearing fast are Jeffersonian ideals of an independent and politically critical press. Reporters and politicians have become bedfellows— albeit uneasy ones—since they often must manipulate and entrap one another for their separate journalistic or political ends. But bedfellows they remain. As a result, in recent years a growing norm of what might be called "presumed democracy" has emerged among news professionals.[4] That is, editors and their reporting staffs increasingly resign themselves to reporting what officials say and do. If circumstances permit, this reporting may carry some critical editorial commentary or news analysis. By and large, however, the ultimate responsibility for making sense of what officials are up to, much less applying critical insights, lies with the public. In other words, the press presumes that giving the greatest share of news space to government views is what the people want, since the people elected the government. And if the people don't like what they see on television or read in the papers, they can elect a different government. But, of course, it is not that simple. In many respects this system of mass-mediated governing has become, in the words of one observer, a "democracy without citizens."[5] Nevertheless, citizen responsibility and democratic accountability seem to be the chief operating assumptions in the media these days (not that journalists are always happy with it, but that is another story). As a result of these reporting norms, a curious pattern enters news content:

• When government elites are divided and in serious conflict about a particular subject, the news pages are filled with controversy and broadly differing points of view. Conversely, when elected officials are silent, or of a single mind, or simply so idiosyncratic and fragmented that no coherent viewpoints emerge at all, the news gates begin to shut down and the media communicate few ideas, voices, or visions to the public.[6] This pattern begins to make some sense of various puzzles about the news. For example, the tendency for the White House and Congress to seek consensus on foreign policy explains why the official ideological line from Washington forms the content of most foreign affairs coverage.[7] By contrast, in other areas—particularly domestic issues—such as abortion, school prayer, and pocketbook economics, the tendency is toward greater elite division. In these areas, the news gates open and the news contains broader ranges of viewpoints, the voices of more ordinary people and grass-roots organizations, and more opinion polls that are cited more often and taken more seriously. In other words, on some issues we have a fairly broad, democratic dialogue in the news, while in other areas the range of voices and viewpoints is exceedingly narrow and unrepresentative. This brings us, at last, to the "electoral connection":

• The overall shape of the news dialogue is thus affected by the way in which campaign financing carves up issue domains in the parties, the Congress, and the White House. (Of course, many other factors influence patterns of elite consensus and division, but none has greater claim to cutting a crazy swath through the circles of power than election money.) In some areas, for example, defense policy, campaign money may forge a narrow Washington consensus that is at odds with competing viewpoints in the society at large. In other areas, for example, budget and tax policies, the centrifugal pull of election financing fragments the official ranks into warring fiefdoms protecting this interest against that. Still other areas, for example, moral issues and gun control, are more typically divided by interest lobbying (and voter pressures) into neat differences of elite opinion. The overall effect, however, is to create so many cross currents in the circles of power that little chance exists for the development of stable coalitions to form around broad political visions and proposals for social renewal.

As this chapter shows, campaign money is given out not just for what candidates say or don't say during elections, but for what they say and do in between (where it really counts, in the governing process). As a result, the impact of elections on the national dialogue goes on around the clock. Because campaign financing undermines the coherence of debate in Washington, elections make the news long after the race is over. Most Washington insiders, both press and politicians, know these things at least at an intuitive level, but the system does not make it easy to talk, much less do anything, about them. Where is the shock, outrage, or just plain discussion from politicians and the media about this widening representation gap between leaders and followers? With polls showing government priorities growing farther out of line with public preferences, it might be awkward for politicians to step forward and explain why.[8] What, after all, would we expect to hear from the one hundred key members of House and

Senate committees who are heavily financed by defense contractors? "Hi! I'm Representative David McCurdy, Democrat from Oklahoma, and my $40,500 in personal honoraria income from defense contractors convinced me of the nation's true priorities. Too bad the public doesn't have the same chance to see things so clearly!" Or: "Hello. I'm Slade Gorton, Republican senator from Washington State, and my $371,191 in recent campaign contributions from defense industry political action committees sure helped me see the light about our national military needs. Too bad the public just doesn't understand."

While these statements are purely fictitious, they illustrate a point: the figures they contain are regrettable facts of political life. The list of the top one hundred congressional recipients of political gifts from the defense industry (from which the above two cases were drawn) makes for eye-opening reading.[9] As noted in Chapter 2, a nice piece of investigative reporting by UPI reporter Greg Gordon showed that in fiscal year 1987, 82 percent ($230 billion) of all military contracts went to one-third of the states that just happened to have members on the Senate Armed Services Committee and the Senate Defense Appropriations Subcommittee.[10]

Although lawmakers frequently cast public opinion aside in favor of more informed judgments, it stretches credibility to think that this system serves some sort of deeper, objective public interest. Even rare cost-cutting gestures by the military itself have been sacrificed to the "special insights" arrived at between politicians and their corporate backers. For example, the *Dallas Morning News* reported that Democratic representative Les Aspin of Wisconsin, chair of the House Armed Services Committee, insisted that the Army buy 3,849 more trucks than it requested at a cost of an additional $500 million more than the Army wanted to spend. The supplier was to be the Oshkosh Truck Corporation, the largest defense contractor in Aspin's state. The Army was adamant against the idea. Still determined to get its interests represented, just two hours before the armed services procurement subcommittee voted on the Aspin amendment, Oshkosh Truck paid six members of the subcommittee "honoraria" of $2,000 each for attending an informational breakfast. Immediately afterward, over the Army's objections, the subcommittee passed the amendment.[11]

Beyond raising questions about the meaning of the term *honor*arium, this system of interest representation returns us to the question of why it hasn't become the object of enduring national scandal and outrage. Quite likely, most people are silently outraged by it but their concerns are hardly expressed regularly in the media. Although the press has produced a handful of good investigative reports like those noted above, the numbers are far from commensurate with the magnitude of the problem.

For the most part, the news brings us the usual political rhetoric about the continuing need for a strong defense or a strong (*fill in your favorite boondoggle here*), along with the usual laments about how there just isn't any money left over to pay for (*fill in your favorite neglected issue here*). The characteristic silence from politicians and the media is broken only by occasional invocations of the myth that the public just doesn't understand the pressures of governing. Politicians are doing the best they can with a nearly impossible system. The only trouble is that the system was created through the muddling and meddling of politicians themselves. . . .

If we can understand the reluctance of politicians to step forward and decry their own fellowship with special interests, the case of the media is a bit trickier. As noted earlier, it helps to understand the business end of news production. Every media organization faces a basic choice: to work out its own unique agenda of what to cover, who to interview, and how to analyze the results, or to fashion most news stories around the readily available pronouncements of government authorities. The first course of action would be a difficult one, requiring news organizations to defend their standards of judgment, compete with each other in defining what's news, hire more (costly) reporting and research talent, and enter into more frequent battles with the powers that be, including, one presumes, their own corporate ownership. Instead, the course of least organizational resistance favors government-issued news, which is more efficient, easily gathered, standardized, and less controversial.[12]

The only way to justify letting the governors define the content of the daily news is to cling to a deep article of faith referred to above as presumed democracy—an article of faith that is more than happily promoted by the governors as well. This everyday working agreement between press and politicians can be stated simply as follows: Elected officials are presumed to represent the broad public interest, and if for some reason they don't, it is, after all, a free country in which disgruntled citizens have no complaint. They are free to elect representatives they like better. The trouble with presumed democracy is that it is too simple to be true. It overlooks the system of campaign financing and gift-giving that makes it difficult for independent-minded leaders to enter politics in the first place. And if they do get in, the same system makes it difficult to promote the new ideas that got them there.

This assumption of presumed democracy is defensible in large part because the system does work fairly well in a great number of small areas. We are not, after all, talking about an Orwellian totalitarian state—just a good system that has developed the bad habit of ducking the big issues that may bring on its downfall. In other words, many issues lend credence to the presumed democracy norm that assures both press and politicians success in their respective ventures. It is easy to think of a host of areas in which the elite is clearly divided and not obviously beholden to organized economic interests. Abortion, prayer in school, the flag salute, and civil rights come to mind. In these and other areas, there are raging debates in legislatures and in electoral campaigns. Obeying the rule of presumed representation, the press eagerly follows these political openings among the authorities and as a result introduces a broader range of street-level opinion into the news. The question is, what do these isolated issues add up to in terms of broad social, much less governing, visions?

The problem of developing a coherent national dialogue is further clouded by those grey and arguably more important areas like defense spending, social welfare programs, foreign policies, wage and labor laws, tax and profit structures, and monetary regulation. On these matters, the elite are more likely to close ranks, resolve their differences as much as possible in private, and present their programs and pronouncements as though the people had spoken with a united voice. In such cases, the people generally know better, but failing to hear their views and dissenting opinions introduced forcefully by the media (either through polls or just by asking grass-roots groups for comment), the silenced majorities and minorities may simply leave the political scene. The resulting political vacuum is quickly filled by abortion marchers or flag burners, creating the impression of a thriving democracy, while a whole range of what may be the most important questions facing the nation have been removed from lively consideration. This vicious cycle, perpetuated by the working agreement of presumed democracy between press and government officials, gives new meaning to Thomas Jefferson's claim that if he were forced to choose between a government without newspapers and newspapers without a government, he would gladly take the latter.

It must be emphasized that the shrinking range of ideas in politics is not the fault of the press alone. Recall that this discussion began with the equally (if not more) important behind-the-scenes factor of political financing. This original condition induces politicians to remain silent while backing unpopular policies on big national issues and then pontificating until eyes glaze over on safe issues like foreign enemies, flag burning, and drugs. To complete the picture, add to this political alchemy of docile media and aggressively well-organized economic interests, a growing industry of media consultants, speech writers, pollsters, and political strategists whose job is to strike the delicate daily balance between the shrinking range of political ideas and the illusion of democracy. And, voilà, we understand how, despite dwindling public confidence in leaders, those same leaders continue to make daily appearances in the media as though they embodied the spirit of democracy itself.

All that is required to make sense of this picture is to accept, as many leaders would have us believe, that we have entered an era of objective political limitations requiring enormous caution. Perish the thought that the national interest has been auctioned to the highest bidders. Believe, instead, that crafty foreign competitors are stealing our economic birthright, that the budget deficit is too big to handle, and that we have a moral obligation to protect the entire world no matter what the cost. Meanwhile, don't ask how Europe, Japan, and (for a brief shining moment) the Soviet Union managed to embark on such bold courses of action against much greater obstacles.

It might serve us better to look beneath these oft-recited but too convenient political limits, to a deeper but, happily, more remediable set of threats to our political creativity. These palpable-but-removable obstacles are the uses of money, marketing, and media to confine the entry of new ideas into the political marketplace and weaken the will of politicians to act in the public interest. The effects of these limiting conditions operate throughout the government on a daily basis, channeling the national potential away from breakthroughs on major problems and into unnecessary holding actions like buying more trucks than the Army needs, or pushing the country into histrionic debate over a flag-burning amendment to the Constitution. Or sending a half million troops halfway around the world to fight a costly war when a long list of domestic problems defies political agreement. If money, media, and marketing affect the whole operation of the political system, their effects are nowhere more pronounced than in elections.

MONEY, MONEY, MONEY

"I've raised millions upon millions for the Democratic Party and I've never seen this happen," said [M. Larry] Lawrence. The 61-year-old chairman of the fashionable Hotel del Coronado in Coronado, California, donated $100,000 of his own to the Democrats in the primaries, and has pledged to raise an additional $1 million for the general election. "We're raising money like it's going out of style. It's beyond comprehension. It's gorgeous. It's so exciting."[13]

In at least one respect, this wealthy businessman and long-time Democratic fundraiser is right: "It's beyond comprehension." The creative interpretations of the Federal Election Campaign Act have showered more money than ever before on the nation's leadership. More importantly, there are now so many points of entry and uses for these huge sums that it becomes difficult to fathom the total effect.

Padding the Presidency

It is now common for presidential candidates' parties to raise far more in soft money than public matching funding provides the candidates. The point of public funding, of course, was to equalize the competition and keep spending within reason. According to one expert, the soft money frenzy drove costs of presidential campaigning to $500 million in 1988, up from $325 million in 1984,[14] and the projections are even higher for 1992. Nowadays, the paltry $100 million or so given in federal funding to the candidates is dwarfed by the soft money escalation. The limit on how much the candidates can accept from their parties ($8.3 million in 1988) if they "voluntarily" take public funding has become a joke. The hundreds of millions in party bank accounts can be spent on a wide array of vote-getting activities as long as the candidate's name is not specifically mentioned. Thus, soft money can be used for voter registration, get-out-the-vote drives, primary and caucus politicking, paying for the conventions (now costing tens of millions), forging alliances between candidates and state and local party organizations, and on and on. Indeed, if the money game is played well, as it was by both Reagan and Bush, there is no need to spend all that soft money on specific name identification advertising. The money ties can end up personalizing the entire party structure. The price of such personalized presidential politics may well be the auctioning off of the various issues that once gave substance to party platforms. As we will see shortly, an even more personalized and fragmented money system has emerged in Congress in the form of members' personal PACs (or leadership PACs as they are known euphemistically).

As noted in Chapter 2, the Democrats learned to play the money game in the mid-1980s, catching up with and then passing the Republicans in congressional wealth, and running close and sometimes ahead of the GOP in the presidential money race. For example, at the presidential level in 1984, the national party campaign was deeply in debt going into the months just before the election. By 1988, the Democratic soft funds easily exceeded the amounts of hard money provided by federal funding. This fact led Bush's chief fundraiser, Robert A. Mosbacher, Jr. (later rewarded with a cabinet post), to remark, probably with tongue in cheek: "The

Democrats are saying they're going for the big money. And I don't think there's much we can do about it but match them."[15]

Mosbacher had the plan to do it: Join the Team 100 club. The membership fee was merely 100 (thousand) dollars to the Republican National Committee (the soft money holding company for the Bush campaign). *Common Cause Magazine* called Mosbacher's Team 100 a veritable who's who of American business:

> The $100,000 contributors include 66 in the investment and banking community, 58 in real estate and construction, another 17 in the oil industry, and 15 from food and agriculture. Team 100 also includes members from the entertainment, cable, insurance, steel and auto industries.
>
> Almost across the board, Team 100 members or the companies they are associated with want something from the government—whether it's broad policy initiatives like Bush's proposed reduction in the capital gains tax or favors more specific to a company or industry. Many gave their $100,000 at a time when they had significant business or regulatory matters pending with the federal government—or knew they likely would under the Bush administration.[16]

Once these donors were on the team, they kept on giving, to the tune of $25,000 a year between elections and another $100,000 in 1992. Thus, each Team 100 member signed checks totaling at least $275,000 for the two Bush elections.[17] Meanwhile, the Democrats weren't doing too badly either. Although slowed somewhat in 1988 by Dukakis' reluctance to solicit corporate funds, the state parties finally decided to join the money fest. At one point the California party chairman boasted that the state campaign was being financed by "every big California corporation you can think of."[18]

Although it is obvious that many big donors hope their checks will get the attention of candidates, party fundraisers walk (and talk) a fine legal line, claiming that these generous souls and corporations are simply overwhelmed with party loyalty. There are several reasons to be skeptical of assurances that soft money is not just a quasi-legal laundering operation for candidates. First, the parties are often so personalized around a particular candidate's politics (and political staff) that giving to the party amounts to giving to the presidential campaign. (This has been more true for the Republicans than the Democrats in recent years.) Second, the key soft money fundraisers are usually insiders in the candidate's campaign. Third, and most importantly, national campaign strategy for candidates ends up being calculated around how to divide up the hard and soft money expenses. In practice, the "ground war" (registration, get-out-the-vote drives, etc.) in a campaign is waged primarily with soft money—money that individual campaigns otherwise would have to spend. Diverting most of the soft money to ground war activities allows candidates to spend more of their personal campaign accounts on the "air war." This drives up the budgets for advertising and marketing, and leads candidates to rely increasingly on the air war as the heart of the campaign.[19]

Cashing In on Congress

The most glaring fact about money on Capitol Hill is that more of it pours in every year. The most visible source is PAC funding, which escalated from $55 million in 1980 to slightly over $150 million in 1990, with the vast majority each year going to incumbents.[20] The figures for election years in this period are as follows:

1980	55.3 million
1982	83.6 million
1984	105.3 million
1986	130.0 million
1988	150.0 million
1990	150.0 million

The slowdown between 1988 and 1990 probably reflects a decline in competitive races, along with the difficulty of top money raisers to explain why they needed so much more money than they could spend.

As described in Chapter 2, the deluge of PAC money allows incumbents to keep their seats by greatly outspending their opponents (by a 2 to 1 margin in the Senate and 3.5 to 1 in the House in 1990). So many interests now walk the halls of Congress that money is handed out even to those legislators who may not vote the right way. A director of a business PAC described this goodwill strategy in these terms: "First, you get to everyone on Ways and Means whether they're for you or against you. Secondly, there's a presumption that we look seriously into giving to incumbents where we have a major facility unless the guy has gone out of his way to urinate on us. And we give money to guys where we have major facilities who vote against us nine times out of ten."[21]

The PAC deluge has atomized Congress. In a column pointing out the broad bipartisan agreement with this assessment, David Broder quoted a former member of the House as saying that Congress "is a rudderless ship, that its members are squabbling all the time and that they are afraid to bite any bullets or make any hard choices."[22] Broder's recommendation, passed along from a number of former solons, is to sweep out the cash. It will take a lot of sweeping, because the cash is not delivered solely in the PAC bundles discussed so far.

In addition to the rain of PAC dollars, members of Congress have to cope with another problem area created by their special interest clients: favors and other considerations. This "ethics swamp" has swallowed one representative after another in recent years. The political treats they are given—the breakfast clubs, party boats, golf trips, book publishing deals, and the like—have become so routine that many representatives seem unaware of their corrupting influences. For example, one of the loudest critics of the savings-and-loan scandal was Massachusetts senator John Kerry. While lashing out at S&L kingpins who stole the nation's savings accounts, Kerry turned out to be a frequent guest of one of those kingpins. According to a *Wall Street Journal* report, one of the S&L operators charged with egregious misuse of over $30 million of his bank's funds was David Paul, the man named by Senator Kerry to chair the Democratic Senatorial Campaign Committee Majority Trust campaign fund. In addition to giving more than $300,000 of his own money to Senate campaigns, Paul personally hosted Senator Kerry a number of times, including several trips on his private jet. At one particularly memorable dinner in Miami Senator Kerry and the other guests were treated to a meal prepared by six chefs flown in from France, a ten-piece orchestra, and caviar, all of which added up to a check for $129,000 picked up by Paul. Although several news reports had surfaced on Paul's growing legal problems by that time, Senator Kerry saw nothing amiss with the dinner, which he thought was a charity affair. "Who could know?" he asked. "In life there are some people who turn out to be bad apples."[23]

As we descend beneath the PAC donations and the special favors, we come to what may be the most serious impact of money on Congress. Chapter 2 briefly noted that one of the growing trends on Capitol Hill is to set up personal leadership PACs. Virtually anyone who wants to be a player in congressional politics has one. These elected fat cats, as Ross Baker has dubbed them, reward and punish their colleagues as party power brokers did in the old days. The competition to rule the roost in Congress is stiff, with more than fifty senators and representatives boasting their own PACs at the start of the 1990s, and the numbers were still on the rise. None of these PACs is called by the name of its owner, of course: the Robert C. Byrd PAC is called the Committee for America's Future; Jesse Helms presides over the National Congressional Club; Dan Rostenkowski controls the purse strings of America's Leaders Fund; and so on.[24] Behind the noble names are large reserves of dollars that multiply the divisions of the PAC system as a whole, splitting Congress internally and further undermining the traditional role of parties and party leadership.

The dilemma is that the system has set in motion a money scramble that won't quit without reforms. Each year the contributions of PACs (both outside and inside Congress) become more important for meeting spiraling campaign costs. The spiraling costs seem endless as increasingly idea-less candidates chase after the votes of increasingly skeptical and disloyal voters.

Media advertising and marketing costs are the main items on campaign budgets. Here, for example, is a fairly typical budget for a Senate campaign. These expenses were not for an incumbent's campaign, but for a challenge by Harriet Woods of Missouri, who raised enough money to put on a credible, though losing, campaign:[25]

Sources of Money		Expense Breakdown	
Individuals in Missouri	1,150,000	TV time & ad production	2,550,000
Individuals outside Missouri	600,000	Polling	200,000
Direct mail & phone solicitation	1,200,000	Staff & operations	875,000
"Bundling" (outside groups collecting individual money)	300,000	Fund-raising costs	775,000
Political action committees	800,000		
Democratic party funds	350,000		
	4,400,000		4,400,000

Running for office, whether on the executive or legislative level, leads candidates into the world of high finance and special interest temptations. Money, not ideas, has become the greatest challenge and obstacle to national leadership. Since there are differing views of how the competition for money affects the production of ideas in Washington, it is worth considering the leading theories carefully.

Two Theories about Money and Politics

As the discussion so far indicates, money has atomized the nation's leadership, eroded the party system, and turned elections into just another part of a grand veto system eliminating new governing ideas as quickly as they begin to develop. This view supports the image of the rudderless ship

cited by David Broder above. It is also consistent with the conclusion of
Ross Baker's study of "The New (Congressional) Fat Cats":

> PACs generally absorb money that has traditionally gone to political par-
> ties. More important, perhaps, PACs also absorbed much of the energy of
> those who formerly worked through the parties to influence public policy.
> If parties with their comprehensive agendas designed to appeal to the
> broadest segments of the population stand at one end of the spectrum,
> PACs with their narrow focus tailored to appeal only to those with a
> special interest stand at the other. PACs have, by their very nature, a
> fragmenting effect on politics. They enable groups with narrow interests
> to contribute money to politicians who have single-issue agendas. Mem-
> bers of Congress are held to no overall philosophical account by most
> PACs. And PACs lavish on legislators the money needed to win cam-
> paigns at a time when the average House race costs almost $270,000 and
> the average Senate race close to $3 million.[26]

The fragmenting influences of PACs are multiplied many times over
when to this indictment of PACs we add the corruption of special favors,
the divisiveness of leadership funds, the covert uses of soft money, and the
increasing reliance on marketing and media control techniques. One significant consequence of the fragmentation, of course, is the vastly diminished production of governing ideas around which leaders and citizens can
develop mutual commitments.

Contrasted with this view is another thesis that states the case somewhat differently: The American parties still represent coherent ideas, but
they are ideologically conservative ones that appeal only to a minority of
voters, leaving the silenced majority without representation or leadership.
In this view, attracting the big money required to win elections has thrown
the whole electoral process into the hands of moneyed interests who have
exacted a right turn in the flow of public debate as the price for their
contributions. As with the fragmentation thesis, the trouble also begins
with money. But in this view political campaigns can be regarded as investment opportunities for more ideologically organized financial interests—
perhaps one of the best investments around. As Thomas Ferguson and
Joel Rogers' investment theory of elections states, the traditional party
conflict between multinational corporate interests (the old Democratic
backers) and domestic manufacturers (the old Republican money) has
been resolved, more or less, over the last few decades.[27] The multination-
als are the big players in the election game today, which means that they
don't need the Democratic party to fight their free trade and nonisola-
tionist foreign policy battles against the Republicans. The Republicans
have come around to the free trade position so completely that the Demo-

crats now must make increasingly large concessions, selling out the interests of their traditional labor and social constituents just to compete for money they once attracted with relatively little effort.

Despite a clear market of voters who are responsive to jobs programs, more favorable labor and minimum wage laws, health protection, environmental actions, budget cuts in defense, and a whole range of other issues, the Democrats have rolled over and played these issues in much the same way as the Republicans. In 1984, Walter Mondale became the first Democrat in modern times to run for office without a jobs program. He proposed a tax increase, but he offered no program of national revitalization to justify the extraction of money from weary taxpayers. In 1988, Dukakis turned his back on the party's traditional constituency of black voters after Jesse Jackson went to the trouble of bringing large numbers of them to the polling place door. In that same year, Dukakis took a weaker environmental program to the voters than did Bush, and neither candidate said anything harsh about corporate polluters, who just happened to be paying the campaign bills.

Can these and a long list of other Democratic right turns be attributed to a rising conservative tide among voters? To the contrary, say Ferguson and Rogers, the long list of government programs on the chopping block during the Reagan revolution would have been spared the axe if left to the decision of voters. Sizable opinion margins favored holding the line on environmental regulation (49 to 28 percent), industrial safety (66 to 18 percent), teenage minimum wage (58 to 29 percent), auto emission and safety standards (59 to 29 percent), federal lands policies (43 to 27 percent), and offshore oil drilling restrictions (46 to 29 percent), among others.[28] Yet government retrenchments in these and dozens of other areas were made with barely a whimper from the Democrats, and virtually no effort was made to rally this opinion in the subsequent elections.

Does public support for corporate interests encourage the parties to run against popular preferences on dozens of issues? This thesis doesn't make sense either. For more than two decades polls have shown a growing public outrage at the favoritism granted to the corporate sector. In a 1969 survey, for example, 61 percent said that too much power was concentrated in the hands of a few large corporations. By 1979, that figure had risen to 79 percent. In 1969, only 38 percent felt that corporate profits were too high; by 1979, the figure was 51 percent. Over the same period, the number of Americans favoring government-imposed limits on corporate profits rose from 33 percent to a startling 60 percent.[29] The most revealing statistic of all relates to the percentage of people who believe that the government is run for the benefit of a few big interests at the expense of the public interest: the figure grew from less than one-quarter of the public in the rosy days of the 1950s to fully three-quarters by the beginning of the 1990s.[30]

As these attitudes would predict, Ronald Reagan's programs favoring big business and undermining social services were anything but popular. Looking through Reagan's confident exterior and past the great deference accorded him by the media, we find that by early 1983 his popularity had plunged to 35 percent, a figure lower than anything recorded for Eisenhower or Kennedy, matching the level to which Lyndon Johnson sank before withdrawing from the presidency in 1968, and exceeding only Richard Nixon's 24 percent approval rating at the time he resigned from office in 1974.[31] Reagan's popularity recovered, of course, but only after his major legislative agenda was finished and, more importantly, only after the economy recovered from the severe recession brought on by his early monetary policies and the interest rate spiral caused by Federal Reserve decisions of 1981 and 1982. Ferguson and Rogers give credence to the idea that political leaders have moved so far out of line with the general public that the performance of the national economy is virtually all that matters these days in the approval of the president. As they put it, Reagan's upsurge in popularity before the 1984 elections "seems to have been caused almost entirely by changes in economic conditions in the country. It gives no evidence of a magic bond between Reagan and the public. Indeed, if one controls for economic conditions, Reagan's popularity does not differ significantly from Jimmy Carter's."[32]

The Reagan magic, it seems, was something concocted between his handlers and a compliant media, with a little help from massive deficit spending and a timely economic recovery. This makes it all the more puzzling why the Democrats in 1984 didn't read their own polls and challenge the fragile bond of media magic binding Reagan to his public support. In summary, there was an ample supply of issues on which Reagan had offended sizable chunks of the public, including many of his own supporters. In light of the Democrats' silence on these issues, we might have received the impression that public opinion was running in just the opposite direction, adding to Reagan's image of invulnerability and popularity, while further undermining any claims the Democrats could make on public approval. Yet silence characterized the Democratic platform on most issues in 1984, accompanied by an embarrassed shiftiness on a host of sensitive moral questions like abortion. Given the lack of hard social or economic issues in the Democratic repertoire, we can appreciate Mondale's unwillingness to run on issues like abortion alone. But the almost furtive avoidance of these moral matters is equally puzzling from a strategic standpoint when we consider an NBC News exit poll on election night, 1984, showing that two-thirds of those who voted favored legalization of abortion, while a subsequent *Los Angeles Times* poll revealed that only 32 percent of those voting for Reagan supported his abortion policy.[33]

According to this view, then, it seems that the Democrats are a party on the run—on the run from their own voters! They continued to run away from their natural constituents in 1988, when, again, numerous polls were available showing large portions of the public favoring more liberal stands than Dukakis offered on education, health, social security, and medicare. And, too, it turns out that Dukakis could have proposed a tax increase for those Americans earning over $80,000 per year and met with the favor of 82 percent of the electorate.[34] Yet the candidate remained silent on these and other issues while he took a pummeling from his opponent for being a *liberal*.

The Ferguson and Rogers right turn thesis is a provocative way of thinking about what has happened to American politics. However, their viewpoint has several troublesome implications that seem inconsistent with other well-known trends on the national political scene. In the end, the fragmentation thesis simply seems to fit more of the data about elections and the national political decline. Consider, for example, one of the more controversial implications of the right turn or investment thesis: that if the Democrats returned to their old liberal agenda they would find a loyal voter following waiting to support them and send them back to the White House with a stable mandate. What Ferguson and Rogers are right about, I think, is that the perception of a solid conservative majority emerging over the last twenty years is quite possibly wrong. This does not mean, however, that there remains a traditional liberal majority waiting in the wings for their cue from a Democratic party once again united behind its old liberal agenda. Recall, for example, the rise of the independent voter. True, a few issues from that old agenda remain popular, but core liberal ideas like the welfare state and government-as-social-problem-solver are dead. Reviving them will not help the Democrats make a come-back. The proof arrived in the late 1980s when Democratic congresses began passing liberal legislation, again, with little notable effect on voter enthusiasm or party fortunes. The point is simply this: while the strength of public support for the conservative visions of Reagan and Bush may have been greatly exaggerated, this does not mean that a return to an old liberal agenda can save the Democrats. With this shift in the argument, we can now take a more productive path toward understanding the Democratic dilemma for the 1990s.

First, however, we must examine how the widespread impression arose during the 1980s of a solidly conservative public. To begin with, a highly vocal, well-organized, and well-funded collection of conservative grass-roots groups had been pushing a variety of religious, moral, social, and economic agendas for more than two decades. Thus, Republican dominance of the White House and many legislative agendas was not accomplished with mirrors or sheer political flimflammery. Rather, the dropout of voters and groups on the left created something of a vacuum in the national dialogue that conservative voices filled quickly. The resulting (and largely correct) impression is that the right wing had the loudest public voice in the media and political campaigns. However, in evaluating public opinion, the loudest voice or the most salient viewpoint is not necessarily the most numerous one. One opinion theorist has described this opinion situation as a spiral of silence in which majorities become politically marginalized because of poor organization or little encouragement from candidates and leaders.[35] These silent majorities hear only the louder voices of other groups and leaders. It is easy for people to conclude from this that they are suddenly in a minority when this is not the case. From there, it is easy to form the impression that those who dominate media debate are in a majority when they are not. In thinking about whether the 1980s and early 1990s brought in a conservative high tide in America, it is useful to recall that both Ronald Reagan and George Bush were swept into the White House on tides of less than 30 percent of the eligible voters.

This much of the Ferguson–Rogers thesis seems to hold fairly well, but the next steps are more problematical. It is not clear that being driven into competition for conservative funding has made the Democratic party more conservative in any ideological or coherent programmatic sense. It has only become more idea-less and fragmented. Nor is it obvious that regaining its old liberal vision would do the party much good. In many ways, the legislative record of recent Democratic congresses (see Chapter 7) has gone back to the old liberal agenda. The investment theory is hard pressed to explain both how this happened and why it generated so little public enthusiasm. What has happened more generally to the Democrats may be even worse: (1) they have bargained themselves out of a solid party identity; (2) the best the leadership can achieve is faint party support for a ghost of the old Great Society vision; and (3) the incoherence of the party makes it difficult to regroup around any new vision at all. This state of affairs becomes even clearer when we look at the party in Congress and in the states.

As an example, let us look at the 1990 elections. (For a more detailed analysis, see Chapter 7.) According to one analysis, fully 382 of the 405 incumbents seeking reelection (the majority being Democrats) were involved in races with either no opposition or ran against opponents who were financially uncompetitive.[36] Congressional incumbents received more than thirty times the amount of funding from political action committees than did their challengers got. At the state level, the picture looks much the same, where 90 percent of state legislature candidates ran unopposed or without viable challengers.[37] Unless a major campaign finance reform movement takes hold soon, these trends will continue well into the future. The result is that individual candidates have little reason for party loyalty. The Democratic state and congressional parties are pulled apart—atomized into individual entrepreneurs with little incentive to worry about the big picture. Pushing popular issues without party support is pointless. Pushing the old liberal vision is, in many cases, suicidal. Above all, having no party vision appears to be of little disadvantage in these days of well-financed individual candidates. So where is the individual incentive or the party potential to experiment with new visions that might disturb the abilities of both candidates and parties to work out the thousands of political financing deals necessary to bankroll winning campaigns? Besides, if we forget about policy and governing and say, as the parties seem to be saying, that winning elections is the real measure of party strength, then the Democratic party is pumping iron at the congressional and state legislative levels.

These considerations suggest at least a couple of changes in Ferguson and Rogers' investment thesis. First, it may be too simple to say that the Democratic party, as some coherent whole, has moved to the right along a neat ideological continuum and that its salvation requires only sliding back to the left again. Second, and related to this point, is a perceptive critique by William Domhoff who argues that the real problem with campaign finance is not moving policies in or out of ideological alignment with the public, but, more generally, disrupting any systematic connections between policies and elections, or voting and government, as it were.[38] This is occurring in a system where vote–policy linkages are already weakened by a winner-take-all, two-party system that works against dramatic candidate differences and ideologically unified parties.[39]

One conclusion is clear: no matter what view of campaign finance we take, structural changes in the electoral system must occur if the parties are to work out anything resembling a broad political vision shared by voters. To return to the case of the Democrats, then, it is tempting but too simple to think that the party can get much mileage out of taking up, one at a time, the collection of scattered issues on which past Republican administrations have been at odds with the public. Without a coherent program or vision, the party has no way to give this loose collection of opinion poll questions any credibility or sense of governing purpose. In the best of times, a symbolic campaign issue or two is about all the party can gain from this wealth of public discontent (as in 1990 when congressional candidates were able to say that the party tax-and-budget package finally put the bite on the rich). As for the worst of times, let us listen to the ideas put forward by the Democratic and Republican candidates in 1988 on just a couple of the big issues:

On Trade

"Now is not the time for Americans or for our trading partners to take refuge in 'economic patriotism'—that's the term for protectionism. Don't we remember what happened the last time that was tried in the 1930's—policies which wrecked the world economy? . . . We need to compete, not retreat."

"We don't need more laws or more amendments or more gimmicks. We need a president who is tough enough and smart enough and experienced enough to use the authority he already has to bring down those barriers to American products overseas."

On the Deficit

"We've got to work that deficit down the old fashioned way, by controlling government spending. I've proposed a flexible freeze, under which total government spending can increase, but only at the rate of inflation . . . Put on that freeze and the deficit will come down."

"We'll set as our goal a steady, gradual reduction of the deficit which will require tough choices on spending. It will require a good strong rate of economic growth. It will require a plan that the President works out with Congress."

Can you guess which statement belonged to which candidate? Unless you have an excellent memory for trivia or a good ear for one speech writer's style over another, there are no other distinguishing features that might be helpful for telling the candidates apart on these or a dozen other major issues. (Answer: The first statement in each pair belongs to Bush, and the second to Dukakis.)[40]

And so the whole spectrum of big questions on which the candidates might stir the public interest shrinks to petty niggling and unconvincing blustering. Why didn't the Democratic candidate propose a jobs program despite his grand promise to "create good jobs at good wages for every citizen in the land"? We must look behind the rhetoric to the candidate's main economic adviser, Lawrence Summers, who stated flatly that unemployment must fall no lower than 6 percent to control inflation. This doesn't leave much room for spelling out a meaningful program difference with an opponent whose economic adviser favors a 7 percent unemployment rate. The only clear truth in all this is that neither candidate nor economist is working for the unemployed.[41]

Similarly, when the candidates have no major disagreement on fundamental defense commitments, the resulting campaign debate becomes tiresome quibbling over this or that weapons program, making the candidates sound knowledgeable about technicalities, even if out of touch with the big picture. Bruce Cummings noted the extent of the defense issue buydown in 1980 with this summary of the debate between Carter and Reagan:

> A straightforward essay on foreign policy debate in the presidential campaign would be brief indeed. It could be summarized as follows: do you want the MX missile, the Trident sub, the Rapid Deployment force, the "Stealth" bomber, the Cruise missile, counterforce targeting strategy leading to a first strike capability, the China card, containment in the "arc of crisis," and a 5% increase in defense spending; or do you want all of the above plus the neutron bomb, the B-1 bomber, anti-ballistic missile systems, civil defense capability and an 8% increase in defense spending? This was Carter versus Reagan.[42]

The overall result of the great political buydown is simple. Candidates just don't have much to say; indeed, they have far less to say than voters would like. Not surprisingly, many voters tune out and leave the political arena altogether. As for those who remain, they represent a tough sell, withholding their preferences, refraining from strong displays of party or candidate allegiance, and requiring all the marketing talents that Madison Avenue has developed through years of selling damaged goods to skeptical and weary consumers.

THE MARKETING CHASE

The arguments on marketing presented thus far can be summarized quickly. Once most of the governing ideas have been wrung out of a campaign, unpalatable issues like defense have been embraced equally, and the candidate dons a flawless if artificial character, campaigns are left with a tricky problem: how to sell what's left to the people. Selling damaged political goods isn't easy. First, voters must be convinced that they have a choice that means something, and then they must be led to accept the idea that within the confines of that choice they can live with one of the alternatives. This is a choice that fully half the electorate won't buy at all, preferring to do something else with the ten or fifteen minutes out of their lives that voting consumes every four years. If we were talking about cars, soap flakes, or deodorants, the marketplace would be in a shambles by now, with one of three obvious results: economic recession, loss of market share to foreign competition, or, as a last resort, improvements in product quality designed to lure consumers back to the market. For better or worse, the voting market doesn't respond like other markets do to declining product quality and resulting consumer unrest.

There is, of course, the danger that a collapsing political market will bring on a loss of political legitimacy, both for the candidates and for the political process that produced them. This decline in faith in the electoral process has various symptoms ranging from chronic dissatisfaction with the candidates to the precipitous decline in voting itself. Yet politics, even more than cars or underarm deodorants, is the realm of illusion. When signs of political illegitimacy begin to appear, image-making techniques can create the illusion of legitimacy to dispel serious consideration of the underlying problem. Elaborate Hollywood productions create the illusion of enthusiasm at the conventions, even as viewers at home wonder what all the excitement is about. All that needs be done is wrap the candidate in the flag—or at least stand George Bush up in front of the world's largest American flag—and have him promise to be more patriotic than his Brand X competition. Viewers at home can only shrug their shoulders and wonder if *they* missed something—if something is wrong with *them*. And who would utter discouraging words in public? Politicians who are trying to make the hard sell in the first place? Journalists who fear rocking the boat without the lead of politicians?

This postmodern version of democracy boils down to a marketing problem. As noted in Chapters 1 and 2, the question of what this means for democracy is lost on the marketing experts who, after all, are only doing a job. It is a job that may not be pretty, but, as they say, somebody has to do it. The first blow to democracy comes with the recognition that since the electoral arena differs from the economic one, the problem of damaged goods isn't so overwhelming. In fact, the first move is to rethink the whole democratic marketplace in order to turn the seeming liability of consumer defection into an advantage. All this requires is lowering the value of democratic participation, and the first big hurdle is cleared easily. Recall here from the first chapter the words of Republican strategist Paul Weyrich who ushered in this democratic devaluation as bluntly as can be imagined: "I don't want everyone to vote. Our leverage in the election quite candidly goes up as the voting population goes down."[43] This is the first principle of the new politics.

Noting this fundamental shift in the democratic tradition, Benjamin Ginsberg observed that "politicians of both parties have turned away from mobilizing voters in an effort to win elections." With predictable, if ironic, results, as Ginsberg points out: "The upshot of all this is that in the United States today the electoral process itself seems to be declining in importance. The electoral arena seems less decisive than we assume it to be under most democratic theories and less decisive than at any other time in our history. We are entering what could almost be called a post-electoral era in the United States."[44] Aiming similar concerns at the wholesale entry of campaign consultants into elections, Mark Petracca said: "The United States faces a monumental challenge to the practice of democratic governance. The challenge stems, in part, from significant changes in the conceptualization and practice of political campaigning and from the revolutionary effects of the technology deployed in contemporary campaigns."[45]

Beyond turning the decline of participation from a problem into a virtue, campaign consultants exert a number of other worrisome influences on the quality of national political life. First, they boost levels of ambiguity and symbolic abstraction in a system already burdened with plenty of both. As Petracca suggests, campaign consultants have turned an annoying tendency toward empty rhetoric into standard, institutionalized procedure.[46] Alongside this trend is a second development of equal concern. In a survey of campaign consultants, Petracca found that candidates have abandoned the content side of campaigning to an alarming extent. Forty-four percent of the consultants said that their candidates were neither very involved nor very influential in setting the issue priorities in their own campaigns. Moreover, 60 percent of the consultants revealed that their clients were neither very involved nor influential in the tactical side of the campaign.[47] Perhaps it isn't surprising to learn that when politicians hire consultants, they abdicate much of their control over campaign content, but it is nonetheless disturbing to think about the implications.

The direct marketing of candidates has dealt a possibly fatal blow to the health of political parties in America. Several prior factors account for the decline of parties as ideological melting pots, grass-roots forums, and leadership development pools. For example, the direct financing of campaigns by PACs and the resulting lack of political competition owing to high incumbency rates greatly reduced the dependence of politicians on parties.[48] However, the dependence of candidates on marketing consultants has blown open the gap between politicians and the last vestiges of ideologically coherent, disciplined, broadly representative party organizations.[49] In the words of former campaign consultant Walter de Vries, perhaps the most important consequence of the new politics is this weakening of the two-party system: "Candidates now deal primarily with consultants. They seldom deal seriously with the parties. . . . During my 25 years as a campaign consultant, I was responsible only to my clients."[50]

Clearly, all these tendencies are on the upswing, following closely the growth of the political marketing industry itself. The American Association of Political Consultants was founded in 1967 with fewer than forty members. Today, there are 800 members representing 400 firms, and this is just the tip of the iceberg. When we include the large number of freelancers and unaffiliated consultants operating in smaller political campaigns, there are, according to de Vries, some 12,000 people earning part or most of their incomes from political consulting. The growth in this industry has been exponential. According to Petracca's survey, fully half the firms have been created since 1980, up from one quarter in 1974 and rising from the tiny 8 percent of today's total that were in business in 1964.[51]

The ripple effects of this strategic industry are beginning to reach well beyond elections into the day-to-day operations of American politics. The services provided by political consultants seldom end on election day as they once did. Having abandoned programs and philosophies to the marketing magic used to win elections, elected officials realize that they have trouble sustaining the public relations atmosphere of the campaign after reaching office. This can be more than a little frightening to the politician who realizes that he (and most of them are still men in this world of power) is in danger of revealing himself to be someone other than the image that was just elected. This moment of shock sends most well-financed politicians back to their consultants for advice about what to do in office—and how to do it. This last trend goes well beyond the effects that political consultants may have on participation, parties, and programs, and into another, perhaps deeper area of concern about their impact on the quality of leadership itself.

Related to this addiction of leaders to their public images is a still deeper problem for democracy: the conversion of the national political scene into an endless election in which the goal is to dodge the problems and issues of the day, keep one's image strong, and make it to the next election with a full campaign chest and no mistakes to live down. Postmodern politicians no longer campaign to win elections and get on with the business of governing. Rather, they govern much as they campaign: to be assured of winning the next election and getting on with the business of staying in office.

The time is past when consultants assumed their jobs were over on election night, writing a termination clause into candidate-consultant contracts to clarify that understanding. Recalling that time not so long ago, former consultant de Vries writes: "Consultants did not expect to be part of the governing process—to go on to the White House, the State House, or other governmental positions. Now, many consultants are retained to advise their candidate/office holders in the course of governing as well as in campaigning. This, to me, is a disturbing trend that raises all kinds of ethical questions. This trend has accelerated during the 1980's elections, and I think it is one that will certainly continue."[52]

As an example, de Vries cites the elevation of Bush consultant/

campaign manager Lee Atwater to the chairmanship of the Republican party. (Atwater later stepped down for health reasons.) While Atwater was left to run the party (presumably without damaging the interests of his man in the White House), the political vacuum inside the executive mansion was filled by appointing glitzy image-maker and former Bush campaign TV producer Sig Rogich to the position of special assistant to the president for activities and initiatives. The job, according to the view presented in the *New York Times,* resembles the same post "raised to a cynical art form in the Reagan years by Michael K. Deaver, [and] entails shaping the president's message and themes, planning his travel schedule and crafting how what he does looks for television."[53]

In addition to producing television commercials for Reagan in 1984, Rogich had a hand in successful 1988 Bush campaign ads featuring the candidate taking environmental shots at Dukakis while standing in front of polluted Boston Harbor. Another devastating spot accused Dukakis of being lenient on crime because of his support for revolving door prison furlough programs. After the election, the White House staff grew nervous that it had lost the "image-edge" it had achieved during the campaign, and wanted to fix the fuzzy image relapse suffered by the president after taking office. And so, they hired Rogich to ghost the president's leadership style.

Who is Sig Rogich? In his spare time, he ran the largest advertising firm in Nevada, worked for clients including Donald Trump and Frank Sinatra (helping Sinatra win a gambling license), served as a Nevada boxing commissioner, acted as a director of Bally's Casino, and helped the Stardust Hotel improve its image after it had been linked to organized crime. With all that behind him, Rogich rose to the challenge of democracy by saying, "I know it sounds corny for someone to tell you they're patriotic and that they feel honored to do something like this. But I believe deeply in this president because he's a good guy."[54]

What exactly do marketing specialists contribute to a campaign? For starters, they accept the limitations on what candidates are willing to say to voters, while taking up the challenge those limits pose for creating voter enthusiasm. Next, they size up the population of people likely to vote and apply basic marketing techniques (polling, focus groups, "people meter" sessions) to evaluate the relative strengths and weaknesses of the client and the opponent, along with themes that generate public interest within the range of topics left open for discussion. Finally, a marketing strategy is devised to deliver favorable candidate images, unfavorable opponent images, and salient themes to key segments of the voting market. These key voter blocs, or target audiences, are determined by applying four criteria:

1. Are they already likely to vote? (There is no point in complicating an already difficult job by stirring up dormant voters.)
2. Are they undecided? (It is nearly impossible to get people to change their minds if they are strongly committed to the opposing candidate or party.)
3. Is it possible to appeal to the resulting groups without creating a backlash in some other group already likely to vote for the candidate? (This would be a very poor return on the marketing dollar.)
4. Which of the finalist groups are located in key states in sufficient numbers that winning their support could make a difference in the outcome of the electoral college vote? (There is no point in turning out people whose votes would not tip the final outcome.)

Running the voting population through these screening criteria helps explain why campaigns can take such strange forms, sometimes seeming out of touch with a candidate's most loyal supporters. "How could Dukakis shrink in shame from the 'L-word,' and sell out the minority vote?" wondered many staunch Democrats in 1988. On the other side of the fence, many Republicans fretted over Bush's apparent softening on defense and the budget, not to mention his dangerous flirtation with environmentalism. The concerns of loyalists in both camps were well-founded reactions to contemporary presidential elections that boil down to spending more than $100 million in hard money and several times that in soft funds to make delicate marketing pitches to groups that may be as small as 10 percent of the total electorate. Yet, in the view of consultants, this tiny percentage of the population meets the four criteria on which campaign strategy is based. Thus, a relatively small number of voters becomes the focus of the entire election. We can appreciate how it is best not to worry too much about what this means for the idea of democracy.

With these marketing considerations in mind, the peculiarities of campaigns begin to make more sense. Consider, first, the Democratic strategy in 1988 which was shaped by the following generalizations. To begin with, Democratic party loyalists are less likely to vote than their Republican counterparts. If we are to believe political scientists, this is because Democrats are less endowed with the requisite amounts of education, income, and occupational status that inspire higher levels of civic virtue. Alternatively, the Democrats may have been less successful in rewarding their followers with prizes like higher salaries, better jobs, and more education that might close both the loyalty and the socioeconomic gap between the party faithful. Whatever the reasons, people who say they are Democrats are less loyal than their Republican counterparts. Compounding the problem, larger numbers of traditional Democrats have slipped into the independent category than Republicans, and many of them go all the way across the line to vote for the other side, accounting for the phenomenon variously described as Reagan Democrats or blue collar Republicans.

The trick, as party strategists saw it in 1988, was to hold the line on those 10 million or so voters and thereby reverse the Republican lock on the presidency. The problem with their analysis was that the party had already lost those voters in the first place because it offered them little in the way of job programs, health care, or other economic incentives to balance the otherwise attractive Republican rhetoric on abortion, welfare, and civil rights—a rhetoric that translates fairly well across fundamentalist, redneck, and blue collar lines.

"But," cried an equally large faction within the highly fragmented party, "what about the black and minority vote?" With a little encouragement, that market segment could also be delivered to the party nominee. The trouble with the black vote, countered the marketing experts, is that it is only one-sixth of the total needed to win, and it is distributed badly over the geography of the electoral map. This means two things. First, a lot of blacks live in the North and East, where the Democrats might do fairly well, anyway, without them. Second, a lot of blacks live in the South, where appealing to them would surely drive those sensitive conservative Democrats into the arms of the Republicans. After all, blue collar Democrats all around the country would be listening carefully to what Dukakis said to black voters, creating the possibility of white flight in places as far away as California and Illinois. Such are the dangers of pursuing a marketing strategy in the media age. An appeal to each targeted group must be weighed against its possible effects on other key groups who may be listening.

After much gnashing of teeth and infighting, the marketers won the day by producing poll data showing that two-thirds of the targeted Democrats strongly opposed Jesse Jackson and were equally opposed to the kinds of campaign appeals that would be required to win over Jackson's constituency.[55] Even though the social programs and defense cuts on Jackson's agenda might have won the support of a majority of Americans, the prevailing wisdom in this age of high finance, mini-market democracy is that majorities no longer rule. Victory goes to strategic market segments.

It was therefore decided to cut the minorities adrift and go after the blue collared birds who were in danger of flying into the Bush camp. The trouble was, Dukakis had nothing to offer them. Undaunted by this apparent Catch-22, the marketers followed their own strategic analysis and tried to win them over anyway. As Gerald Pomper observed, "Dukakis presented no striking new programs, nor did he provide any content to his promises of 'the next American frontier,' and 'a new era of greatness.' The values he stressed were uncontroversial: economic opportunity, pride in ethnic traditions, good jobs at good wages, honesty among public officials, community concern."[56]

While having little to offer his target audience, Dukakis at the same time opened himself up to attacks on his exposed moral flank: abortion, school prayer, civil rights, and the flag salute. It was painful to watch him as he took one Bush campaign ad after another right on the chin. By the time he decided to counterattack and admit that he was, after all, a liberal and proud of it, he resembled a punch-drunk fighter barely able to remember why he was in the ring. In his famous stammering performance on Ted Koppel's "Nightline," it would have been more humane for Koppel to have declared a TKO and gently turned out the television lights.

Not only did Dukakis step into the powerful right hook thrown by the Bush marketing people (one wonders if the Democratic marketing strategy could have been more damaging had it been left to the Republicans), but also the decision to sell out traditional party constituencies like the black vote further undermined what was left of the party itself. As Dukakis doggedly pursued the strategy laid out by his marketers, daily newspaper headlines watched both the decline of his lead and the growing rift with the black community. Beneath a *New York Times* headline saying, "JACKSON AIDES SAY DUKAKIS WANTS HIM TO LIMIT CAMPAIGN," those Jackson aides averred that their man had been told to stay out of Mississippi, Alabama, Michigan, New York, and Texas.[57] These states had lots of black voters but equal numbers of the white swing voters designated as the favored targets of the Dukakis campaign strategy.

Even after it became clear that the chosen marketing strategy was not a winning one, Dukakis was slow to give it up. The chair of the House Democratic Caucus, William Gray of Pennsylvania, recounted what initially appeared to be a fence-mending session between Dukakis and eighteen black religious leaders toward the end of the campaign. Everything went well until after Dukakis left and Gray began looking around outside for the usual press members waiting for a comment from the participants. A Dukakis aide told Gray there would be no press coverage, signalling that the candidate was still more concerned about losing the votes of conservative white Democrats than winning the black vote.[58] At that point, Dukakis' determination to breathe life into a dead campaign strategy only added insult to injury, there being little he could have done to change the outcome of the election. As Willie Brown, speaker of the California Assembly, put it, "By this stage, people have given up on Dukakis. When you manage to go from a 17-point lead to an 11-point deficit in a matter of 8 short weeks, they're not inclined to buy a lottery ticket from you, never mind electing you president."[59]

There is both good news and bad news for democracy in the fact that Dukakis played out this kind of "death wish" marketing strategy to the bitter end. First, the good news: there are some things that marketers, no matter how sophisticated their technique or strategy, just can't sell. There was more than a little hubris in the notion that you could get a working-class and redneck audience to buy a cowering liberal with no substantive promises and the contrived image that, beneath the Boston technocratic exterior, he was really just "an average guy, with a 25-year-old snow blower, a modest duplex, a loving family. He was Joe Suburbia ennobled—worthy of the White House."[60]

But before breathing too deeply in relief that the threat of an Orwellian democracy has been lifted, consider the bad news. So binding is this gospel of candidate marketing that campaigns embrace it all the way through, even in losing causes. Candidates simply don't know what to do without their consultants. Even when Dukakis realized his scripted strategy was failing, he could do no better than fire one set of marketers and hire another who served him no better. This brings us to the worst news about the universal hold of political marketing on the electoral process: even when one side's marketing strategy is inept, the other side's marketing strategy is winning the day. Whether the strategies are good, bad, or indifferent, one of two marketed candidates will always win the election.

And now for a few words about the strategy used to elect George Bush under the masterful planning of "the three marketeers": campaign manager Lee Atwater, chief pollster Robert Teeter, and top media man Roger Ailes (with strong assists from pollster Richard Wirthlin and the aforementioned Sig Rogich). This impressive lineup of heavy hitters illustrates de Vries' observation that, as consultants hold more sway over campaigns, their roles become more specialized and their ranks more numerous:

> The early consultants—in the campaigns of the 1960's—were generalists. They knew something about every piece of a campaign and advised candidates on everything. What you have now increasingly is more and more specialized consultants who deal only with television production, media buys, fund raising, polling and so on. Today, a campaign can have as many as three, four, or five consultants and I'm not just talking about presidential campaigns; I'm talking about statewide and even lesser campaigns.[61]

Saddled with a candidate who had an overwhelming image problem of being "a wimp," the Bush team went to work fashioning tough-guy attacks on the opposition. Bush attacks on crime, abortion, prayer, and the flag salute weren't pretty, but given the diminished confines of what the candidates were willing to talk about, they were effective. The heart of the Bush strategy was to keep the blue collar Reaganites in the fold with a host of shrill attacks summarized by conservative columnist George Will as the "Eeeeek!—a liberal!" campaign.[62] *New York Times* reporter Mark Green dubbed the Bush strategy the *slur du jour* approach.[63]

Pollster Teeter dignified the approach by explaining that "People don't decide based on some great revelation. They form their views based on thousands of little bits of information that shake out from television ads and news stories, from pictures of the candidates' wives, kids, dogs and homes."[64] Knowing how to deliver those bits of information in a range of styles from family pictures to the *slur du jour* is made easier by working up what Teeter calls a perceptual map, which is a psychological model of how people see the candidates and what happens to that perception when this or that bit of information is added or subtracted.[65]

It turned out that adding the slurs about crime, the flag, and other liberal quagmires both solved the Bush wimp problem and exposed Dukakis' greatest weakness with his target audience. The Bush consultants worked with focus groups of Reagan Democrats and gradually found the image that drove them away from Dukakis and toward Bush. The most effective image of all was the story of a prison furlough program in Dukakis' home state that released a black convict named Willie Horton for a weekend. Horton, a convicted murderer, raped a white woman during his weekend release. The story was rich. Some said it appealed to deeply held racism among the targeted blue collar Republicans. Beyond the racial overtones, it was clear that the Willie Horton story evoked the image that Dukakis, like all liberals, was soft on crime. After observing the effects of the Horton story on focus groups of targeted voters, Atwater is reported to have said, "If I can make Willie Horton a household name, we'll win the election." He is reported to have followed up that remark at another Republican gathering by saying, "There's a story about a fellow named Willie Horton who, for all I know, may end up being Dukakis' running mate."[66] Willie Horton did become a household name, and Dukakis never recovered. Later stricken with a terminal illness, Atwater repented the Willie Horton ad, but the system that creates such political communication lives on.

To counter the danger that the Bush image would become too tough and mean-spirited as a result of all this negativity, the attacks on Dukakis were limited to about 50 percent of the content of the media campaign. The other half of the messages showed Bush exuding sympathy: playing with his grandchildren; promising relief for the poor and the overtaxed alike; and occasionally pointing out that he really liked Dukakis, who was a decent human being underneath that regrettable liberal exterior. In the end, Bush would forgive his poor opponent for being hopelessly out of step with America—that is, with that tiny slice of the American public for whom most of the campaign was staged.

When Bush was not slashing away at Dukakis or issuing campaign promises in Clint Eastwood, "read my lips" rhetoric, he spoke of a "kinder, gentler nation" illuminated by "a thousand points of light." At first, the candidate expressed some discomfort with the new persona fashioned for him by his consultants. Roger Ailes summarized Bush's early reactions to the negative ads and the attack days on the campaign trail by saying, "He hates it, but he knows we'd be getting killed if we didn't go negative."[67] Although expressing a preference for the "kinder, gentler" days, the candidate acknowledged that the sweet and sour personality was having its desired effect on those voters for whom it was created. "I like the mix," Bush told *New York Times* reporter Maureen Dowd in a tone that she described "as though he had just sipped a martini or tasted a pasta sauce and found the ingredients perfectly blended."[68]

In this age of the mass-marketed candidate, it no longer matters who the real George Bush is, just as it is beside the point to ask what the real Michael Dukakis stands for. Candidate marketing shapes a candidate's personality and rhetoric. The key to it all is the ironic human capacity that leads voters to make sense of almost any available information. The hardy souls who stay tuned to the contest must strive to make the whole experience credible. As Hershey put it, these "voters respond to the political stimuli they receive"[69]—even, it seems, when those stimuli are offensive, contrived, or devoid of political consequence. Thus, in the words of one analysis, "The public's response to symbols—the flag, tanks, liberals, and criminals—dominated the 1988 campaign."[70]

MEDIA CONTROL

"Damage control" has taken its place alongside "spin doctor" and "sound bite" as the favorite phraseology of contemporary politics. Many journalists understand that the contemporary election has made the final transition from logos to logo, from the spontaneous to the contrived, from real to realistic. They lament covering "The Speech" day in and day out while searching desperately for something new or interesting to offer their audiences. They write increasingly of how candidates and their consultants try to manipulate news content. They note declining voter registration and growing distress among those who remain in the voting ranks.

They grow angry and frustrated, waiting to pounce on a candidate mistake—eager for a chance to unleash the press in a spontaneous question and answer session with the candidates.

If the marketed candidate is to survive in this volatile atmosphere, the name of the game is to control the media. The good news for campaigns is that the press is easily controlled because it depends on content generated by the candidates themselves—a dependence reinforced by the growing conservatism in corporate media ownership. As Mark Hertsgaard has noted, contemporary campaigning follows the media control strategy developed in the Reagan White House: "Control your message by keeping reporters and their questions away from a scripted candidate; capture TV's attention with prefabricated, photo-opportunity events that reinforce the campaign's chosen 'line of the day.' "[71] This strategy only works, however, if the media remain willing to let the politicians dictate the content of the news. Hertsgaard noted, for example, that considerable documentary evidence contradicted Bush's denials of involvement with the Iran–Contra scandal and the Noriega fiasco in Panama, creating an obvious opportunity to break out of the media control trap and raise a challenging issue that the candidate would have to address. In this connection, recall here from Chapter 1 the words of the network producer who revealed that he turned down a hard-hitting piece from one of his reporters, saying simply "We don't want to look like we're going after George Bush."[72]

The result of this syndrome of a restless but often controllable press is that we enter an Alice-in-Wonderland world where the media savage the candidates who can't control them, while offering grudging respect for those who can. The spin doctors, marketers, handlers, and other damage control experts have become the political antiheroes of the age. In this upside-down world, the campaign becomes evaluated according to a perverse aesthetics of media mastery. For example, Marjorie Hershey observed that the press judged the debates in 1988 largely in terms of the candidates' media demeanor. This observation provoked her equally disturbing conclusion that the post-debate news commentary of 1988 "was a landmark in the development of politics as a spectator sport. Media values had almost completely supplanted the values of governing."[73]

Meanwhile, the grumbling press continues to be led around by the campaign's story of the day, no matter how contrived, empty, or repetitive. Veteran journalist David Broder describes a typical scene on the early morning press plane as sleepy reporters sink into their seats, downing Bloody Marys to steady the nerves from late-night complaint sessions in the bar the night before. The only activity is in the forward cabin where the candidate's speech writer works feverishly on The Speech to be delivered that night, knowing that the reporters must have advance copies to make their filing deadlines. As each page is finished, mimeo stencils are cut, run off, and collated. At last, the one hundred copies are completed and handed out. Broder notes the transformation in the press section as pandemonium breaks out: "Now their sloth disappears, and they quickly read through the offering. 'Where's the lead?' someone asks. 'Bottom of page six!' shouts a wire service man, who took a course in speed reading. Everyone underlines the designated passage."[74] Suddenly, the press corps is hard at work writing up The Story. Soon after the plane lands for its first stop of the day, The Story is flying over the wires to the major news organizations and syndication services in the country.

And so it goes. The press complains, the consultants calculate, the spin doctors spin, and the candidates are wheeled out on cue in front of the visual backdrop of the day. Bush appears before the world's largest American flag, walks down the runway with the just-landed crew of the *Discovery* space shuttle, and points at a polluted Boston Harbor while warning spectators not to open their mouths if they fall in. Meanwhile, Dukakis claps his hands awkwardly to the beat of a black gospel choir, rides around in a tank like a slightly demented child, and provides a dowdy contrast next to actress Daryl Hannah on a stage. The difference between these campaign stories of the day is that one candidate managed to look more comfortable with his part. That's all.

Is there an alternative? Apparently not. Even the Dukakis camp preferred its awkward media control efforts to the early days of the campaign when the candidate was allowed to mix it up with the press. Reporter Michael Oreskes explained:

> There is no reason to speak through the news media, and the campaigns say, no particular punishment for avoiding the reporters. In fact, Dukakis campaign officials say that before they isolated their candidate the campaign suffered greatly for being accessible. Mr. Bush would launch attacks and Mr. Dukakis, confronted by reporters, would answer. He looked defensive, Mr. Bush looked in control. Mr. Dukakis plummeted in the polls.[75]

What responsibility do the media assume for constructing an independent agenda of issues and challenges to bring the candidates out of hiding? Apparently, they have none. In response to Oreskes' analysis above, *Chicago Tribune* editor James Squires voiced the popular belief among media executives that it was up to the voters, not journalists, to deal with candidates who hide from reporters.[76] Even when media reports become more critical, their impact on cynical voters may be to reinforce the cynicism.

Meanwhile the media remain locked in a vicious cycle of electoral politics that only a serious round of reforms can change.

We come full circle. In the end, the election process falls under the political loophole of presumed democracy. No matter how they are financed, marketed, or mediated, the electoral choices presented to the public are presumed to constitute some outpouring of democracy, and if there is something amiss, it is for the public to fix. One wonders, however, who will finance the popular reform movement, how it will be marketed to politicians, and who will publicize the efforts.

PART II

Political Culture
at the Crossroads

From the White House to Capitol Hill, the critical weakness of American
politics and governance is becoming woefully apparent: a frightening
inability to define and debate emerging problems. For the moment, the
political culture appears to be brain-dead. —*Kevin Phillips*

CHAPTER 5

Running on Ritual

Society revolves around a calendar of rituals: planting and harvest; birth and death; graduation, career, and retirement; marriage and family-building; gift-giving and economic exchange; power-sharing and political succession; religious worship and spiritual rebirth. These ritual events mark the passages and cycles of life. From grand public occasions like coronations and elections, to the private celebration of bar/bat mitzvahs and weddings, rituals mark time, create order in moments of change, and recall the meanings and messages of civilized life.

Rituals suspend the ordinary course of daily existence and invite us to become spectator-participants in larger-than-life events. Well-performed rituals are at once familiar in script and caricature, and at the same time full of drama, mystery, and surprise. Actors who are given over to the dramatic possibilities before them call up the great traditions and truths of society with an eye to the contemporary concerns of the participants.

Taken seriously, these dramatic affirmations of society and culture bring the wisdom of the ages to bear on thought and action in the present. Creative leaders speak the emerging truths of the day, sowing the seeds of myths for future generations to live by. Yet rituals also can fall victim to cynicism and neglect, becoming little more than instruments to bedazzle and manipulate a people. Brittle and transparent, they break apart under the strain of apathy and popular disbelief.

The trouble with rituals, then, is that they are easily reduced to empty exercises in which people simply go through the motions. The actors become cardboard characters—objects of secret scorn and mockery rather than the embodiments of wisdom and virtue. When leaders no longer bring new life to old litanies, prayers, vows, and myths, the meaningful links between past and present, society and the individual, are broken. Contemporary problems and concerns are paid lip-service. Visions for the future grow dim.

Decaying rituals are confusing to people who still try to find meaning in them. Like fading images whose parts remain clear enough to suggest the whole, they are reminiscent of something meaningful, but ultimately elusive and unsatisfying. In American elections, the party conventions still have the balloons, the music, and the demonstrations, but political conflicts are suppressed in favor of harmony for the television cameras. Platforms have dissolved into so many words on paper, binding none to their spirit. Meanwhile, on the campaign trail, candidates continue to invoke themes and symbols from the grand American mythology, while assiduously avoiding applying those principles to initiatives for change that might bring the people back into the governing process.

In an age when political consultants regard voter apathy as a strategic advantage, there is no reason to revive the grand dramas of the political culture. The need to control image and communication frustrates collective actions that might breathe life into a dormant citizenry. Thus, the grand problems and promises that might inspire and ignite a people are ignored in favor of the low-cost, manageable symbols—prayer, abortion, race—that discourage and divide. Low-powered groups—the poor, the minorities, the elderly—are eased out of the political picture. Society becomes an awkward place in which public life finds disparate groups moving uneasily around each other.

This is not to suggest that well-functioning rituals are celebrations of peace and harmony. Embedded within most cultures are conflicting traditions, class and ethnic differences, and competing human values. It is within the relatively safe confines of ritual performances that these tensions can be expressed, explored, and resolved, however tentatively. The problem arises when rituals are no longer used as safe, and even playful, contexts in which to express social strains and problems. When constituent groups and their traditional concerns are ignored, the social fabric begins to tear apart. Society becomes dispirited.

The transformation of elections into marketing situations reduces the grand ritual to a propaganda battle that is often cynically narrow in its social appeal. Not that elections are always (or even often) social free-for-alls from which great coalitions emerge to change the course of history. Like a structured dance or a familiar piece of music, all ritual contains a patterned core. However, in healthy rituals there is also the potential for spontaneous exchanges with the audience that may open up surprising opportunities to rewrite the historical script of society. It is this potential that is being drained from American elections. When people sense that rituals have become empty, whether through corruption or neglect, they hear the familiar words and see people going through the old motions, but doubt their relevance to the everyday life of society.

In charting the decline of the election ritual, it is useful to analyze a transitional contest in which the old patterns from history are evident but in which they also run up against the forces of historical change. The election of 1976 was such a case. In that year, the rules and well-known litanies of campaigning chafed against the pressures of marketing and media control that have since driven spontaneity, bold initiatives, and popular enthusiasm out of American political life. In this contest Jimmy Carter and Gerald Ford battled for the nation's top office, while Ronald Reagan learned the hard lessons that enabled him to emerge four years later as America's first postmodern president.

In many ways, 1976 was a year ripe for political renewal. The war in Vietnam was over. The ordeal of Watergate and governmental corruption was laid to rest by congressional investigation, reform legislation, and purging the worst offenders from government. (It is perhaps significant that through his resignation in 1974 Richard Nixon and the public did not engage in the grand purging ritual of impeachment.) In addition, campaign finance reform was being tried out for the first time, without the specter of PACs that would come to dominate the political scene in the next decade.

Yet, an independent and suspicious electorate remained understandably mistrustful of politicians and parties. Not surprisingly, Jimmy Carter's main campaign theme that carried him to victory was "trust me." In Carter's march toward victory we see clear signs of transition from the old politics to the new: for example, the marketing of independent voters and the blurring of distinctions between political advertising and news. At the same time, however, we also find in the primaries that year a great deal of spontaneous exchange between the candidates. Surprisingly, the most spontaneous of all was Ronald Reagan, who learned a bitter lesson that year: *the emerging election game requires leaving content and public performances to the media consultants to script.* It was a lesson that he applied with great success throughout the 1980s (see Chapter 2). Ironically, the candidate who learned this lesson best in 1976 was Jimmy Carter, who then abandoned it later in office. Not until Ronald Reagan in 1980 and 1984 did we see a president whose advisers understood the importance of playing the new political game both during elections and in office.

In short, in 1976 the first signs of the new system (the rise of independent voters, the decline of party, the emergence of independent candidates, the changing communication game, etc.) began grating uneasily against the old electoral system. For that reason, it is an ideal case to show how the political culture itself—the guidance system or national idea forum of American politics—began to break down. Let's drop in on Election '76 for a look at a political culture at the crossroads.

RIGHT TIME, WRONG ELECTION

In the midst of the 1976 presidential campaign, senior American states-
man W. Averell Harriman journeyed to the Soviet Union to brief Soviet
premier Leonid Brezhnev on the election. The major purpose of the visit
seemed to be to assure Brezhnev that he need not take the candidates'
statements too seriously. Harriman said of his mission: "It's awfully hard
to understand the workings of an American campaign, but I think I did
some good. I think he was somewhat relieved by what I had to say. I'm
sure he wasn't totally satisfied. I'm not sure I was able to persuade him
that everything that was said was of no importance."[1]

It is unlikely that Harriman meant that the candidates' pronouncements on various subjects during the campaign were of *no* importance.
However, as everyone knows, candidates often say things just to win
votes. Moreover, they have to say things just to appear plausible as people
engaged in a familiar ritual. In other words, the same symbolic appeals
that win or lose votes for the candidates also establish the election ritual
itself. All this means that the candidates' vote-getting or pragmatic language (campaign rhetoric) must also serve as the ritualistic symbols
through which citizens work out tensions and satisfy needs for security,
order, leadership, and control over the future. These basic human concerns are addressed by elections and all other rituals of political succession. Thus, if we are to understand how elections have traditionally
worked, candidate rhetoric must be interpreted at two levels: the set of
pragmatic symbols that attract votes, and the ritualistic symbols that give
the ceremony its impact and the contested office its importance.

Although these two levels of campaign rhetoric are easier to deal with
separately for analytical purposes, it is clear that they operate together in
the real world. It makes sense to think a sort of cultural logic underlies
campaign appeals. This logic permits certain pragmatic advantages to flow
from properly constructed ritual acts, and, at the same time, it assures that
the ritual will be served by well-constructed pragmatic appeals. This dual
logic guides the participants in any established cultural ritual to act in ways
that both accomplish practical ends and affirm important principles, values, and community identities. For example, the spring (fertility) and
autumn (harvest) rites of agricultural communities assure the timely performance of practical activities—planting and harvesting, respectively.
They also dramatize community concerns about survival and affirm beliefs
about the means of survival.

The key to a successful or humanly satisfying ritual is whether the
participants sense that the script is also open to them and their everyday
needs.[2] In sum, the question is whether the performance is open to

change, new leadership, the expression of popular discontent, and a search for insights that might apply to the uncertainties of life in today's society. There is always a fine line between order and chaos, stability and change, in the political arena. Rituals are the settings in which that line is discussed, explored, drawn, and redrawn.

The 1976 election is an interesting case because the ritual order was displayed in all its finely drawn etiquette, yet pressures for new ideas and bold initiatives were held in check by the emerging technologies of marketing and media control. Jimmy Carter emerged the victor but an enigmatic one. Was he the new leader to guide the nation out of its period of moral decay following Vietnam and the Watergate crisis? Or was he an elusive, if cleverly drawn, media image, carrying his garment bag from the campaign plane and walking down Pennsylvania Avenue to his own inaugural? It was hard to tell from the campaign performance whether Carter had the "right stuff" to mobilize the public in an effort to move an unwieldy political system in some new direction. Ultimately, most people turned away from him, sensing that his presidential call for moral stock-taking lacked a political vision to go with it.

Carter's ignominious exit from office in 1980 was the last act of a ritual drama that opened full of hope and expectation in the snows of Iowa in 1976. It was a year in which the people wanted more from their leaders than simply going through the motions. Carter won because he was the outsider in a time of inside corruption. He seemed sincere in an age of deceit. His strong religious code promised morality in an age of cynicism.

But something was missing. Even though Gerald Ford, the incumbent Republican opponent, displayed an astonishing penchant for blundering and ineptitude, and despite his being marked as the handpicked successor of the disgraced Richard Nixon, the 1976 election ended as a close contest with Ford nearly seizing victory from the jaws of defeat. In the end, the slim margin of Carter's victory can be attributed to his promise of change, even though there was little beyond the media image to give foundation to that promise.

The election ritual of 1976 was in the end too manipulated, too closed, too empty. It was a strange and unsatisfying contest in light of the public clamoring for a new national agenda, the avoidance of tired symbols, and candidate accountability. The conditions favoring these possibilities looked promising during the primary elections. Both party nominations were contested vigorously. The Republican race involved a challenge to the incumbent president (Ford), with the challenger (Ronald Reagan) pledging repeatedly to address specific policy questions of major consequence. On the Democratic side, the large number of candidates should have diminished pragmatic pressures to hedge the rhetoric in order to win centrist voters.

Moreover, many of the candidates claimed independence from both party and political establishment. These factors, combined with the waning public faith in government following Vietnam and the Watergate scandal, led many of the challengers to promise they would face serious problems, ask real questions, take uncompromising stands, and offer voters clear choices.

Given the number of candidates, the new faces in the race, the challenge to a sitting president, and the general backdrop of scandal in government and ebbing public faith in leaders, there seemed to be some basis for taking these promises seriously in 1976. Despite all these conditions, the political rhetoric of the primaries and the general election was restricted campaign fare. Election '76 might have been any election, and the candidates might have been any candidates. The analysis of statements made by these contestants reveals the capacity of marketing and media control techniques to hold the election ritual—even when there is great pressure for change—to the bare minimum requirements of ritualistic and pragmatic rhetoric. In short, an empty ritual.

THE RITUALISTIC BASIS OF CAMPAIGN RHETORIC

The pragmatic or vote-getting communications among participants in a ritual must also establish the ritual itself. A ritual is properly established when the actors are able to communicate through their ordinary dialogue (1) that they are doing some familiar social activity, (2) that they are doing it in a competent fashion, and (3) that the participants and observers, therefore, can respond properly to the situation by assuming familiar roles. In other words, as candidates go about the business of getting elected, the way they do it reminds voters—if the ritual is still healthy— that an important opportunity for the exchange of ideas and the evaluation of leaders awaits their participation.

The contestants must establish, first of all, that they are serious candidates who seek the office out of concern for the public good. The most obvious way to establish legitimacy is to claim expertise in certain policy areas. Policy rhetoric thus becomes both a means of attracting voting support and a basis on which to make a credible entry in the race. Candidates then link their policy concerns to claims about the personal deficiencies of the other candidate or party. Personal and party competition also gives the ritualistic appearance that serious choices are offered based on free and open disagreements between the candidates. It is a small step from themes of personal competition in campaign rhetoric to the general subject of leadership. Thus, to the extent that public debate emerges in an election the requirements of the ritual generally restrict it to (1) the policy visions of the candidates, (2) the personalities of the contestants, and (3) the need for a change in party or leadership.

In summary, both pragmatic and ritualistic communication in a campaign are organized in three general areas: policy issues, personal issues, and leadership issues. Ritualistic demands to define the electoral situation create the familiar, highly patterned nature of these pragmatic appeals. However, the demands of marketing and media control determine whether the familiar rhetorical categories become empty or full of meaning for voters. In other words, rituals would not be rituals without their familiar patterns of language and behavior. The question is, what makes some rituals full of meaning and others, as the saying goes, empty?

Policy

A concern with policy problems represents the most acceptable, if not the only, justification for a candidate's entry in a race. This invocation of concern for the issues can be quite direct as was the case in most of Ronald Reagan's justifications of his candidacy. For example, in Reagan's first nationally televised speech during the 1976 primaries, the candidate began his campaign by saying simply, "Good evening to all of you from California. Tonight I'd like to talk to you about issues. Issues which I think are involved—or should be involved—in this primary election season."[3] Reagan used this often repeated theme of concern about "neglected" policies to legitimate his challenge to the incumbent president of his own party.

The following statements illustrate Democratic challenger Jimmy Carter's embrace of the issues:

> "I don't make these commitments [on the issues] idly. . . . When I say we need a national health insurance program, I mean to do it. Nobody's ever done it. It's been talked about by very fine Democratic presidents ever since as early as Harry Truman. That will be the difference."[4]

> "I'll never tell a lie, I'll never make a misleading statement, I'll never avoid a controversial issue. . . . Watch television, listen to the radio. If I ever do any of those things, don't support me."[5]

As far as this ritualistic component of an election is concerned, the subsequent naming or definition of issues merely serves to make candidate statements plausible. It is the act of paying obeisance to the issues, not their detailed definition, that matters. It is the gathering together of issues under a general theme or vision that makes the voting choice meaningful and the generation of governing visions possible. Jimmy Carter ended up offering little vision but won (barely) anyway.

Personal Attacks

After legitimate grounds for running have been established, the competitive aspect of an election must be dramatized. The practice of making an issue of an opponent's record, views, or competence is another area in which detailed discussion is both superfluous and undramatic (i.e., counterproductive to the ritual). A number of stylized formats can be used to attack one's opponent (e.g., Democrats spend money, Republicans cause unemployment, the incumbent has thwarted progress, the challenger has no experience). To step much beyond such simple and familiar phrasings of the issues is unnecessary and risks damaging the dramatic buildup of the entire performance.[6]

These personal issues can be constructed in either direct (offensive) or indirect (defensive) formats. Offensive formats directly accuse an opponent of taking an irresponsible stand on an issue or of exhibiting some undesirable personal trait (lack of candor, indecisiveness, fiscal irresponsibility, membership in an ineffectual party, etc.). Defensive formats place the same general charges in the context of responding to the opponent's prior (and, no doubt, uncalled for) attack, which moved the respondent to issue a defense of his honor. As a rule, underdogs are granted more latitude with offensive formats, and front runners generally utilize indirect or defensive formats.

This rhetorical pattern is central to the broader cross-cultural practice of exchanging ritual insults—a feature of leadership and status struggles in many cultures in which competitiveness and self-reliance have high values. Consider, for example, the insulting practice of low-status chiefs giving lavish gifts and feasts to higher status chiefs in the potlatch ceremonies of the Kwakiutl Indians of the Pacific Northwest. Or the pattern of insulting rhetoric in the complex verbal game called Playing the Dozens, played, among others, by urban American youth who vie for status and membership in street gangs. In another historical time, chivalrous knights of inferior status challenged knights of superior status by throwing down a gauntlet. All these symbolic exchanges involve the initiation of a personal challenge by a lesser contestant and the opportunity for the higher status recipient of the challenge to respond in a manner befitting his dignity. The point is not that candidate attacks during elections are just like gift-giving by tribal chiefs or insult exchanges by urban youth, but that they may be governed by ritual conventions.

Jimmy Carter's use of personal attacks in the 1976 campaign illustrates the basic rules governing ritualized personal attacks. To begin with, Carter pledged to conduct a campaign that was above personal attacks. Such pledges, of course, are obligatory for those planning to engage in personal recriminations. In the Michigan primary, Democratic opponent Morris "Mo" Udall, a colorful member of Congress from Arizona who also pledged a campaign based solely on the issues, challenged Carter by running an intensive media campaign that accused the front runner of being fuzzy on the issues. The ads labeled Carter "The Waffler." As an underfunded underdog in the race, Udall utilized an appropriate offensive format for these attacks. As the front runner, Carter responded appropriately by defending his honor and accusing the opponent of vindictive and vituperative campaign practices. The advertisements, he said, represented a "breakdown in the relationships that have been maintained between candidates."[7] Even though everyone knew what candidate he was referring to, Carter felt it would be improper to mention him by name. This is a good example of an indirect attack on an opponent that defended Carter's honor while remaining consistent with his front runner's claim to being above personal concerns.

His reluctance to mention names also permitted Carter to generalize his attacks to other opponents who, he claimed, sought only "to maintain at all costs their own entrenched, unresponsive, bankrupt, irresponsible, political power."[8] It is noteworthy that these speeches were delivered in Ohio, a state where opponents Jerry Brown and Frank Church were not on the ballot. When asked if he referred to all his opponents in these speeches, Carter preserved his claims to being above petty personal concerns by saying, "I don't attribute that kind of motivation to Jerry Brown or Frank Church." These opponents, he argued, were "very good men and very worthy candidates."[9] Despite this caveat, Carter had encountered one of these "worthy opponents" (Brown) in the Maryland primary ten days earlier. In that primary Brown was the front runner and Carter was the underdog. Carter assumed an offensive posture by airing a statewide television commercial containing a direct attack on Brown and his entrenched power motive: "My opponent has the backing of almost every machine politician in Maryland. They want a brokered convention where powerful people can horse trade in the back rooms and pick the nominee. They don't want to let the people of Maryland make that decision for themselves."[10]

In each race where he ran as an underdog, Carter followed the basic rules for direct personal attacks. For example, in the early Florida primary Carter's personal polls showed him running third behind George Wallace and Henry Jackson. Carter attacked the front runner directly by describing Wallace as a "perennial candidate who's forever running and losing and who will probably still be running for president in 1988, if he's able."[11] This veiled reference to Wallace's poor physical condition was usually followed in Carter's speeches by an elliptical barb about Wallace's "odd" campaign style. Carter repeatedly told audiences that "He raises a lot of money and spends very little."[12]

In general, the use of personal attacks by all the candidates conformed to the three basic rules that (1) the underdogs use the offensive format, (2) the front runners use the defensive format, and (3) the candidates claim to be above these personal concerns at all times. The dramatization of personal competition is so basic to an election that candidates who chose to be largely unresponsive to the attacks of opponents (e.g., Eisenhower in 1952 and Nixon in 1972) generally find it necessary to send their running mates into personal skirmishes with opposing candidates.[13] These symbolic tests of personal mettle involve substantial precision in the use of negative or attack rhetoric. A failure to observe the norms can throw the ritual out of balance, resulting in damage to social understandings about the proper personal code of a leader.

Although the rules governing personal attacks were observed in 1976, respect for the formal etiquette of ritual insults had crumbled by 1988. George Bush began his negative campaign against Michael Dukakis as a proper underdog, issuing direct attacks on Dukakis' liberalism, patriotism, and religious convictions. Also befitting the front runner, Dukakis chose to ignore the mudslinging, maintaining the image of being "above it all" (an acceptable alternative to the indirect counterattacks issued by Carter when he was the front runner in 1976). However, after Bush took a commanding lead in the polls, he continued to push his negative offensive against Dukakis—an approach that disturbed many voters seeking a degree of decorum in an otherwise empty ritual. To compound the problem, Dukakis finally launched his own negative campaign against Bush but did so in the rhetoric of the front runner, appearing stoically above the fray despite a seventeen-point deficit in the polls. It is worth considering that public dismay at the negativism of the 1988 race was due not so much to the spectacle of the candidates attacking each other, but to their disregard for the etiquette that once governed the exchange of ritual insults.

Leadership

The electoral drama resolves personal battles by designating a new leader or affirming faith in the old one. The familiar litany of leadership is therefore a basic component of campaign discourse. If elections are about nothing else, they entail the dramatization and resolution of voter concerns about security, governmental succession, and the future. In order for candidates to play their roles properly, they must address these concerns by defining leadership as the basic campaign issue and by transmitting personal images of leadership in the process. The rhetoric of leadership is so standardized that a few examples are adequate to illustrate it:

"The American people deserve a leader they can trust."[14]

"A president should describe a future."[15]

"Well, I think where Ford is most vulnerable is the absence of leadership capabilities he has demonstrated since he's been in the White House . . . his timidity about dealing with domestic problems . . . the absence of policy . . . his lack of comprehension . . . his deferral to the Secretary of State. . . ."[16]

"When I was sworn in, I said our long national nightmare was over. And it is."[17]

"I have followed a course that has led us to rising prosperity, renewed trust and a lasting peace. . . . I want to lead our country away from a wasteful preoccupation with what's wrong with America and get on with the job of making things right with America."[18]

These banal words hardly display the sophistication normally associated with persuasive appeals.[19] It makes more sense to think of such standard pronouncements as the sort of thing one must say in order to establish the proper definition of the election ritual. Once the candidates have established the proper concern for policy, personal competitiveness, and leadership, they can develop each of these issue areas in more pragmatic directions. It is in this realm of pragmatic, vote-getting rhetoric that we see the inhibiting effects of candidate marketing and media control strategies most clearly.

THE PRAGMATIC FORMS OF CAMPAIGN DISCOURSE

By converting ritualistic incantations into pragmatic vote-getting appeals, elections open up possibilities for meaningful public involvement in national dialogues about the problems of the day. In 1976, there was a constant tension between meaning and marketing, with the edge going to marketing. By the late 1980s, that tension had disappeared, and marketing held complete sway; even the ritual forms were enacted badly and were virtually devoid of meaningful pragmatic content.

Personal Attacks

The news media devote a disproportionate amount of attention to personal exchanges between the candidates. One study showed that in 1972 the major television networks devoted 60 percent of their coverage to crowd scenes, public performances, baby kissing, personal portraits of the candidates, and, most importantly, the exchange of personal attacks.[20] It is clearly in a candidate's interest to translate the ritual forms for displaying personal virtue and attacking the opponent into carefully staged performances designed to capture the attention of the media and, in turn, the voting public. For example, challenger Udall's attacks on front runner Carter during the Michigan Democratic primary received heavy (and free) television coverage on the evening news programs. Such exposure was particularly important for Udall's financially troubled campaign. Udall's attacks on Carter were covered so regularly that, toward the end of the campaign, Udall strategists designed a daily appearance for the candidate in settings that were chosen both for visual qualities and for their compatible, documentary-like relationships to the issue of the day on which Udall accused Carter of waffling. For example, one of these appearances was staged in front of a field of oil storage tanks. Udall accused Carter of fuzziness in his positions about the regulation of the big oil companies. Another appearance was staged in front of an auto equipment plant (recall that the primary was in Michigan) that had closed and moved south to avoid union shop regulations. Udall accused Carter of being inconsistent in his policies on right-to-work legislation.[21]

While personal attacks are a central feature of the election ritual, refining them through marketing and media manipulation removes the traditional sense of play from candidate exchanges. In 1976, at least some of these attacks conformed to the familiar outlines of the ritual. They also served a vote-getting purpose because they interested television audiences and provided an occasional glimpse of candidate character in the bargain. By contrast, in the more recent contests of the 1980s and 1990s, the playful, open qualities essential both to the spirit of the ritual and to meaningful voter involvement have been steadily killed off. Contestants no longer mix it up in half-serious, half-playful personal exchanges. The elements of danger and spontaneity are thus removed, as candidates walk through carefully staged performances that reveal little about their own wits or their personal abilities to handle attacks in pressure situations. As a result, audiences lose their sense of dramatic involvement in these exchanges and see them as purely negative. (This is, of course, an accurate perception of the intent of the media consultants who design contemporary campaign attacks.)

Leadership

Appeals to popular leadership images are an important part of the vote-getting pragmatics of any campaign. However, the creation of a following is seldom accomplished through intellectual discourse on leadership. The representation of leadership in a campaign evolves through actions and through displays of skill or virtue that invite the attribution of competence by the followers. Direct campaign statements about leadership are, by contrast, almost exclusively ritualistic.

A common pragmatic approach to leadership occurs when incumbents blur the distinction between their images as candidates and their images as public officials. For example, the majority of Republican incumbent president Gerald Ford's television spots during the 1976 primaries showed still shots of Ford acting as president (holding conferences, signing bills, studying reports, giving speeches, etc.) within official settings like the Oval Office, aboard Air Force One, and in the chamber of the House of Representatives where he served before being appointed vice president by soon-to-resign President Nixon. Included in the soundtracks were excerpts from Ford's 1976 State of the Union Message and the recurring strains of "Hail to the Chief." In some of these ads the word "president" was used more than a dozen times, including the repetitious closing lines that ran, "President Ford is your President. Keep him."[22] In addition to such advertising, the official activities of the president were exploited for their leadership imagery. The most notable of these activities was an international economic summit conference that Ford initiated and hosted shortly before the Republican nominating convention. Relatively little was accomplished at this conference, but front-page pictures appeared almost daily in which Ford was shown in the company of the leaders of the major capitalist industrial nations.

Even when the Ford campaign abandoned its Oval Office advertising format late in the primaries in response to gains by challenger Reagan, the new marketing strategy preserved the focus on images of presidential leadership. The new ads were created around a slice of life format. The basic Madison Avenue scenario for such commercials involves a friend giving an enthusiastic recommendation for a product to another friend. The recipient of the recommendation then becomes converted into a satisfied buyer during the course of the commercial. In the commercials run by the Ford campaign during the June primaries, the product was Gerald Ford and the satisfied buyer was a housewife who was pleased with lower food prices. The commercial began with two women (carrying bags of groceries) meeting in front of the supermarket:

Friend: Ellie! Are you working for President Ford?

Ellie: Only about 26 hours a day. Notice anything about these food prices lately?

Friend: Well, they don't seem to be going up the way they used to.

Ellie: President Ford has cut inflation in half.

Friend: In half? Wow!

Ellie: It's just that I'd hate to think where we'd be without him.

Announcer's Voice: President Ford is leading us back to prosperity. Stay with him. He knows the way.[23]

Even though the format is a radical departure from the Oval Office motif, the basic symbolic appeal is much the same. Candidates who lack this symbolic resource (incumbency) must develop other devices if they are to convert their obligatory attention to leadership into a pragmatic consideration as well. Endorsements by other political leaders and celebrities is probably the most familiar device of this sort. However, more novel formats may surface in the course of a campaign. Among these were Jimmy Carter's efforts to develop an image as a national leader and a foreign policy expert. An ingenious tactic was a leak from his staff claiming that Soviet officials had made repeated efforts to contact and consult with the candidate. A Carter aide was reported as saying that "Since February or March, and especially in the last month or so, they have been lighting up our switchboards and coming over regularly."[24] This leak came on the eve of a speech on international nuclear energy policy that Carter delivered at a privately sponsored conference held in the United Nations Building. The leak drew considerable attention to both Carter and his speech. In news reports, the speech became "a major policy statement" that was delivered "at the U.N." The leak also gave Carter the opportunity to respond to reporters' predictable questions by saying, "They [the Soviet officials] believe I have a good chance to be the Democratic nominee, the next President."[25] He added that he didn't think it would be appropriate to hold direct negotiations with foreign governments until the nominating process was over. The moral of this scenario, it would seem, is that short of being the president the next best strategy is to act in a presidential manner.[26]

Policy

In the days before TV news provided instant accounts of what candidates told followers, candidates could make quite different appeals to diverse audiences. In particular, candidates who had a governing vision to offer could always justify bringing distinct groups in under various parts of the big social picture. With the rise of the nightly news and the decline of visions, however, candidates had to be more careful about what they told diverse audiences. As marketing and media management techniques improved over the years, campaigns developed rhetorical strategies to restore special appeals to target audiences whether or not the candidate had a governing vision to go along with those appeals. For example, in 1976, even though he had figured out how to market effective special appeals to different segments of the voter audience, Carter offered little general vision in the bargain—unless, of course, we consider themes like "trust me" and "a government as good as the people" to be visionary.

What we witness in this case is the rise of communication strategies that fill the minimum pragmatic and ritualistic requirements of elections without requiring candidates to introduce ideas or controversial visions into the public dialogue. In particular, 1976 saw the introduction of three communication strategies (used most skillfully by the Carter campaign) to get around the lack of a governing vision and, at the same time, to escape charges of inconsistency and crass marketing of votes:

Special appeals: through which focused but potentially volatile appeals were constructed for homogeneous and isolated audiences.

Disclaimers: through which these special appeals were qualified or given "tag lines" that make it difficult for opponents to take them out of context. This allowed candidates to advocate different, often contradictory, policies to different audiences.

Vague generalities: through which special appeals were summarized in broad or vague terms that allowed diverse constituencies to form different interpretations of the candidate's position.

The use of these rhetorical strategies may help generate the appearance that common understandings and goals exist between a candidate and his or her diverse electoral following. The combined use of these three rules also protects candidates against the opposition's charges that they represent narrow interests or that they are inconsistent. Such charges reflect the ritualistic pressures in American elections for legitimate candidates: they must represent a broad base of the population; they must address the general welfare even though they represent partisan interests; and they must try to reconcile contradictions within their visions for the national future. In other words, the traditional pressures in the ritual are to unite voter coalitions under broad governing visions. The emergence of the new marketing-oriented rhetorical strategies makes it possible to create voter coalitions in the absence of visions that have broad popular or institutional support. This is not to say that the traditional election system always worked or often achieved high pinnacles of meaning. It can be argued that, even under the best of conditions, the old system made specific policy pledges hard to pin down and left candidates vulnerable to bargaining over policies with various support groups after the election. However, this seems preferable to the current system in which there is little of substance worth pinning down, and there are few voter groups that even hold inside bargaining positions.

Selective appeals in practice. Carter's critical upset victory in the 1976 Florida primary may well be credited to his judicious use of selective appeals. The Carter campaign spent more than a year before this primary isolating different media audiences and designing appeals for them. For example, a tape of Carter saying that the Civil Rights Act was "the best thing that ever happened to the South in my lifetime" was aired on black radio stations through the state. This message was withheld from other audiences. The rationale is obvious: Carter had a good chance of attracting black voters but did not want to risk losing conservative whites to George Wallace, the front runner. Spots showing Carter talking about togetherness and the mood of the country were regularly aired on "Sara," a television program with a middle American audience. Liberal renditions of Carter's stands on welfare and employment were broadcast during episodes of "Maude," a program with a young and comparatively liberal following. Other selected appeals were presented to blue collar audiences on "Hee Haw," to professional viewers on "Today," and to senior citizens on "Lawrence Welk."[27] As this list indicates, care was taken to target programs that attracted fairly homogeneous audiences and that had relatively little overlapping viewership.

Another good example of selective rhetoric also comes from the Carter campaign. In the early primaries, opponent Henry Jackson, a powerful senator from Washington State, appeared to have attracted the majority of Jewish Democratic voters. Private polls indicated that Jackson would probably control this group of voters in the remaining primaries and that Carter had little support among them. A Carter speechwriter reported that after this pattern crystallized, his candidate issued an instruction saying, "I don't want any more statements on the Middle East or Lebanon. Jackson has all the Jews anyway. It doesn't matter how far I go, I don't get over 4 percent of the Jewish vote anyway, so forget it. We get the Christians."[28] When Jackson withdrew from the primaries following his defeat in Pennsylvania, Carter began to make special appeals to Jewish audiences once again. For example, he appeared before a large Jewish audience in New Jersey. Wearing a blue velvet yarmulke[29] for the occasion, Carter said, "I worship the same God you do. We study the same Bible you do." He also noted that when the United States recognized Israel in 1948, "the President of the United States was Harry Truman, and Harry Truman was a Baptist."[30] In this and other speeches following

Jackson's withdrawal from the race, Carter began making major policy statements on the Palestinian question, the Middle East situation, the status of Jews in the Soviet Union, and other issues of potential concern to Jewish voters.

Carter was not, of course, the only candidate to engage in the standard practice of appealing directly to special interests. For example, Gerald Ford told the convention of the California Peace Officers Association that he favored a mandatory imposition of the death penalty "upon conviction of sabotage, murder, espionage, and treason in certain circumstances."[31] Two days later, Ford's opponent Ronald Reagan told the same convention that "Piously claiming defense of civil liberties and prodded by a variety of bleeding hearts of the society we have dismantled much of the intelligence operations of law enforcement that we must have if we are to protect society."[32] When Ford addressed the San Diego Council of the Naval League, he criticized Congress for its "political interference with our national security needs."[33] When Reagan spoke to the Economic Club of Detroit, he said that "The automobile and the men and women who make it are under constant attack from Washington."[34]

Not all selective appeals are politically risky. For example, Reagan's remarks to the auto workers were fairly safe. They were also open to more diverse interpretations than most selective appeals. In contrast, Carter's statement on the Civil Rights Act and Ford's pronouncement on the death penalty could alienate potential supporters if they were taken out of their initial contexts.

Disclaimers. The volatility of selective appeals can be reduced by affixing disclaimers, or tag lines, to them. These symbolic appendages have little impact within the immediate context, but they make it possible for a candidate to defend a statement if it is taken out of that context. A classic example of the use of tag lines was Richard Nixon's political abdication speech of 1962. In this speech, delivered after his loss in the California gubernatorial race (which followed his earlier loss of the presidency in 1960), Nixon claimed that he was leaving politics and that the press would not have him to "kick around" anymore. The speech was both emotional and bitter. In 1968, however, Nixon returned to politics as a candidate for president, claiming there was a "new Nixon."[35] Strategists for his Democratic opponent, Hubert Humphrey, hoped to use excerpts from the 1962 speech in commercials designed to combat the new Nixon image. However, upon close attention to the speech, they discovered that, despite the obvious sentiments of the performance, not a single damaging line could be taken smoothly out of context. Each of Nixon's charges against the press was coupled with some statement of faint praise.[36] This was all the more remarkable since the speech was both spontaneous and emotional, attesting to the degree to which some political actors may internalize the use of disclaimers.

Disclaimers and tag lines were numerous in 1976. For example, Gerald Ford's rather extreme statement on the death penalty carried the tag line "in certain circumstances." This disclaimer was rather simple in comparison to many of Jimmy Carter's uses. In one speech Carter told a group of wealthy oilmen at a Houston, Texas, fundraising banquet that he perceived an "unwarranted inclination on the part of politicians and the people to blame the oil industry for inflation and fuel shortages."[37] In the same speech he also addressed the sensitive issue of governmental regulation of oil monopolies. He said that he would support a partial breakup of the oil industry "only as a last resort." These sentiments could have been perceived by other Democratic groups as direct contradictions of two major planks in the party platform concerning the protection of consumers and the breakup of oil company monopolies. As if to guard against this interpretation, Carter included two tag lines in the speech. The first one stated that, unless he was satisfied that adequate competition existed in the industry, he would favor legislation divesting the big companies of their wholesale and retail outlets. The second tag line was even more subtle: "I want to be sure we have a minimum of interference of government in the affairs of business provided we can assure that consumers are adequately protected from a violation of the competitive commitment that's got to be part of all our lives." Should the occasion arise, it could be shown that these lines were virtual quotations from the Democratic party platform. One plank in the platform that (at the time of Carter's speech) had been submitted for adoption by the party convention read: "When competition inadequate to insure free markets and maximum benefit to American consumers exists, we support effective restrictions on the right of major companies to own all phases of the oil industry."[38] Thus, the speech could be defended as a statement of party policy, even though the contextual references to oil policy were a considerable departure from the party line. Carter's rhetoric showed that the party platform had become another empty element of the ritual that was not worth fighting for, much less introducing into the campaign itself.

Vague generalities. The use of tag lines permits candidates to make fairly pointed statements to isolated audiences with relatively little risk that the statements will alienate other groups. However, on numerous occasions candidates must present their policy positions to a broad spectrum of voters. Covering specific appeals with a rhetoric of vague generalities allows the consensual requirements of American democracy to be affirmed, even as the emptiness of those generalities raises public doubt about the grounds and the quality of the consensus.

The rhetorical principles underlying all vague generalizations involve two categorical properties of language. First, words that appear together in the same context lead people to search for relationship categories that provide common meaning for the words.[39] Sociolinguist Harvey Sacks provides a nice illustration of this principle with his analysis of a child's statement, "The baby cried. The mommy picked it up."[40] Sacks argues that the terms *baby* and *mommy* can be located, in the abstract, within several different categories of relationship: family, stage of life, human beings, and so on. Their particular relationship in this context is best satisfied by the interpretive use of the category family. Sacks claims that as a result of this categorization we "hear" that the "mommy" in this utterance is the mommy of the baby, even though their relationship to one another is not stated explicitly.

The second property might be called the projection principle; that is, a highly specific word permits people to hear a small number of possible categorical relationships, while a more abstract word for the same thing may evoke a larger number of relationship categories. The use of more general words therefore invites people in heterogeneous audiences to project multiple interpretations that fit their different political circumstances.

As an example of the first principle, recall Jimmy Carter's reference to George Wallace in the Florida primary as the perennial candidate who would run until 1988 if he was "able." This is a classic political statement. Carter did not have to specify precisely what he meant by "able." In the abstract a number of links can be drawn between the symbols "run" and "able." For example, we might think of such connections as financial support, age, political backing, physical health, and mental health. In referring to Wallace (who had been partially paralyzed after being shot in an earlier campaign), it was clear that the state of the candidate's physical health was the most appropriate connection to draw. Not only was this the connection most interpreters were likely to make, but it was also the one that Carter did not have to make explicit. As a result, the candidate could defend the statement in later situations by substituting any of the other category connections available for interpreting the two symbols. This practice permits candidates to take their own words out of context on subsequent occasions if it is useful to claim that other connections were intended.[41]

The second (or projection) principle is well illustrated by a variety of policy statements made on the issue of turning control of the Panama Canal over to Panama. Consider Ronald Reagan's ill-fated suggestion that we should stop responding to blackmail (i.e., stop negotiating) and simply tell the Panamanian dictator that we own the canal and "we're going to keep it." Compare this highly specific usage to Jimmy Carter's categorically more general position that he opposed "relinquishing actual control of the canal." This usage permits a large number of inferences to be drawn (through the symbol "control") about possible relationships between the United States and Panama.

On rare occasions, the internal logic of vague generalizations is exposed to public view. For example, at a press conference during the energy crisis of 1973 a reporter asked a White House official how the administration planned to deal with the crisis. The gist of the official reply was "whether we have an energy crisis or not is just a matter of semantics. Whether it's a crisis or an emergency, we have an energy *problem*. Our efforts in the future must be directed at solving this problem."[42] A similar effort to shift the definition of an issue from specific and politically damaging terms to more general symbols occurred during the Reagan–Ford contest in 1976. Ronald Reagan had succeeded in making an issue of the defense and foreign policies of the Ford administration.[43] At the core of Reagan's attack was his criticism of the conciliatory foreign policy of Secretary of State Henry Kissinger. Reagan referred to this policy of détente as "a one way street," "a concession of weakness," and an "approval of Russia's enslavement of captive nations."[44] In the face of the popularity of Reagan's definition of détente, Ford made a curious speech in which he revealed the recategorization process at work: "I don't use the word 'détente' anymore. I think that what we ought to say is that the United States will meet with superpowers, the Soviet Union and with China, and others and seek to relax tensions so that we can continue a policy of peace through strength."[45]

Most uses of the generalization rule are more subtle than these two cases. For example, in a campaign statement on the busing of schoolchildren, Ford implied that his opposition to busing had some relationship with obtaining "quality education." He said, "I don't think forced busing to achieve racial balance is the proper way to get quality education."[46] In his speech before the National Press Club, Carter used the general symbols of preparedness and efficiency to organize audience inferences about his proposed defense policy: "Our nation's security is obviously of paramount importance, and everything must be done to insure adequate military preparedness. But there is no reason why our national defense establishment cannot also be efficient."[47] In answering his rhetorical question "What is the cause of crime in America?," Ronald Reagan first dismissed a possible specific category reference (poverty) and then provided a string of general symbols that permitted his audience to hear any number of possible relationships among them: "If you want to know why crime proliferates in this nation, don't look at the statistics on income and wealth; look at statistics on arrests, prosecutions, convictions, and prison population."[48]

Jimmy Carter made excellent use of categorical generalization in the 1976 campaign. His standard format was to use specific terms of reference to describe conditions or values on both sides of a political issue and then to define his policy in general terms that spanned the range of specific symbols. This is a very sophisticated tactic that requires great care in the choice of specific and general symbols. For example, in his standard campaign statement on welfare, Carter began by referring to specific conditions in the welfare system. He noted that there were 12 million people "chronically on welfare and 2 million welfare workers, one worker for every 6 recipients." He also cited the figure of the 1.3 million people who "should not be on the welfare rolls at all."[49] Then, on the other side of the issue, he cited the specific problem of the "unfortunates" who both deserved welfare and who should be "treated with respect, decency and love." He then invoked the general reference for his welfare policy by saying that when he became president he would "reform the welfare system."[50] The term *reform* in this context clearly means many different things politically. This general tactic was very successful: opinion polls taken during the primaries showed that conservatives viewed Carter as conservative, moderates saw him as moderate, and liberals identified him as liberal.[51]

In contrast to Carter's strength at turning special appeals into vague generalities, the leading Republican candidates, Ford and Reagan, showed a certain ineptitude in this area, each taking advantage of the other's rhetorical vulnerabilities. Reagan's greatest triumph was a national television speech in the middle of the primary campaign. The broad generalities in that carefully written address contrast markedly with his string of shoot-from-the-hip specifics in other, less controlled campaign appearances. By 1980, Reagan's handlers had convinced their man to stick to the script and avoid thinking on his own in public, giving most of his 1980 performance the tone of broad generality achieved in this 1976 speech:[52]

"Our nation is in danger and the danger grows greater every day."

" 'Wandering without aim' describes U.S. foreign policy."

"We're Number Two in a world where it is dangerous, if not fatal, to be second best."

"We're Americans and we have a rendezvous with destiny."

Ford made the initial mistake of responding to these general statements in specifics. Among his responses were the public abandonment of the term *détente* and his confession in numerous speeches that Reagan had shifted the focus of the campaign from Ford's economic achievements to his foreign policy. Ford also made numerous public defenses of his secretary of state.[53] He even delayed the signing of a nuclear testing treaty with the Soviet Union shortly before the crucial Michigan primary. Ford aides reported that the delay was designed to avoid giving Reagan something else to criticize.[54] Another indicator of Reagan's early success in defining foreign policy issues to his advantage came in a speech delivered by Vice President Nelson Rockefeller during a trip to West Germany. A speech that had been drafted by the State Department was replaced at the last minute by a speech written by Rockefeller and his staff. In contrast to the State Department speech, the last-minute substitution was filled with cold war rhetoric that described the Soviet Union as an imperialist nation whose growing superiority had to be countered with force if necessary.[55] Such a speech might have been delivered by Reagan himself. This move may have been another effort to deny Reagan possible objects of criticism. Thus, Reagan's focus on foreign policy had been successful. Not only had Ford responded (thereby making the issues valid ones), but also he had responded defensively. This defensiveness allowed Reagan to cite Ford's responses as evidence of the validity of his (Reagan's) claims. For example, after Ford made the public statement that he would stop using the term *détente*, Reagan was able to remark in a national speech that "Now we are told Washington is dropping the word 'détente' but keeping the policy. But whatever it's called, the policy is what's at fault."[56]

Reagan accomplished all this without articulating his own basic policies in these areas. However, as Reagan's success in the primaries grew, he began to make an increasing number of specific policy proposals. As often happens under such circumstances, his opponent was able to take advantage of these statements. Among Reagan's violations of the generalization rule that Ford was able to turn to his advantage were the following:

> *January 15, 1976, on Angola:* "[Tell the Russians to get] out. We'll let them do the fighting, or you're going to have to deal with us. . . . It's time for us to straighten up and eyeball [the Russians]."
>
> *February 27, 1976, on Panama:* "I don't understand how the State Department can suggest we pay blackmail to this dictator, for blackmail is what it is. When it comes to the canal, we bought it, we paid for it, it's ours, and we should tell Torrijos and company we are going to keep it."
>
> *May 22, 1976, on Vietnam:* "Never again should this country send its young men to die in a war unless this country is totally committed to winning it."
>
> *May 31, 1976, on Vietnam:* "Can anyone think for a moment that North Vietnam would have moved to the attack had its leaders believed we would respond with B-52's?"
>
> *June 2, 1976, on Rhodesia:* "Whether it will be enough to have simply a show of strength, a promise that we would [supply] troops, or whether you'd have to go in with occupation forces or not, I don't know."

These statements were of such categorical specificity that they permitted dispute on ideological, logical, and even empirical grounds. Toward the end of the primary season, the Ford staff built an effective propaganda campaign around these statements. An important element of the campaign involved a number of conservative Republicans attacking Reagan's policy statements as irrational, extreme, and factually incorrect. For example, in a series of radio commercials aired before the important Nebraska primary, Senator (and former Republican presidential candidate) Barry Goldwater told Nebraska voters: "I know Ronald Reagan's public statements concerning the Panama Canal contained gross factual errors. . . . He has clearly represented himself in an irresponsible manner on an issue which could affect the nation's security."[57] The categorical difference between saying that we owned the canal and saying that we had interests or rights in the area allowed Reagan's opponent to make this effective attack on his ability to take competent and responsible positions on foreign policy issues.

The resulting shift in Ford and Reagan's strategic positions was illustrated in their exchanges over Reagan's statement on Rhodesia shortly before the California primary. Ford's public response to the Rhodesia statement was: "Any indication that a President might send American troops to southern Africa, I think, is irresponsible."[58] This response turned the remark into an issue that Reagan had to defend repeatedly in public appearances. On numerous occasions he reiterated the statements, "I'm not going to start a war in Rhodesia," and "I made a mistake of trying to answer a hypothetical question with a hypothetical answer."[59] However, as had been the case earlier with Ford's abandonment of "détente," even Reagan's disclaimer about starting a war became a resource for Ford's propaganda campaign. Ford strategists produced a series of radio and television commercials that were aired during the California primary. The narration in these ads ended with the admonition: "When you vote Tuesday, remember: Governor Ronald Reagan couldn't start a war. President Ronald Reagan could."[60] These commercials did not keep Reagan from winning the California primary.[61] In the long run they may even have been detrimental to party unity, but they crystallized Reagan's narrow definitions of a number of foreign policy statements into major campaign issues. For the first time in the campaign, Ford was able to assume an offensive posture. This turnabout in the late stages of the campaign was crucial because the outcome was decided by the candidates' abilities to persuade uncommitted Republican delegates to support them at the nominating convention. The irony here is that while the Republican candidates were waging a fairly traditional election battle, Jimmy Carter was running a much more controlled, marketed, and mediated campaign. And he won.

RUNNING OUT OF RITUAL

Despite the clear influence of marketing and media control in the 1976 campaign, there were still moments in which the ritual threatened to become meaningful for its voter audience. Even though Carter was cautious in his appeals to minorities and the poor (hedging them with disclaimers and vague generalities), he still made those appeals. As a result, the Carter victory in 1976 came without sacrificing the party's traditional constituency. By contrast, Mondale in 1984 and particularly Dukakis in 1988 all but abandoned appeals to traditional groups of poor and minority voters. The result was not just a loss of meaning in the pragmatic relationship between candidate and voters, but a notable sacrifice in the broad democratic appeal of the election ritual itself.

Beyond narrowing the ritual's appeal to broad voter groups, there has also been a notable decline of open policy debate among candidates since 1976. For all the use of marketing and media control techniques in 1976, there was still a tentativeness about their intrusion into the nation's most sacred political context. Reagan actually spoke his own mind on a number of occasions. Ford actually shifted his foreign policy position during the campaign in response to Reagan's criticisms. These glimmers of open debate offered voters the hope that something meaningful might be transpiring on the political stage.

After 1976, the role of political consultants and candidate handlers became unashamedly intrusive. George Bush's 1988 claim that Michael Dukakis was a liberal was probably effective only because Dukakis took the advice of his handlers and denied it for months. It did not require a particularly enlightened voter to see that Dukakis was denying the obvious. Adding insult to injury, the Democrat finally took the advice of a new consulting team and admitted that he was, after all, a liberal and proud of it. Such slavish scripting robs any meaning or vision that terms like liberal might have, while turning elections into painfully staged affairs.

Candidates are now ordered to stick to their scripts, while avoiding spontaneous outbursts of public thinking and shunning contact with the media. These dictates of campaign strategy may enable campaign consultants to apply their techniques with greater precision and effect, but the resulting damage to the ritual is great. As campaign content is increasingly filled with the results of marketing research, the central ritual of American democracy grows increasingly empty.

CHAPTER 6

Failing the Presidential Character Test

Most students of the presidency stress the personal qualities of candidates. In one view, even if candidates have a vision, they must be evaluated in terms of their strength of character to carry it out.[1] In another analysis, the lack of a vision (or credible issues) may not prove fatal if the candidate communicates personal qualities worth voting for.[2] The trouble is that the new electoral system plays havoc with these personal considerations in voter choice. Not only do money, media control, and marketing undermine political visions, but they also reduce the chances that voters will catch useful glimpses of the personalities behind the campaign masks. This chapter explores how the new election system makes it difficult for voters to make satisfying judgments about candidate personalities.

A stranger to American politics might conclude that nearly everything a candidate is subjected to during an election is degrading in some way. Political campaigning is grueling. Presidential candidates often spend eighteen-hour days carrying their messages and their campaign personalities into as many media markets as possible. A typical day's itinerary may contain twenty or more entries.[3] The events on the schedule are often as tedious and humbling as the schedule itself. The time, place, supporting cast, and audience may change from hour to hour and day to day, but the activities and performances fall into a pattern. The campaign becomes a numbing blur of repetitious action.

The attention of press and public seems to shift from the monotony of the campaign to any activity that represents a departure from the routine. The most newsworthy and, perhaps, the most noteworthy departures from electoral routine are those occasions when candidates blunder, lose control, or otherwise reveal embarrassing flaws in their carefully staged performances. Not only are gaffes by candidates and the often degrading episodes that follow them a major focus of press coverage, but also candidates spend a good deal of energy explaining their mistakes in efforts to repair their images. Some blunders are repaired effectively, while others are handled in ways that only seem to confirm suspicions about the candidate's incompetence or deceitfulness.

Since gaffes have been such prominent features of elections, it is important to understand them. Although pundits and purists often bemoan the media fascination with candidate blunders, gaffes are not easily dismissed as trivial preoccupations of a frustrated press and a bored public. To the contrary, gaffes can be shown to be the basis of clearly identifiable character tests or what we define later in the chapter as degradation rituals in campaigns. These rituals contribute both to the definition of the electoral process and to the information needs of voters who must make decisions within that process.

PRESIDENTIAL CHARACTER

Many analysts have noted the connection between gaffes and the generally grueling and personally challenging nature of campaigns. For example, James David Barber has described the campaign as a stress test. The measures of performance on this test are the incidence and handling of gaffes. In Barber's words, "The campaign stress test reaches its apex in the gaffe."[4]

Gaffes seem to be defining features of campaigns, and the attention paid to them hints at the possibility that they convey some sort of useful information. In light of all the issues, policies, and personal attacks that were deftly handled by the candidates in the 1976 debates, for example, why was so much attention devoted to Gerald Ford's gaffe about there being no Soviet domination in Poland and his unsuccessful efforts to repair it?[5] Why does it seem that a campaign event is of diminished significance if a gaffe does not occur within it? For example, gaffes did not figure in the 1980 Carter–Reagan debate, and so the press seemed hard pressed to pick a winner. *Washington Post* reporters Lou Cannon and Edward Walsh called the debates "bloodless" and noted that "each candidate remained carefully in control of his emotions throughout the 90-minute forum."[6]

Perhaps the most glaring trend in presidential debates since 1976 is their general lack of gaffes. This, I would argue, is due less to the nomination of unerring humans to candidacy than to the increased control of campaign consultants over the coaching and directing of candidates before their every public appearance. Not that we can expect complete elimination of gaffes in the race for the presidency. To err, after all, is human, and no candidate is thoroughly programmable. However, the coaching, directing, and scripting of candidate performances are making a visible impact on the incidence of candidate mistakes. The contemporary campaign is less a test of character than a display of public relations techniques.

The disappearance of the campaign character test represents a serious blow to the integrity of the election ritual. In the past, popular histories of campaigns were often written around gaffes and their consequences. Nineteen hundred and seventy-six was the year of Gerald Ford's bumbling and memorable malapropisms, of Ronald Reagan's "shoot-from-the-hip" statements on foreign policy during the primaries, and of Jimmy Carter's admission that he had "lusted in his heart" and his remark about "ethnic purity." The election campaign of 1972 began with Democratic contender Edmund Muskie crying in the snows of New Hampshire and ended with George McGovern, the Democratic nominee, feverishly subtracting from his 1,000 percent support for troubled running mate Thomas Eagleton while blundering through an unconvincing series of explanations of his welfare proposals.

Despite the importance of gaffes in elections, when they do occur critics often regard them as the concerns of a simpleminded public and sensationalistic press. In a typical comment on gaffes during the 1980 campaign, one columnist criticized NBC News for trying (unsuccessfully) to make something of Ronald Reagan's defense of the Vietnam War as a "noble cause." The critic alleged that "by leading the newscast with this story phrased this way, NBC News was giving the clear impression that Reagan's remark was wildly insensitive and that he didn't quite know what he was saying. It cast doubt on his fitness as a leader, if not by implication, on his sanity."[7] This was precisely the point, of course.

Another critic in 1980 resurrected the standard charge that candidates seem to get away with creating new personae for each campaign and are then held accountable for the smallest deviations from their contrived characters. Judging candidates against their fabricated claims rather than against their historical records, so this criticism goes, reduces campaign discourse to "a bunch of 'lashings out' and 'strikings back' and this one 'charged today' and that one 'counter-attacked with'—and, finally, who cares? It is exciting without being interesting, which is what happens when there is neither memory nor history nor whole people nor even any sense of time."[8]

In a narrow sense these criticisms are correct.[9] That is, candidates are permitted a remarkable degree of freedom to invent their campaign personalities and then are held accountable for the faithful portrayal of those characters.[10] However, in the age before campaign management held a near total grip on candidate performances, gaffes gave voters an opportunity to see if candidates were truly comfortable with their transformed selves. Now, comfortable or not, candidates are taught how to play their chosen roles to the hilt. Witness, for example, George Bush who, by his own admission, felt awkward and estranged from his tough guy image in 1988, but who recited the obligatory lines in flawless if unconvincing performances. Then, there is the continual preparation of Dan Quayle. Who knows? Perhaps by 1996 or inaugural day, 2001, a character will emerge that does not experience technical difficulties before the television cameras.

With the rise of gaffe control (media consultants call it damage control) as a prominent feature of campaigns, voters no longer get a candid look at leadership skills like knowledge, sensitivity, awareness of social norms, and the ability to think and act under pressure. In traditional campaigns where candidates had greater spontaneous contact with the press and with each other, gaffes regularly became campaign issues when they could be plausibly defined as violations of public norms about leadership and democratic accountability. Then, the success or failure of candidates in redressing the violations became a basis for practical voter judgments. Well-understood norms of public accountability guided voter judgments about the importance of the violation. In complementary fashion, candidate responses confirmed the importance of the norms in question.[11] Nowadays, on the rare occasions when candidates depart from their scripts or get caught in questionable activities, they just ignore reporters' questions, while smiling over the heads of the snarling press to the viewers at home. In the congressional races of 1990, for example, incumbents accused of doing special favors for the owners of failing savings and loans responded as though there was no difference between pulling strings for fat-cat campaign contributors and helping little old ladies find lost social security checks. The danger in all this is that we may be losing the all-important public accountability that keeps our political norms and values (along with the rituals in which they are displayed) meaningful for citizens and politicians.

Character Tests in Other Social Settings

The once-familiar efforts of candidates to restore lost status, morality, or competence in the eyes of skeptical voters are similar to what sociologists call degradation rituals that occur in almost any setting in which new members are socialized, status is conferred, and character is tested. As Harold Garfinkel noted in his seminal article on the subject, there is probably no society or institution with a moral order to uphold that does not contain some sort of degradation ceremony to test and affirm members' commitments to that order.[12] Degradation rituals literally certify that an individual's public persona meets the standards of the group or the institution. Certification is granted if individuals who are alerted to features of their behavior that violate the norms for their public roles can then repair the violation in ways that indicate understanding and acceptance of those roles. People who fail to repair their indiscretions suffer status degradation by being rejected as suitable players for their chosen social careers.

Degradation rituals, according to Garfinkel, always display several defining characteristics. First, other actors must regard the offending behavior as a departure from the norm and a damaging blow to proper role behavior. Second, and more importantly, the group leaves to the transgressor the task of repairing the damage. Third, and most important of all, the offender must select a rhetorical gambit (an account, a reinterpretation, or an apology) that (1) indicates recognition of the nature of the problem, (2) demonstrates an understanding of the proper behavior, and (3) indicates a convincing ability to display the proper behavior.

If concluded successfully, degradation rituals accomplish a number of important social functions, including the socialization of new members, the rehearsal of social norms, the affirmation that roles and norms are binding on the individuals in the setting, the promotion of solidarity in the group, and the display of command or ineptitude on the part of various actors. These social accomplishments of degradation rituals explain why they are so central to so many social contexts. For example, "total institutions" like prisons, asylums, and the military use degradation rituals to uproot individuals from former life contexts and induce the radical transformation of identity necessary for successful conduct in the new setting.[13] Degradation rituals also occur in not so "total" institutions like street gangs, business firms, families, universities, and, of course, political campaigns.

In these and other social contexts, degradation rituals, when they work meaningfully, subordinate individuals to the norms and values that define institutions and guide the proper behavior of their members. For example, the norms of machismo and male superiority are challenged when one member of a street gang dates the girlfriend of another.[14] In another setting, unemployed black males suffer painful degradation when unemployment officers force them to seek low-paying jobs that underscore their failed status. As a result, groups of chronic unemployed may celebrate the rejection of work with a language of social solidarity and secret status.[15]

Status and social norms must be negotiated rhetorically from moment to moment in street corner settings that lack formal institutional rules. Street corner language games like Playing the Dozens are responsible for creating ongoing social order.[16] For example, sociolinguist William Labov cites an exchange in which Rel, a low-status gang member, commands the floor from Stanley, a high-status member, by "degrading" him with a convincing insult:

Rel: Shut up please!

Stanley: . . . 'ey, you tellin' me?

Rel: Yes. Your mother's a duck.[17]

In this exchange, Rel's failure to deliver a clinching insult would have forced Stanley to affirm his higher status in the group by asking Rel to fight. As it was, Rel's apt rejoinder served as a grounds for Stanley to acknowledge that he had been bested temporarily and that Rel could have the floor. Rel's rhetorical move was not unlike the skillful exercise of parliamentary procedure.

Presidential candidates do not refer to their opponents' mothers as ducks. However, they routinely exchange insults, and, as noted in the last chapter, they exchange them according to a very special set of ritualistic rules. At least they did before the ritual began to fall apart. In the traditional election ritual, candidates were also held accountable for alleged violations of political norms and for apparent inconsistencies in their contrived characters. The following discussion addresses the questions of how gaffes are identified, how they are formulated into complaints, how candidates respond to them, and how political audiences assess the responses. Afterward we turn to the problem of what it means when these character tests disappear from the electoral process.

Patterns in Electoral Character Tests

Turning gaffes into legitimate campaign issues is a problem of rhetoric involving language categorization: finding the words to describe a questionable candidate action in a way that is consistent with both observed reality and some relevant political norm. Testing candidate actions against various political norms enables voters to make two kinds of judgments. First, gaffes that violate important norms can be distinguished from gaffes that represent minor slips of little or no political importance. Second, finding a normative category for a particular gaffe enables voters to anticipate how a candidate should repair the violation.

As these guidelines suggest, not all candidate errors provide good material for campaign issues. Some slips and blunders are hard to categorize within accepted political norms. For example, when Jimmy Carter slipped during his 1980 acceptance speech at the Democratic party convention and referred to former vice president and party heavyweight "Hubert Horatio Hornblower Humphrey," he was not called into account for his statement. Neither was Carter called into account following a poor performance in the 1980 presidential debate with Ronald Reagan when he thanked the people of Cleveland for showing such hospitality in the "last hours of my life." A simple slip of the tongue may blemish the delivery of a line in a speech, but it is not easily taken as a sign of serious character or leadership problems. A chronic problem with delivery, pronunciation, or coherence, may, on the other hand, lead to the formulation of complaints about leadership skills. Gerald Ford's slips in 1976 became notable because they exceeded what many observers regarded as normal or tolerable levels in a leader.[18]

There are, of course, no precise rules for determining exactly what constitutes a normative violation. The existence of such rules would miss the point of the gaffe-repair ritual. It is through the playing out of each situation that agreement is negotiated on the nature and gravity of violations. Without this element of spontaneity and surprise, rituals become, as the saying goes, "empty."

Thus, a candidate's choice of repair rhetoric has a big effect on public judgments about the severity of the violation and the possible remedies that might be in order. For example, concern seemed to die quickly following the Carter charge in 1980 that Reagan was a "warmonger." Carter staff people answered questions about the propriety of the remark with the concession that the word may have been a bit harsh. Suggesting the relatively minor normative category "momentary loss of temper" was enough to satisfy NBC's John Chancellor, who described the incident as a mere case of the president "having some trouble with his rhetoric today."[19] In contrast, Carter's 1976 remark about the merits of preserving the "ethnic purity" of neighborhoods was less easily dismissed and, instead, was taken as a possible violation of major norms about race relations in America. A president's failure to adhere to such norms would undermine his credibility as a national leader. As a result of the more serious nature of this violation, Carter was forced to engage in an elaborate series of attempts to demonstrate his commitment to social equality and integration. He finally surrounded himself with a group of black leaders who offered personal endorsements at a televised press conference.

Transforming a gaffe into a campaign issue requires not only a linkage to some political norm, but also the introduction of the public as the party to whom the accounting is directed. There are various ways of doing this. For example, an opponent may discount the personal hurt of an insult and suggest, instead, that it lowers the standards of campaigning (implying that the public deserves better). In other cases, leaders of a social group may register a complaint, as when black leaders initially denounced Carter's ethnic purity statement. In still other cases, a neutral political leader may speak "in the public interest," as Barry Goldwater did in 1976 when he issued a statement (no doubt, on behalf of Gerald Ford) pointing out the factual inaccuracy and irresponsibility of Ronald Reagan's Panama Canal position. In other cases, the press reports a gaffe in such a way that its offensiveness is made clear.

The ways in which gaffes are formulated constrain, to some extent, the ways in which candidates can respond effectively to them. For example, a gaffe that is poorly categorized under a norm of only minor importance leaves the candidate the option of simply denying the validity of the charge. In contrast, a clear normative violation increases the pressure for some form of apology to satisfy an offended audience. The gambit from "denial-to-apology" is, of course, very general. The art of apology involves a variety of ways to save face.

In their discussion of the rhetorical genre of apologia, rhetoricians B. L. Ware and Wil Linkugel argue that attempts to restore character and affirm social norms involve much the same techniques that are employed in resolving belief dilemmas in general.[20] The voter's dilemma in elections involves the simple problem of reconciling expectations about a candidate with an apparent violation of those expectations. To the extent that candidates respond in ways that minimize the expectation gap, the voter's dilemma is resolved with a minimum of damage to the candidate's credibility.

Ware and Linkugel suggest the suitability of Robert Abelson's typology of resolutions for belief dilemmas which includes the four symbolic operations of denial, bolstering, differentiation, and transcendence.[21] Under some circumstances, candidates simply deny charges against them. At other times, they try to separate or differentiate an offending action from one normative category so that it can be thought of in other, less damaging terms or as a special case. Sometimes an extenuating circumstance or motive will be emphasized, or bolstered, in an effort to highlight a more positive interpretation. Finally, candidates may try to transcend the entire situation by showing that the unfortunate incident served some larger purpose or lesson. Candidate responses often combine more than one of these repair techniques, as in the case of Richard Nixon's Checkers Speech, or Edward Kennedy's Chappaquiddick defense.[22] (In these notorious cases Nixon was accused of accepting gifts during his vice presidential campaign in 1952, including a cute cocker spaniel puppy named Checkers, and Kennedy was faced with the possible end of his political career when a car he was driving went off a bridge in Chappaquiddick, Massachusetts, and a young female companion was drowned.)

CANDIDATES WITHOUT CHARACTER

Candidates still go through the ritualistic motions of exchanging attacks and insults but in ways that are far removed from wit-testing spontaneity. If voters are put off by the new negativity in campaigns it is probably not because it is unfamiliar in form, but because its content has been so contrived as to be pointless, and the chances to witness spontaneous candidate reactions are all but eliminated. It is worth considering, for example, whether Campaign '88 might have been different if Michael Dukakis had taken the risk of responding personally and emotionally to Bush's attacks on his patriotism and his state's prison release programs, or to a reporter's hypothetical question about "what if" a released prisoner raped Dukakis' wife. Instead, Dukakis pursued a rhetorical strategy of controlled, calculated responses that revealed little about his humanness.

Psychologist Harold Zullow studied the rate of verbal slips among presidential candidates in high-pressure debate situations. He found that Dukakis displayed an astonishingly low verbal error rate of 5.5 percent compared to Bush who made errors in 20 percent of his sentences during their first debate.[23] Such a button-down character style leaves voters little to go on, and perhaps explains why by the end of the campaign Bush scored higher than Dukakis in a number of preference scenarios, ranging from being the person most preferred to handle a crisis situation to the person most people would prefer to invite over for dinner. Voters did not apparently label Bush's slips as serious enough to be gaffes; instead, they revealed the humanness of a candidate who was slightly shy and flustered under the television lights. Most people were evidently able to laugh with Bush rather than at him when he declared September 7, Pearl Harbor Day, and when, as president, he struggled to gain command of that elusive "vision thing," and when he made a speech to an AFL–CIO convention in which he referred to the organization in the context of its foreign labor organizing efforts as the AFL–CIA.

As media guru Roger Ailes said, the goal of modern campaigning is to maximize visuals and attacks while minimizing mistakes. Damage prevention is the word of the day, and damage control is its constant shadow. Following his first campaign trip of 1988, Democratic vice presidential candidate Lloyd Bentsen did not point to his policies, programs, or stirring oratory as the mark of success on the road. Rather, he marked the success of the trip with these words: "We just haven't had any serious slip-ups that I know of. If we have had them, the staff has masked them well."[24]

The exceptions to the rule of the well-controlled candidate are worth noting. One of these exceptions involved a Democratic candidate in the 1988 presidential primaries, Joe Biden, who recited plagiarized lines from a speech by British Labor party leader Neal Kinnock. Clearly, in this case true campaign professionals were not on the job. Similarly, we have the case of Democratic hopeful Gary Hart who singlehandedly elevated the term *bimbo* to the top of the American political vocabulary for a few weeks. His much publicized affair with Donna Rice was a gaffe royale. Yet even in this case, the error was an exceptional one. Hart did not really violate a clear public political norm, for in the past the press had always covered up candidate and even presidential indiscretions with a cloak of public secrecy. Journalists did not cover for Hart because he personally challenged them to follow his movements and report whatever story they discovered, no matter how tawdry. That sort of taunting proved too much even for the ordinarily indulgent press to tolerate. Joe Biden and Gary Hart, for all we know, may have been better leaders than Michael Dukakis and George Bush, but they were not as well managed. In the final analysis, victory went to the leader with the best director, which is hardly the same thing as the leader with the best sense of direction.

What is the connection between the character of leaders, particularly presidents, and society's ongoing efforts to define and solve its problems? The answer begins with the recognition that elections in America were not designed with policymaking in mind. With the notable exceptions of Jefferson and Paine, most of the nation's founders lived in fear of ignorant and unruly, not to mention unpropertied, masses holding sway over the course of government. As a result, unlike most other liberal democracies we do not have a parliamentary system. Our undisciplined and beleaguered political parties have had little success in hammering out detailed programs and holding members to the party line after the voting is over. Thus, the United States stands in sharp contrast to systems in which party loyalty is the key to power and ideological clarity is the key to votes. Fortunately, the nation's founders also suffered an equal fear of each other; as a result, we also have a fairly reliable, if unwieldy, set of checks and balances against the rise of an enduring oligarchy. This process of eliminating the unacceptable alternatives produced a system unusually dependent on folk heroes and strong leaders to make it go. Our quadrennial political spectacle is first and foremost a leadership competition with no binding connection between what candidates promise voters and what actually might happen after the victor takes office. Yet the election ritual also has an important policy and agenda-setting potential if left open to spontaneous communication between candidates and voters.

RECYCLED CULTURE

As a result of the breakdowns in American politics, when old problems come up again and again to haunt Congress and the chief executive, the remedies proposed give us a powerful sense of déjà vu. New political situations seem to fall quickly into old symbolic molds.[25] The persistence of old political solutions is remarkable in light of their repeated failure to resolve the social and economic problems they address. When issues fit so readily into familiar but dubious symbolic formats, the reason may be found in some cultural logic that organizes the political communications between elites and the general public.

To summarize the argument from the last two chapters, culture consists of the basic beliefs, values, and behaviors that organize social interaction and communication. Culture produces the common social understandings that guide people through everyday life situations, help them respond to new social conditions, and enable them to accept their positions in the social order. The most important aspects of culture are the basic models of (values, beliefs, and stories about) society, called myths, and the social routines through which they are brought to life, called rituals. In the absence of formal political ideologies, another notable characteristic of American politics, political myths and rituals guide the processes in which policies are made and public opinion is formed.

Political myths are difficult to analyze because they are such integral components of everyday perception. They are like the lenses in a pair of glasses: they are not something people see when they look at the world; they are the things they see with. Myths are the truths about society that are taken for granted. These basic cultural principles are woven throughout everyday social communication from dinner table conversation, to the morals of television programs, to the lofty policy debates of Congress.

In the process of growing up in society, most people encounter hundreds of myths that gradually slip into their subconscious thinking. For example, young children are exposed to a battery of folk tales through school, parents, and the mass media. Some myths recount the exploits of groups such as the Puritans, the Founding Fathers, the slaves, the western pioneers, or the European immigrants. Other myths convey their social lessons through the acts of individual heroes like George Washington, Daniel Boone, Andrew Jackson, Abraham Lincoln, Mother Jones, John Kennedy, Martin Luther King, Jr., or Muhammad Ali. Through these cultural models people first encounter the ideals of free enterprise, honesty, industry, bravery, tolerance, perseverance, and individualism. Myths also explain the causes of poverty and other social adversities and show how people overcome them. That is, myths explain the principles of politics and the nature of society. The range of different myths allows cultural perspectives to be transmitted in ways that fit the experiences of different social groups. This mythology is the basis of political consciousness in American society.

Myths condition the public to respond to the symbols used by politicians. In times of stability, myths underwrite the status quo, and in periods of upheaval they chart the course of change. In the day-to-day business of politics, they set the terms for most public policy debate. When mythical themes and myth-related language are stripped away from policy discourse, very little of substance remains. Most political controversy centers around disagreement over which myth to apply to a particular problem.

It is difficult to talk about this underlying structure of public thinking because myths are seldom learned as complete stories that individuals can recall at a conscious level. Myths are assimilated through fragments of movies, books, school lessons, news stories, and personal experiences— inputs that blend fact with fantasy and confuse history with legend. They are transmitted as much through dramatic imagery and emotional associations as through concrete words or ideas. Their core symbols are reinforced throughout the social environment where individuals continue to encounter fragments of them in books, advertising, songs, religious ceremonies, youth organizations, business associations, school, family activities, the workplace, sporting events, and in numerous other everyday contexts.

As a result of their pervasive reference to life experience, myths become deeply embedded in consciousness as associative mechanisms linking private experience, ongoing reality, and history into powerful frameworks of understanding. This suggests that they are employed in communication and opinion formation through primary process thinking. In contrast to secondary process or rational thought, primary process thinking is characterized by projection, fantasy, the incorporation of nonverbal imagery, a high emotional content, the easy connection of disparate ideas, the failure to make underlying assumptions explicit, and the generation of multiple levels of meaning. The most notable features of myth-based thinking are:

- The absence of formal logical connections between political beliefs and values and understandings about specific issues.
- The power of simple political symbols to evoke strong but unarticulated mythical understandings.
- The capacity of individuals to hold divergent, even contradictory, myths, which explains American voter tendencies to switch parties and candidates, the regular mixing of liberal and conservative views on different issues, and high individual tolerance for a range of political outcomes.

Consider an example of myth-based thinking in an interview with a veteran of the Revolutionary War battle of Concord and Lexington. The following interview was conducted by a historian some sixty years after the event. The interviewer was interested in the question of what motivated the patriot to risk his life in a struggle for independence:

Q: Why did you? . . . My histories tell me that you men of the Revolution took up arms against intolerable oppressions.

A: What were they? Oppressions? I didn't feel them.

Q: What, were you not oppressed by the Stamp Act?

A: I never saw one of those stamps . . . I am certain I never paid a penny for one of them.

Q: Well, what about the tea tax?

A: Tea tax, I never drank a drop of the stuff. The boys threw it all overboard.

Q: Then, I suppose you had been reading Harrington, or Sidney, or Locke, about the eternal principles of liberty?

A: Never heard of 'em.

Q: Well, then, what was the matter, what did you mean in going into the fight?

A: Young man, what we meant in going for those red-coats, was this: we always had governed ourselves and we always meant to. They didn't mean we should.[26]

The dictates of rational or logical analysis would have us dismiss such ramblings as meaningless. However, discounting the significance of ordinary political thinking not only robs individuals of a dignified basis for their actions, but it also frustrates any possibility of understanding how politicians mobilize public support. The cryptic remark about self-government at the end of the interview is the key symbol that anchored the individual's thought and action within the mythology that dominated public consciousness at the time of the Revolution. Self-government was a popular translation of the Liberty myth that mobilized public support for the insurrection. Contemporary historians are beginning to recognize that the Liberty myth was not communicated to the masses in terms of ideological analyses of stamp acts or tea taxes. As Catherine Albanese noted in her excellent book on the mobilization of support for the Revolution, the myth of Liberty permeated the environment through the symbolism of poems, songs, posters, emblems, statues, and, above all, religious preachings.[27] When the myth was expressed in political terms, it was generally embedded in dramatic performances at public gatherings. In a common political ceremony described by Albanese, church bells gathered the townsfolk in the village green to witness a somber funeral procession carrying the casket of Liberty to its burial site. When the first spade began throwing dirt on the coffin, the Sons of Liberty swarmed over the landscape to rescue the symbol of self-government from an early grave. Historical accounts of this oft-repeated ritual note the attention of the audience, the impact of the plot, and the emotional release at the climax.

Just as drama, literature, and other forms of popular culture are often the most profound carriers of insight in everyday life, these forms also operate in politics to leave their impressions in the deepest levels of consciousness. This is why the formal structure or logic of myth remains hidden in ordinary political discourse. Only a few key symbols are needed to evoke meaningful responses.

Where do leaders and candidates for public office fit into this picture? They are the ones responsible for putting on the dramas, telling the national stories, suggesting the symbols through which understandings are to be found, and connecting the wisdom of mythology to the dilemmas that bedevil daily life. The fate of the United States perhaps more than that of any other first world nation has depended on the rise of great leaders to preside over the rituals and invoke the myths of state—especially in elections.

How candidates approach the election ritual largely determines the course the nation will take after the voting is over. Will candidates seize the chance to be creative in telling the national story—blending new insights with old wisdoms, suggesting time-honored rationales for new programs, rallying public opinion behind powerful symbols, and inviting continued support for the changes to come? Or will they choose to play it safe— reciting tired phrases with little concern about their contemporary relevance, content to turn citizens away at the door of political understanding?

The American system's curious dependence on strong leaders to articulate the consciousness of the nation is both its greatest strength and its greatest weakness. The strength lies in having a society that is relatively free of the ideological tensions that create explosive animosities and paralyzing political divisions. Leaders with an eye to national renewal and an ear for the American mythology can mobilize support across party and class lines. The weakness is its vulnerability to political candidates who have neither a vision nor an interest in mobilizing popular participation. When getting elected is the main goal and vision is narrowed by commitments to backers, the election ritual loses its vitality. Society stagnates and people lose hope. Times of failed leadership are particularly distressing in the American system because there are no traditions of strong parties or guiding ideologies to reverse the decline. Instead, people must rely on slow and often exhausting social movements to bring about reforms. Even these movements are heavily dependent on strong leaders, although they often attract a leadership relatively free of obligations to special interests.

This overview of myth, leadership, and public consciousness does not imply that bold leadership alone is sufficient to move the nation. The irony of American politics is that effective leaders generally move the public in new directions by finding creative applications of old mythologies. The memorable failures of Barry Goldwater on the right and George McGovern on the left suggest that radical ideas not cloaked in the proper mythology seldom capture the popular imagination.

The public rejects radical alternatives not because of their calculable impact on life quality, but because they cannot be assimilated meaningfully into the spectrum of myth. Intolerance in this sense is quite literally a fear of the unknown and the unimaginable. This sort of intolerance is illustrated in Karl Lamb's study of members of a wealthy conservative California community. Even though Lamb found people scattered all along the spectrum of political myth, he discovered that none of them could imagine political solutions that fell outside that range of myth. For example, Lamb concluded that his respondents "cannot really imagine a society that would provide substantial material equality." One of the people he interviewed had the following incredulous response to the idea of guaranteed economic equality: "It would be like everyone going out for a track race and saying, 'Okay, everyone can run this race in the same time,' so eventually there would be no more records to be gone after."[28]

For example, in the 1972 election Democratic presidential candidate George McGovern provoked strong public rejection by proposing a guaranteed minimum income for every American. McGovern's failure to cast his plan in familiar mythic symbols elicited a hostility based on confusion. One of Lamb's respondents expressed his confusion by posing the rhetorical question of why superwealthy people like Howard Hughes would need an extra thousand dollars. In contrast to this popular rejection of the McGovern plan stands the overwhelming public approval of Republican president Richard Nixon's earlier proposal for a guaranteed annual income. Shortly after taking office in 1968, Nixon proposed a Family Assistance Plan to the public and to Congress. The most significant difference between the Nixon and McGovern plans was not the amount of the stipends or their probable impact on society and economy, but the way in which the plans were symbolized. In his presentation of the Family Assistance Plan to the public, Nixon did not even mention the concept of a guaranteed income. Instead, he stressed the work incentives and other conditions attached to the financial assistance. Recipients were required to accept job training and a job while they were in the program. As an incentive to work, they would continue to receive a diminishing stipend until their income brought them above the designated poverty line.

The symbolism in Nixon's proposal aimed at the very center of the mythological spectrum bounded by the characteristic American themes of individualism and equality of opportunity. The result was an impressive one from a political standpoint. An overwhelming 78 percent of the public supported the plan.[29] Even more revealing is the fact that Lamb's respondents discussed the program and the social problems it addressed in a vocabulary of symbols that was a perfect parallel to Nixon's myth-based references.[30] This suggests that normal political communication is referenced in myth. Elites use, and the public looks for, key symbols that carry implicit mythological meanings.

The vitality of elections lies not just in choosing leaders, but in making those choices meaningful for as many voters as possible. Unless presidential candidates can dramatize their goals to the satisfaction of large numbers of people, the importance of elections for the political system is greatly diminished. Without strong leadership emerging from the electoral arena, and without continuing popular support for the political vision embodied in that leadership, the curious and cumbersome American system of checks and balances remains unworkable.

The dilemma of American politics is in finding strong, creative leaders at the precise time we need them. In the past, the nation has been blessed with a remarkable number of visionaries who emerged from the wings to mobilize both Congress and the people through the ordeals of crisis and change. The question today is whether the current system of campaigning discourages strong leaders from seeking office in the first place or, if they do run, from taking the risks necessary to mobilize people behind bold courses of action. We may have reached an impasse in which the very leadership qualities necessary to the functioning of the system have been screened out by the rules of the contemporary campaign game. Even when promising leaders choose to play the game, they may have to bend their rhetorical talents and ideas to the dictates of campaign consultants who are, after all, the experts on how to get elected these days. And when those candidates are elected, they face the unhappy prospect of having failed to cultivate the public understanding and support necessary to carry out their political goals effectively. If the rules of the current election game systematically work against the rise of leaders with clear and sustainable visions for future action, what will the future bring for a nation poised on the brink of great historical changes both at home and abroad? This is the question to be explored in the next part of the book.

PART III

The Future of Electoral Democracy

I get home at night and wonder, "Why can't we do things in the best interest of the country?" —*Robert H. Michel (Republican, Illinois), House Minority Leader*

The American people go to the polls today, or anyway some of them will. It seems apposite to reflect on the state of their democracy, and any reflection must start with two observations: First, the palpable sentiment of the electorate is discontent with the status quo. . . . Second, the most likely outcome of today's ballot is that nothing will change. . . . It could scarcely be otherwise. Of the 435 races of the House, barely more than 80 are effectively contested. In any event, probably only around 35% of potential voters will show up at the booth today; citizens no longer see voting as an effective way to voice their discontents. —Wall Street Journal *Editorial, Election Day, 1990*

You would think the more secure you are the more of a risk taker you would be. But it's the reverse. Sometimes the longer you are here, the less capable you are of determining what you stand for. —*Thomas J. Downey (Democratic Representative, New York)*

CHAPTER 7

Politics and Elections
in the 1990s

As we round the postmodern bend to examine the governing system of the 1990s, it will help to have the argument clearly in mind. The main points from Parts I and II are these:

• Money in the form of campaign financing has entered the marketplace of political ideas as a highly decentralizing force. Without getting into sticky questions of corruption, conspiracies, or "right turns" in the party system, it is possible to argue a simpler point: parties, politicians, and political programs are being pulled apart by well-financed interest organizations in pursuit of narrow political goals. Elevating a host of narrow-gage goals to the top of the national agenda effectively eliminates the possibilities for stable power blocs (e.g., voters and parties) to line up behind broad programs for national renewal. In short, money undermines the emergence of what can be called "governing ideas."

• Having no credible governing ideas to stand behind, politicians have made an overwhelming commitment to the use of advertising and marketing strategies to sell themselves to voters (and to maintain public approval later on during their terms in office). The result is a short-circuiting of the public give-and-take in political rituals, such as elections, where candidates and ideas have been tested in the past. As a result, most Americans today experience elections as empty rituals that offer little hope for political dialogue, genuine glimpses of candidate character, or the emergence of a binding consensus on where the nation is going and how it ought to get there. Thus, the political culture has been robbed of its creative communicative potential by the imposition of packaged messages that inspire little interest, faith, or involvement from the people.

• Aware of their role in delivering these unwelcome messages to the masses, the news media have become increasingly critical of election content. The faint distress signals sent by journalists to their audiences in 1988 were amplified in 1990, as illustrated later in this chapter. This point should not be generalized to any larger conclusions about the emergence of more critical or activist mass media. On most other issues and news topics there is considerably less public consensus of the sort that invites the growing chorus of complaint about elections in the media. The more important point, however, is that media criticism within the current electoral system creates a strange political result: candidates and public officials are inclined all the more to withdraw behind curtains of media management techniques, while the public is taken on cynicism-producing media tours behind these curtains.

Increasing exposure to the inner workings of electoral politics may have fueled the sense of hopelessness that ushered in the 1990s. However, media criticism could equally well become a positive force for reform if journalists and the attentive public work out understandings of the problem that can serve as models for change. As a first step, it is helpful to recognize the link between the decline of elections and the crisis in governing. Many connections exist between elections and governing, but most of them involve sacrificing political leadership in order to get elected by marketing. As noted earlier, winning elections by marketing often leads—particularly in the case of prominent leaders with national ambitions—to bringing the marketing consultants to Washington after the election. After all, somebody has to figure out what to do in office. The result is a gradual reversal of traditional assumptions about the relationship between elections and governing. Where people may have assumed in the past that politicians ran for election in order to govern, today politicians generally create the appearance of governing in order to win elections. To underscore the importance of this reversal in the role of elections, this chapter opens with several intentionally provocative sketches of leadership, public policy initiatives, and legislative politics surrounding a typical election of the new era, the 1990 congressional contest.

THE FUTURE OF LEADERSHIP

Given the present course, it is not too farfetched to imagine the ideal candidate of the future being selected precisely for a lack of ideas, the absence of strong personal character, and a corresponding willingness to be scripted, directed, and marketed down to the last detail. This is a frightening possibility, but it is not absurd. In this connection, Dan Quayle, the man the polls have repeatedly featured as America's worst nightmare in the presidency, comes immediately to mind. Larry Sabato, a political scientist concerned about the growing impact of media control and candidate marketing on the democratic process, reports a story attributed to Quayle's best friend in college. Quayle and his friend had gone to see Robert Redford in *The Candidate,* which is a film about an attractive but directionless politician who is packaged and marketed all the way to the presidency. In Sabato's account, "The friend reported that Quayle said it was the greatest film he had ever seen, and Quayle was so excited about it that they talked for eleven hours straight after the movie. Of course, this movie became in some respects the story of Dan Quayle's life."[1] Upon hearing of Quayle's fascination with *The Candidate,* the film's screenwriter, Jeremy Larner, tried to point out that real-life candidate Quayle had failed to grasp the whole point of the movie. In Larner's words, "I am amazed to have inspired Dan Quayle. Inspiring such candidates was not our intention and I don't think [he] understood our movie. . . . [He] missed the irony. Unless, in a way we never could have foreseen, [he *is*] the irony."[2]

Whether or not The Candidate of the future turns out to be Dan Quayle, the moral of the story remains the same. Failing to grasp the point of a simple movie may not be a liability in the candidate of the future. To the contrary, it may represent a great advantage, rendering the candidate wholly malleable and uncompromisingly marketable. Indeed, this sort of Frankenstein fantasy may have crossed the minds of political consultants who may be tempted to test the limits of their art. Sabato suggests, for example, that George Bush's surprising choice of Quayle as a running mate came largely at the urging of Bush's managers: "It's pretty well known that George Bush did not have a close and continuing relationship with Dan Quayle; they didn't know each other very well. So how did the Quayle pick happen? Well, Bob Teeter, Bush's pollster, and Roger Ailes, his media consultant, had both handled Dan Quayle's previous congressional campaigns in Indiana. And they knew just how attractive and malleable Dan Quayle was. . . . It's clear that not only did they put his name on the list, but at least in the case of Roger Ailes, they became advocates for the candidate."[3] In this view, the only trouble with such perfect media candidates is that "they may be better at running for office than governing."[4] This only appears to be a problem, I suppose, if one insists on some nostalgic link between elections and the idea of government.

THE FUTURE OF POLICY:
THE WAR ON (fill in your favorite issue, problem, or country here)

It has become part of the American way of politics to declare war on national problems. Wars on crime, poverty, and drugs have occurred and recurred in the past several decades. Wars make for good symbolic politics, at once turning public concerns about a dreaded problem into support for the leaders fighting it, and at the same time reassuring people that something is being done about those problems that aroused their fears to begin with.[5]

At least since Machiavelli began advising his prince, politics in most societies have had strong symbolic and public relations overtones. In postmodern America, however, there may not be much substance left after the election is over and the marketing consultants move into staff positions with the politicians they helped elect. There are, of course, lots of government activities still going on: crises, bailouts, stopgap measures, and the like. But would there be so many crises to manage, or gaps to stop, or disasters to bail out if a bit more governing was going on at the center? Indeed, when administrations and congresses try to look ahead and take concerted action against social problems these days, the superficiality of governing becomes most apparent. The wars on various public problems increasingly resemble the one-dimensional gargoyles and other design details on postmodern buildings: stuck onto the facades as ironic, ghostly reminders of times when the pieces fit the whole and the edifice stood for the kind of human activity that was going on inside.

Again, this is not to imply that political symbol-waving was ever an entirely useful, straightforward, or public-spirited activity. However, some of the grand symbolic wars on social problems as recently as two decades ago displayed notable differences with those of today, including: a better fit between the war symbolism and the surrounding policy program; the uses of symbols to generate helpful levels of public support and enthusiasm; and last, but not least, occasionally attacking targeted problems in ways that made a difference in solving them. In this light, consider Lyndon Johnson's grand War on Poverty in the 1960s. That war was actually part of a larger social vision (a governing idea, as it were) called the Great Society. Whatever one's ideological feelings about this Democratic-driven idea, fighting poverty in the context of a larger program of health, education, social services, and civil rights legislation actually ended up reducing poverty levels by about half (from 22 percent to less than 12 percent of the U.S. population) during the period from the early 1960s to the mid-1970s.[6] Many Americans objected to the welfare system that grew out of this war and therefore condemned the vision as flawed. As a result, the war was canceled, the welfare system was cut back, and poverty rose fairly steadily through the 1980s and into the 1990s. The point is not whether the poverty war was part of a 20–20 vision of social problems, for such clarity of insight is hard to come by in politics. Rather, the idea is that, for all its symbolic hype, the War on Poverty was part of a larger political program—however flawed—that made a difference.

Or take a Republican-driven example of an earlier social war: the Nixon-era battle against drugs. Once again, critics were quick to charge that it was just another symbolic crusade—this one, with sinister law and order, or police state, overtones. This is perhaps so, but the larger point is that at the same time that drug-related law enforcement efforts increased, the government also supported expansions in surrounding social programs for health, education, counseling, and social work. One result was a decline in reported drug use in all monitored categories (marijuana, cocaine, and hallucinogens) by the mid-1970s.[7] Like the earlier War on Poverty, levels of the problem rose again after the official fight was called off.

The drug war of the 1970s was canceled because of Richard Nixon's exit from office, successor Gerald Ford's somewhat short and rocky regime, and the next president Jimmy Carter's de-emphasis on conservative law and order politics. The levels of casual or recreational drug use had peaked and were in decline again by the time Ronald Reagan came into office in 1981. In the early years of his administration, the spotlight was not on drugs, but on cutting many of the social programs that provided a broad policy context for the drug wars (particularly against hard-core drug use) in the decades before. Only after much of this programmatic context had been whittled away did the Reagan advisory team discover a symbolic use for another drug war. The Reagan remake of *Drug Wars* was devised in considerable part as a marketing strategy not for the popular president but for his less beloved wife, Nancy. White House polls showed that the First Lady's reputation for designer clothing, hobnobbing with the rich and famous, and expensive White House entertainment and decorating tastes all mixed poorly with her general lack of social concerns. As a result, Nancy Reagan's negative public image grated uneasily alongside the president's easygoing popularity. Even worse, the First Lady's uncaring image seemed to be rubbing off on her husband. Marketing research conducted by Richard Wirthlin turned up drugs as an issue that could be used to reach out and touch (image-wise, that is) real people—particularly children—caught up in what was obviously a serious social problem.[8] And so, Nancy Reagan was cast as the media star (with husband Ron in a strong supporting role) in a prolonged national war on drugs. The script of this long-playing political commercial was reduced to a single sound bite: "Just Say NO" (to drugs). It was simple, clear, and, above all, successful—not in reducing drug use but in elevating the First Lady's public image to its proper (positive) place alongside that of her already popular husband. For these and other masterstrokes of marketing and media manipulation during the Reagan presidency, Richard

Wirthlin was crowned Advertising Man of the Year in 1989.[9] It was an industry Oscar given not for his creative work for General Foods or Mattel Toys, but for his career-capping achievements as director of consumer research for Ronald Reagan.

The above analysis in no way doubts that drugs were (and are) a major national problem. To the contrary, wars on social problems are more likely to enlist public support if people are inclined to see the problem as serious to begin with. Following the cocaine epidemic of the early 1980s, public concerns about drugs and related problems of crime, gangs, workplace drug use, and so on, were on the rise. Typical of the emotional escalation following a declaration of war, media images of Congress and the White House leading the nation into battle pushed the issue of drugs even higher up the public agenda of most important national problems. However, the main point here is one about politics in the current era: like the "designer" issues filling space in elections, the issues that later emerge within the government itself are increasingly likely to be pure spectacle, devoid of links to larger programs, and, therefore, incapable of changing much of anything in the social world. In the end, of course, these symptoms of postmodern politics end up feeding public cynicism and withdrawal, leading to rejection of government and distrust of leaders. In the short run, however, new marketing strategies often fool (or otherwise move) still-attentive publics into forming opinions, expressing feelings, and making marginal political choices like voting. As a result, test-marketed issues get candidates elected and, once elected, give politicians (and even First Ladies) the appearance of doing something with their time in public office.

It may be too simple to say that wars on social problems unguided by larger governing ideas have few effects other than image-building for politicians. Indeed, a more critical look at the Reagan round of drug wars leads to the conclusion that there were many political effects, but few of them related to the intended goal of reducing drug use. The most tangible results of the drug wars of the 1980s may have been the creation of a larger police apparatus, the erosion of constitutional guarantees, the provocation of paranoia in tens of millions of citizens who have been counted among the enemy, and the contribution of endless material for "just say no" (just say mo') jokes among the underclass and the youth who suffer the drug problem most painfully. And then there is the curious self-fulfilling—we might even say addictive—effect that largely symbolic political campaigns can have on those who take them seriously.[10] Images of a besieged society create a fortress mentality in which the good burghers retreat behind the castle walls awaiting the daily supply of symbolic reassurance to calm their fears about the state of siege outside. Leaders bereft of hard political issues are only too happy to fill the public demand for symbols.

Why has this governmental failure occurred? The political culture has become stuck—unable to do much more than to recycle the symbolic scripts of old solutions and apply them melodramatically to new problems. The drug epidemic, like dozens of other items in the political crisis inventory, has its origins in a stagnating society burdened with serious problems at the core. Yet politicians who are both dependent on and divided by campaign financing, political marketing, and media management are unable to contemplate the programmatic reforms that might actually bring about social renewal. This is a classic vicious cycle. Because politicians are unwilling to address long-term solutions to the big social problems, they must launch ever grander symbolic crusades against symptomatic social crises, like drugs, that spin off from the core problems. As the political paralysis worsens, symbolic crusades become the only recourse for politicians. To appear to be doing nothing would further antagonize the dwindling numbers of citizens who remain involved in the political process.

So we come to George Bush and *Drug Wars, 1990*. Having little in the way of domestic programs to implement, White House media advisers and marketing specialists decided to stage yet another revival of what has become by now a modern (and postmodern) political classic. For its part, being little affected by the Reagan crusade, the drug problem was still around. Boding well for the chances of victory, several categories of drug use were declining on their own. *The decline in those categories had been going on steadily since before the Reagan team declared war.* These figures are always a bit slippery both because they are based largely on self-reports of drug users, and because the main decline has occurred since 1979 in the rates of casual drug use, while the rates of hard-core addictive use—particularly in cocaine—have held steady, and, according to some studies, even increased into the 1990s. In symbolic wars, however, slippery figures only improve the chances for declaring symbolic victories. Equally important, the plot changed enough in the late 1980s and early 1990s, with the increased use of crack cocaine and growing gang involvement, to justify a new symbolic offensive.

Typical of political issues that do not have governing ideas behind them, the drug war of the Bush administration was also largely an image device. This time, George Bush replaced Nancy Reagan in the starring role, and the specific image objectives were altered to suit the new star's political needs. Ms. Reagan was in need of warming up—an image achieved by casting her in media events surrounded by schoolchildren and rehabilitating Americans of all races and social backgrounds. Bush, meanwhile, was still haunted by his image as a wimp. Although his wimpiness was fairly well overcome during the election by negative campaigning and Clint Eastwood sound bites, drugs offered the chance to continue playing Mr. Tough Guy in office. This anti-wimp image was further enhanced by creating a special office for drug-fighting, filled initially by another tough guy, William Bennett, whom the media dubbed the drug czar. Thus, the same social problem was used to create a softer, more likable image for one political figure and a harder, tougher image for another—both transformations were brought to the public through the wonders of market research and political advertising techniques.

For their part, the media played a less passive yet more opportunistic role in covering the Bush remake of *Drug Wars*. On the opportunistic side, television networks conducted their own ratings wars with dramatic and often frightening coverage of gangs, violence, drug lords, addicted children, and cities turned into murder capitals. At the same time, the news was surprisingly critical of Bush's symbolic crusade, pointing out that its law and order emphasis (including guerrilla warfare in the cocaine fields of Bolivia) was more likely to win political cheers from conservatives than get at the roots of a serious American social problem. Thus, although the media could be faulted for turning the urban drug scene into police drama "infotainment" on the nightly news, there were also a few hopeful signs that news organizations were resisting the White House's management techniques. Publications no more radical than *Time* magazine began to recognize the symbolic foibles of the age. Journalist Walter Shapiro explained to *Time* readers how the latest take on the symbolic drug crusade worked:

> Begin with public officials who have exploited the issue for 20 years, advocating phony feel-good nostrums like the current fad for drug testing in the workplace, as if mid-level bureaucrats were society's prime offenders. Joining the politicians in the dock are those anti-drug crusaders who have either squandered credibility with exaggerated scare talk or strained credibility with prissy pronouncements. The media are culpable as well, for sensationalized coverage that has often served to glamorize the menace they are decrying. Then there are the social-policy conservatives who purport to see no connection between the flagrant neglect of the economic problems of the underclass and the current crack epidemic. And sad to say, well-intentioned parents can also contribute to the hysteria by viewing drugs as the sole cause of their children's problems, rather than as a symptom of family-wide crisis.
>
> For drug use, as [drug czar William] Bennett argues, is indeed a reflection of the nation's values. And as long as American society continues to place a higher premium on titillation than truth and on callousness

than compassion, the latest attack on drugs may prove, like all the failed battle plans of the past, to be mostly futile flag waving.[11]

Perhaps sensing that his symbolic credits had been spent, Bennett left his post after less than two years in charge of the war. As for the problem, drug abuse itself will ebb and flow, perhaps inviting another drug war or two from future administrations. Then, if we are fortunate, the problem, like many other symptoms of deeper social distress, will eventually go away on its own. There is little hope for serious solutions when the chances for a national dialogue about governing ideas are preempted time and again by political image campaigns. These symbolic crusades inspire volumes of chatter and sloganeering that fill the airwaves from talk shows to religious cable TV channels. In the Bush drug crusade, a somewhat more critical media took a few tentative steps toward breaking down what Walter Shapiro described above as the social network of politicians, preachers, press, pundits, and parents dedicated to making symbolic sense out of political absurdity. It is always possible that journalists are regaining their grip after their long, perilous slide down the Teflon slopes of Reagan rhetoric. Perhaps making the connection between their own unpopularity and that of the national leadership, reporters and editors began figuring out that it can't really do them any harm to stop swallowing whole whatever politicians feed them.

It may take nothing short of a "new journalism," however, to counteract the media management strategies of political gurus like Bush advisers Sig Rogich and Roger Ailes. Still, it is noteworthy that a publication like *Time* made the following statement in its lead news article about the much-ballyhooed Bush drug program:

> The big joke is that Bush proposes to do all this with pitifully little money. The administration will tout a $7.8 billion program. But only $1 billion will be new money, including $600 million for education and treatment. Almost $6 billion consists of funds the government is already spending, and an additional $1 billion-odd constitutes double counting of cash . . . that Bush has already asked for as part of his anti-crime program.[12]

These are strong words for a news article, but one wonders about their effect on a war-weary, cynical public. It is not clear, for example, what effect, if any, followed the *Washington Post*'s investigative report in 1989 about a bag of crack cocaine held up by George Bush the night he declared war in a nationally televised speech. Bush offered the bag of crack as evidence that the drug problem could be found right across the street from his own home at 1600 Pennsylvania Avenue. The president told a national television audience that the crack had been purchased by undercover agents in Lafayette Park, across the street. The *Post*'s investigative efforts revealed that even this tiny skirmish in the national drug war had been staged to bring the real world in line with the political script of the media consultants. Here are the opening paragraphs of the *Washington Post* story that received wide media play:

> *Washington.* White House speech writers thought it was the perfect prop for President George Bush's first prime-time television address to the nation—a dramatic one that would show how the drug trade had spread to the president's own neighborhood.
>
> "This is crack cocaine," Mr. Bush solemnly announced in his Sept. 5 speech on drug policy, holding up a plastic bag filled with a white chunky substance. It was "seized a few days ago in a park across the street from the White House," he said, adding, "It could easily have been heroin or PCP."
>
> But obtaining the crack was no easy feat. To match the words of the speech writers, Drug Enforcement Administration agents lured a suspected Washington drug dealer to Lafayette Park four days before the speech. They made what appears to have been the agency's first undercover crack buy in a park better known for its location across Pennsylvania Avenue from the White House than for illegal drug activity, according to officials familiar with the case.
>
> In fact, the teen-age suspect, when first contacted by an undercover agent posing as a buyer, seemed baffled by the request.
>
> "Where is the White House?" he replied in a conversation that was secretly tape-recorded by the drug agency.
>
> "We had to manipulate him to get him down here," said William McMullen, assistant special agent in charge of the agency's Washington field office. "It wasn't easy."[13]

All in all, when Bush took his turn at commanding the drug crusade, the press seemed more determined than usual to point out that the emperor had no clothes. Or as cartoonist Pat Oliphant parodied the president's famous "read my lips" cliché, "The emperor has no lips." The trouble was that Bush applied the Number One damage control rule to the situation and sealed his lips. He may well have learned the art of muffling damaging lines during his years as understudy to Ronald Reagan. The Great Communicator's most effective response to spasmodic outbursts of press criticism was simply to smile, wave good-naturedly off in the distance beyond the snarling reporters, and say nothing.

To his credit, Bush added a small touch of his own to the Reagan communications philosophy. From time to time, his approach was to "go ballistic" with the press—not a full-out nuclear strike, but more of a limited tactical launch—and then lapse into silence. Following his celebrated bout with Dan Rather during the campaign, when the newscaster

pushed Bush on his former ties with drug profiteer and former Panamanian dictator Manuel Noriega, Bush handlers discovered that a bit of
bristle with the press made the candidate look tough and committed. It
was a tactic of immaculate media manipulation that toned down the wimp
factor by playing to popular dislike of the way journalists operate. After
that, silence on an issue could be golden.

Shortly after the *Washington Post* story on the staged drug bust appeared, the president took an image trip to a Maine tree farm to demonstrate his environmental concern. (A proposed trip to Valdez, Alaska, was
nixed by advisers because they didn't want the chief even remotely associated with the disastrous Prince William Sound oil spill or its unsuccessful
cleanup. Baby trees were regarded as better image material.) Rather than
conduct dutiful interviews about the president's relations with baby trees,
the press hounded him about the staged drug bust that dramatized his
national speech. The president suggested testily that questioning his methods in such a holy crusade made reporters antagonists in the drug war: "I
don't understand," he complained. "I mean, has somebody got some
advocates here for this drug guy?"[14]

In this day of managed news, it is doubtful that many people were
shocked or even surprised when the bag of cocaine held up by the president turned out to be a theatrical prop. The irony of press criticism these
days may be in confirming suspicions about how unresponsive leaders
have become to reasonable public expectations about their conduct.
There is something more the press could do to promote responsible political leadership: formulate its own agenda of national issues. Editors and
producers may sense that it is risky for the press to do anything beyond
allowing government officials to define the *crisis du jour,* and then respond critically if the winds of public opinion and elite opposition are
blowing in the right direction. Yet, keeping the heat turned up on a few
widely recognized big problems like the budget deficit, defense boondog-
gling, campaign financing, or rebuilding the economy just might meet with
more public approval than a superstitious media establishment imagines.

Until the idea of assuming a national leadership role overtakes the
editorial offices and press rooms, we can expect a steady stream of symbolic crusades like the drug wars. A defender of the current press system
may argue that journalistic fire occasionally brings down a stubborn (Michael Dukakis), poorly handled (Joseph Biden), or stubborn and poorly
handled (Gary Hart) politician. However, the important question is
whether these attacks, even when successful, do anything to alter the
conditions that are currently stagnating the governmental system. To the
contrary, political outsiders who fall to press criticism may be the very
ones most likely to bring new ideas into the electoral process and, eventu-

ally, into the government itself. It is simply their misfortune not to have better media handlers on the payroll.

Until the press ups the political ante, politicians will continue to tackle issues that are safe, surefire nonlosers. The drug war fills the bill neatly. To begin with, its reassuring familiarity makes it easy to pass off as a widely accepted problem. Indeed, almost every politician in the past twenty years has addressed it. Equally importantly, this means that few political opponents will openly expose the issue as a sham or a fruitless distraction when everybody else is scrambling to jump on the political bandwagon. If these features are not enough to make drugs the perfect "can't lose" political issue, the war imagery is rich with rhetorical possibilities ranging from poor, addicted children and terrorized neighborhoods to despicable enemies, foreign and domestic.

Leaving absolutely nothing to chance, Mr. Bush guaranteed himself victory in the opening night declaration of war speech by announcing an annual goal of 5 percent reductions in the number of drug users. That figure just happened to coincide with the rate of natural decline in drug addiction at the time, meaning that doing nothing would have satisfied the announced goals equally well.[15] In another stroke of good timing, a little over a year later (and just a few weeks after William Bennett resigned), the National Institute on Drug Abuse released the results of a survey showing a huge drop in casual cocaine use since the start of the drug war. President Bush hailed the findings as evidence that his troops were winning the war.[16] Critics charged that the survey was so badly designed that the reported dramatic (45 percent) drop in recreational cocaine use in two years was meaningless.[17] But reality in such symbolic debates is beside the point. Leaving aside the nagging suspicion that not much ever changed in the inner cities, or in the futures of the children growing up there, the George Bush production of *Drug Wars* had a successful curtain at the end of Act I. Once again, drugs had become the perfect political issue—just what the political consultant ordered to get by from one election to the next. And so, Bush prepared the nation for his reelection campaign in 1992 by doing nothing on the domestic front but doing it very well— except for one small detail that threatened to dash all the president's images against hard and unavoidable realities.

THE CASE OF THE MISSING GOVERNMENT: THE 101ST CONGRESS

Presidential politics is not all or even the greatest part of government; it is merely the most visible part. But the same lack of programmatic focus that is evident in the White House is also abundant in Congress. This is not to say that nothing is going on in Washington these days. To the contrary, the lights are burning late in the offices of hundreds of committees, commissions, and regulatory agencies where politics is increasingly focused in recent times. The fragmentation of the governing system has at once produced a decline in broad, programmatic national policies and an increase of what might be called government in the trenches. Both on Capitol Hill and in the executive branch, committee and agency personnel are working overtime writing the rules and regulations that bring thousands of small fragmentary policies on line consistent with the interests of the groups that have pushed them into legislative and bureaucratic agendas. This flurry of micro politics belies any suggestion that government has ceased activity. Rather, government has become even more dedicated to the writing and rewriting of rules and regulations and haggling over where federal responsibilities lie for increasingly uncoordinated politics. The point is simply that government is less and less occupied with passing laws backed by the force of governing ideas.[18] A look at Congress in recent years amply illustrates this claim.

In the popular view of national politics these days, the Democratic and Republican parties have contented themselves with dividing the executive and legislative branches of government between them, leaving the potentates in each party with plenty of power, lots of services to deliver to clients and constituents, an unprecedented degree of job security, and a merciful escape from being blamed for national calamities because they can each truthfully say that they lacked the full governing power to prevent them. While the past several decades do seem to have produced a rather neat division of legislative and executive power between the Democrats and the Republicans, respectively, the reason may have less to do with willful corruption and cynical complacency than with the corrosive effects of money, marketing, and media management on the evolution of governing ideas. The result is that neither party can muster a leadership quorum around any broad governing program worth implementing, much less offering it to the electorate as a basis for renewed party loyalty. Viewed in this light, the recent volume of talk from both parties about searching for a new vision or social agenda to offer voters may not be all hot air. Perhaps some aspiring party leaders would really like to capture the national imagination but can't figure out how to do it since their own political imaginations have been captured by organized interests. Accordingly, the performances of the parties in Congress in recent years begin to make sense. The Democrats are the better case to begin with here because their solid majorities in both the House and Senate have given them the chance to show what they can do by way of forging a legislative agenda.

At first glance, it would seem unfair to charge the party with squandering its incumbent majority for several consecutive congresses (the 100th, 101st, and 102nd running from 1986 to 1992) and promising to continue into the future. A more charitable assessment might be that it is surprising that the Democrats succeeded in passing as much legislation as they did, considering the influences pulling at the center of the party. The 101st Congress (1988–1990) is a good example. Beyond voting itself a pay raise and approving the appointment of a new Supreme Court justice, this Congress passed legislation in a number of areas, including clean air, child care, farm subsidy reforms, a ban on flag burning, increasing the minimum wage, bailout of the savings and loans, expansion of civil rights for disabled people, revision of oil spill cleanup procedures, employment rights for minorities, and medical leaves for workers in medium and large companies. (President Bush vetoed the last two bills.) As the *Washington Post* said in a "faint praise" editorial, there were "some pretty good things" in this list, particularly compared to most of the congresses of the 1980s.[19]

If we look beyond the flag-burning law and strain to find a pattern in the above list, what begins to emerge is a ghostly vision from the Democratic past. We see a sort of dim replay of civil rights, child care, and environmental concern without the accompanying force or feeling of the Great Society of the 1960s. Looking to the future (and, again, assuming sincere intentions), the best the party could do with its secure power base in Congress was to recycle the past—too little, too late, and without the visionary force or the social support that made those legislative fragments part of a meaningful whole the last time around. The best we can hope for from the present government, it seems, are a few "pretty good things."

It is little wonder that prominent members of Congress like those quoted at the opening of Part III began to complain about the legislative record they took into the elections of the 1990s. The spirit of the laws (and the lawmakers) appeared to be broken by interest group domination, party fragmentation, and crisis management—all of which placed serious limits on how far any piece of legislation could go to really make a difference. Said a legislator who retired after twenty-eight years in Congress, "This is the worst I've ever seen it. There is just a complete breakdown of the process."[20] Reflecting on the absence of guiding leadership in Congress, political scientist Ross Baker described his classroom talk on the subject as "one of the all-time short lectures in political science. There are too many guys calling themselves Mr. Chairman."[21]

The signs of a special interest– and campaign finance–dominated Congress were equally apparent in the legislation that was not passed. For example, none of the bills concerning election and campaign finance reform became laws. Although few of these proposals threatened radical changes in the system, one in particular (a Senate bill to eliminate political action committees) might have threatened the incumbent Democrats' lock on the House of Representatives and was, thus, rejected by that chamber.

The deeper legislative workings of those coveted campaign funds were illustrated in a series of gun control and decontrol laws that the gun lobby alternately blocked and pushed. The National Rifle Association (NRA) succeeded in blocking legislation that would have banned semiautomatic assault weapons and imposed a one-week waiting period on handgun purchases. The cherry on the NRA cake was congressional approval for the domestic manufacturing of semiautomatic weapons. The public interest watchdog group Common Cause estimated that key House members involved in this gun decontrol package received approximately $1.4 million in campaign contributions from the NRA over the previous three elections.[22]

Then there was the budget spectacle of 1990. Like many other accomplishments of the 101st Congress, the 1990 budget package was the best performance in many years. But like the legislative record discussed above, the best that could be said of the heroic efforts to pass a budget and reduce the deficit that year was "pretty good," "not bad," "better than nothing." Indeed, "nothing" was what the past several congresses had done while budget deficits soared and the national debt (the sum of deficits past) soared to over $3 trillion. After passing the Gramm–Rudman budget law in 1985 requiring Congress and the president to meet reduction targets designed to reach a balanced budget after five years, the national leadership managed to suspend and/or amend the law each year without hitting even one of the targets. In fact, Congress and the White House dodged the budget bullet so skillfully that the deficit at the end of the five-year plan was at a five-year high of almost $250 billion in 1990.[23]

The moment of truth also arrived in 1990. The public outcry over the budget was dragging any remaining faith in government to the bottom of the polls. Perhaps worse, from the standpoint of poll-hardened politicians, was the fact that the huge American debt and world economic uncertainty began scaring Japanese and European investors away from buying the treasury securities that Washington was forced to sell in order to keep the country running. Paying higher interest rates to lure investors to buy shares in the national government meant dedicating an increasing share of the annual budget just to interest on the debt. As it stood, roughly 15 percent of the budget was going for interest payments—slowly squeezing social programs out of existence and further alienating public support for government. This desperate picture showed only part of the country's deepening difficulties: a $500 billion price tag for the savings-and-loan bailout; the even higher sums estimated in deferred maintenance on national bridges, highways, airports, and nuclear weapons facilities; the impending crisis in the national banking system (with no money left in the government insurance till); and the wild card costs of a huge U.S. troop deployment in Saudi Arabia with the threat of war on the horizon. Even politicians who had avoided looking at the big national picture for years were forced to take a peek at budget reality.

After months of summit-like negotiations within and between the parties and between Capitol Hill and the White House, a package of tax increases and budget cuts was finally worked out. The initial fanfare promised to cut about $500 billion off the deficit over a five-year period. Compared to governmental performance of past years, this (like the legislative record of the 101st Congress) sounded "pretty good." Indeed, the media were reluctant to be too critical of the results, often noting, instead, how remarkable it was for Congress and the president to reach any responsible budget agreements at all. Yet, buried within the faint praise editorials and news analyses were some pretty gloomy assessments of this budget agreement. When all was said and done, it appeared that the reductions might do no better than hold the deficit at its current annual $200 billion–plus levels, with little hope of a balanced budget at the end of the latest five-year plan. The economic assessments became even worse when the costs of the savings-and-loan bailout, the military intervention in the Middle East, or any of several other high-cost or reduced-revenue scenarios was added to the bottom line.[24] Within several months of the much-heralded budget breakthrough, both White House and congressional budget offices conceded that a record deficit of around $300 billion (not counting the off budget items) awaited in 1991.

Probably the worst news of all was the six months of news coverage of foot-dragging, niggling, summit meetings, and finger-pointing among the national leadership in the process of producing this modest step toward national economic responsibility. The still-attentive public watched the spectacle of powerful leaders pulling this way and that to save pet programs or spare their preferred constituents the inconvenience of higher taxes. This time, however, they could not perform the budget trick with mirrors, and so George Bush's lips finally began to move slowly around the dreaded "T-word." In the end, he moved them so often and changed the words that came out so regularly that the media revived the wimp label and had a field day with all the flip-flopping going on in the White House. In fact, some instant analysts were quick to declare the budget spectacle a victory for the Democrats, because Bush not only moved his lips, but also held out for unpopular tax advantages for the wealthy. Perhaps this topsy-turvy state of national politics was best summarized in a *Wall Street Journal* front-page headline: "How the Democrats, with Rare Cunning, Won the U.S. Budget War."[25]

It is true that Bush created an easy campaign issue for the Democrats on the eve of an election by eating his sound bite and then inviting the Democrats to appear to be the enemy of the rich. In the end a crisis-weary public declared all parties losers. They had, after all, witnessed too many other culprits during these six months of political agonizing it took just to pass a responsible national budget. In the process, the government was shut down once and revived twice more with emergency funding—all because an agreement could not be reached when the fiscal year (and the money) ran out on October 1. During this protracted crisis, a parade of news stories about special interest protections made it clear that President Bush and the Republican leadership were not the only ones suffering a lack of vision or a reluctance to govern responsibly at the expense of personal political interests. Indeed, as one news account put it: "The end product of months of negotiations—a package of new taxes and spending cuts—reads like a who's who of congressional clout."[26] Among the congressional leaders (mostly Democrats) who shepherded special interests safely through the entire process were the following:[27]

- Senate Finance Committee Chair Lloyd Bentsen (D-Texas) won $2.5 billion in tax breaks for oil and gas interests and $5.9 billion for other programs.
- Senator Robert Packwood (R-Oregon) protected small wineries from a tax increase.
- Representative Sam Gibbons (D-Florida) spared big cigar companies from the tobacco tax increase.
- Senator Robert Dole (R-Kansas) eased the luxury tax on private airplanes.
- House Ways and Means Committee Chair Dan Rostenkowski (D-Illinois) saved state and local government workers from paying increases for medicare insurance.
- Representative Henry Waxman (D-California) saved $2.3 billion in medicaid for children and low-income senior citizens.
- Representative Mary Rose Oaker (D-Ohio) saved a $1.1 billion medicare breast cancer detection program.

The point is not whether these are good or bad programs and tax breaks. Depending on one's point of view, some may seem worthier than others. And that's the point: when government feels its way along without governing visions, all politics is reduced to battles of special interests that are ultimately decided by power brokering and deals. The result is that even budgets become difficult to pass. And, no matter what the final outcome, there is little coherence to offer the public to explain what the government did or why. As William Pfaff has suggested, public hostility to government and taxes may have simple roots. Unlike their European counterparts, Americans sense they are getting little benefit from government.[28] They have no confidence that tax increases will translate into lower deficits and many see voting as only a gesture of encouragement to a poorly performing system.

In any event, the public decided that none of the actors looked good during the budget crisis. In a national poll taken at the height of the budget follies and less than a month before the 1990 elections, the respondents allocated "some or a lot of blame . . . for current problems in reaching an agreement on a federal budget" as follows:[29]

President Bush	69%
Republicans in Congress	74%
Democrats in Congress	71%
Special interest/lobbying groups	66%
Voters opposed to higher taxes or spending cuts	60%

There was, it seemed, plenty of blame to go around. Moreover, the public had a pretty clear sense of the big political picture. According to Republican party pollster (and chief Reagan–Bush marketing analyst) Richard Wirthlin, "Americans are very angry and cynical about the system. They think government is simply not governing."[30] It is little wonder that many members of Congress expressed reluctance to go home and campaign on the record of the 101st Congress—even though by (post) modern standards it was a better record than most.[31] "Pretty good," some even called it, but the voters were not buying it. Therefore, with nothing better to sell, it was once again up to money, marketing, and media management to rescue victories for the incumbents in the 1990 election.

THE ELECTION OF 1990

Eating his sound bite on taxes and appearing even weaker than the Democrats, George Bush became the focal point of a midterm election that did not even involve his office. At stake, however, was the coherence of the Republican party itself, which some alarmists charged with having fallen into greater disarray than the Democrats.[32] Also at stake were many state legislatures and governorships around the country, responsible for drawing new national political maps for congressional districts based on the population changes in the 1990 Census. As a result, "the president's waffling," and the Democrats standing up and "taxing the rich" (a faint echo of the New Deal pledge to soak the rich a half century before), became the early campaign issues.

In the end, neither issue moved many voters to the polls. The turnout of 36.5 percent tied 1986 as the lowest recorded since 1942.[33] However, for those still tuned into the media campaign, the almost daily spectacle of the president trying to coin a new sound bite was, if nothing else, amusing. During a morning jog, Bush fended off reporters' questions about moving his lips in agreement to tax increases with a grimaced quip of "Read my hips." In another awkward moment, he claimed that the Democrats had forced him to "pay a ransom."[34]

Nothing seemed to work. Even when Bush escaped the capital for the soothing remove of a small-town America, he left a trail of unsettled words behind him. In towns like Omaha, Nebraska, and Glen Ellyn, Illinois, the president confided, "Oh, how nice it is to be out where the real people are, outside of Washington, D.C."[35] He expressed relief at leaving behind the political "hogwash" "inside the beltway" of the nation's capital. The press corps was quick to point out that George Bush was, if nothing else, a Washington insider whose string of high-level appointments and Ivy League ties (Yale graduate, ambassador to the United Nations, envoy to China, U.S. representative, CIA director, vice president, chair of the Republican National Committee, president, etc.) hardly left him in a position to cast stones (or even sound bites) at Washington insiders.[36]

The president was so consistently unable to find the right thing to say that one news magazine humorously suggested he might really be a spy for the Democrats, bent on sabotaging the Republicans from within. In the article, the political director of the Democratic National Committee confided, "The President has been our best ally. We're just trying to stay out of his way."[37] Also mentioned was a memo from the co-chair of the Republican congressional campaign committee faxed to candidates with the encouragement: "Do not hesitate to oppose either the president or proposals being advanced in Congress."[38] To make matters worse, several Republican congressional candidates took this advice seriously and distanced themselves from the party figurehead. Some even ambushed Bush with criticism after he showed up to campaign for them. It was not long before the media began to use those words again: "wimp," "indecisive," "distant," and "out of touch."[39]

Dan Quayle to the Rescue?

Improbable as it may seem, when the commander-in-chief began to falter, the vice president was sent out to do battle with the media. After a rocky first couple of years in office, Dan Quayle was still being schooled in the finer arts of media management. Even if he had yet to graduate from Press Relations 101, the hour of need was great—and, so, off he went to "Face the Nation" and "Meet the Press." Apparently trying to act presidential on the first program, he responded to CBS correspondent Leslie Stahl's questions about Bush flip-flops in a distant, magisterial style. The more Stahl pushed for a simple answer about why Bush waffled on taxes, the more Quayle launched into numbing reviews of the administration record. Stahl finally snapped in exasperation, sending the vice president back to his media advisers with a tongue-lashing: "Please, Mr. Vice President, we don't have time for history . . ."[40]

Undaunted, Quayle took another tack and went on NBC's "Meet the Press" a couple of weeks later.[41] This time, trying a more flip media style, the vice president announced that "this is truly a great day, because Congress has finally left town and America is now safe." He followed this remark with a widely reported charge that the Democrats would pay the electoral price for the budget embarrassment because, as he put it, "The American people are fed up to here. . . . [They] are sick and tired of what they have seen going on here in Washington." David Broder, who was a panelist on the show, wrote in his regular *Washington Post* column the following week: "On 'Meet the Press' Sunday, I very nearly disgraced NBC and *The Washington Post* by busting out laughing when Vice President Dan Quayle tried to peddle the line that the Republicans now have the Democrats right where they want them. Hearing Mr. Quayle say that Democrats would pay a political price for Mr. Bush's tortured budget dealings was very much like the apocryphal line credited to General George Custer at Little Big Horn: 'I'd hate to be in Sioux shoes tonight.' "[42]

My Kingdom for a Sound Bite?

It appeared that the White House emissaries needed to go back to media school. Indeed, that was the kernel of the problem. The White House image team had fallen into disarray, leaving the administration looking for all the world as if it had no domestic policy agenda of its own, beyond the words put in the president's mouth by his former media consultants.

To begin with, the speech writer (Peggy Noonan) who wrote the original "Read My Lips" speech was not on the scene. It was later disclosed that a Bush campaign adviser wanted that infamous sound bite about taxes taken out of Bush's acceptance speech at the Republican National Convention in 1988, but Noonan reportedly won the argument, saying "Don't touch those lines. They're good."[43] The irony is that the adviser (Richard Darman) reportedly objected not on economic principle, but on stylistic grounds that the words were "phony macho." He turned out to be wrong on that score, but had he worried a bit more about policy substance, Darman might have had an easier time dealing with economic realities later on after he became the White House budget director. Then there was the curious absence of campaign pollster and marketing strategist Robert Teeter from the Bush inner circle—possibly a result of White House chief of staff and main domestic adviser John Sununu, who wanted to run the domestic game plan on his own.[44] Sununu's lack of media finesse turned out to be a tough lesson on the indispensability of the marketers when, in reality, there is no game plan. Finally, long-time Bush confidant and domestic political analyst James Baker was off around the world as secretary of state trying to hold the allied coalition together around the building military crisis in the Persian Gulf. The president, too, was undoubtedly distracted by his involvement in the first big world crisis after the end of the cold war. As a result, Bush took his key political advice from Darman, Quayle, and Sununu. Not exactly a public relations brain trust.

To make matters worse, the president tried winging it on the campaign trail. The word flips and finger-pointing at the Democrats reinforced the growing impression among journalists that behind all the well-crafted sound bites and media strategies of his past, there had been no substance, no vision, or, as a Democratic pollster put it, no course: "Bush's problem is that he has no economic message. There's no 'Stay the Course.' There's no 'Change the Course.' There's no course."[45]

Live by the sound bite, die by the sound bite. The moral is as short as its subject. Jostled by unanticipated realities intruding on neatly packaged images, the Bush political performance began to unravel. His popularity plummeted from record highs to disturbing lows, particularly in economic areas where presidential elections are often decided in the absence of other issues. But the president had two years to reassemble his marketing team and learn some new lines. This was, after all, a congressional election, not a presidential year.

Despite a few dire predictions of Bush costing his party seats in Congress, or voter anger finally spilling over into a rout of incumbents in both parties, nothing much changed in Congress when it was all over. The system held. Incumbents used their fat campaign chests to run test-marketed media campaigns. Cynical voters stayed home in droves, and a majority of those who went to the polls rationalized their choices by deciding that their own incumbents were somehow better than the rest of the rascals in Congress—and in any event, better than the few rascally opponents able to raise enough money to mount effective campaigns. As a result, more than 96 percent of the incumbents running for reelection were returned to Washington. Only 15 of 406 incumbents who stood for reelection in the House were defeated. Just 1 of 32 incumbent senators suffered a loss in 1990. And so the 102nd Congress looked much like the 101st, which looked much like the 100th, which looked . . .

Are the Voters Rascals, Too?

To some extent we can only conclude that voters, too, have bought into this system by recognizing the overall corruption of government but allowing themselves to be bribed by their favorite representative who "brings home the pork barrel" to the local district. There is no denying that members of Congress have learned how to stay in office by catering to the needs of their supporters.[46] It is also true that incumbents ease the minds of their voters by blustering about waste and special interests elsewhere in Congress, while quietly passing the pork to voters and handing legislative favors to campaign contributors. The media noted more than a few examples of such hypocrisy in 1990:[47]

- Senator Mitch McConnell called for abolishing the PACs while taking $900,000 in PAC money for his 1990 campaign.
- Representative Newt Gingrich called for free world markets and domestic budget-cutting, while voting "yea" for trade protection laws favoring textile manufacturers and "yea" again for domestic agricultural subsidies.
- Representative Bill Frenzel called the free mailing privilege in Congress "an outrageous use of the peoples' money" while mailing out $120,000 worth of political messages to his constituents. (Mr. Gingrich, too, condemned the mail privilege while leading his state delegation in its use.)

Voters should be able to detect such hypocrisy in their own representatives, and they might be expected to resist supporting it with their votes. To the extent that they do not do these things, the electorate, too, has become part of the system. Indeed, to put it even more bluntly, the system would not be a system if substantial numbers of voters had not bought into it at some level. Since, however, it is a system we are talking about, it would be unreasonable to point the sole finger of blame at the voter. There are several reasons why voters, though certainly not blameless, are not the sole culprits:

1. While many of those who continue to vote overlook the hypocrisy of their relations with their representatives, it is increasingly clear that voters understand the system well enough to know that throwing one rascal out is likely only to bring another one in. In the meantime, many voters seem willing to accept whatever favors their incumbents can give them, even though it is the sum total of these political favors that has paralyzed the larger system of government.
2. The steady decline in voting combined with the steady rise in anger at the system seems to indicate that many people see no choices and have stopped voting as a *principled* reaction. In other words, they left the system rather than buy into it. Now, it may be said that these folks have an obligation to do something more meaningful than withdraw from politics at a time like this. Fair enough. (The next chapter goes into this subject in more depth.)
3. Voters and nonvoters alike express a strong desire for choices other than the ones they are given. Remember the data on voter dissatisfaction from the 1988 campaign? The 1990 elections were a replay, suggesting that voter discontent has simply been absorbed like an angry wound into the larger system. For example, the candidates for governor in Texas spent a whopping $32 million in the 1990 race, yet polls offering the alternative "None of the Above" repeatedly showed both candidates losing badly to "nobody."[48] A voting clerk at a Texas polling place reported many voters asking "Do you have a place where I can push 'None of the Above'?"[49]

Unfortunately (or fortunately, as the case may be), election ballots do not offer "None of the Above" as an official choice. Even if they did, angry voters would succeed only in getting rid of government rather than reforming it in useful ways. As a result of having no meaningful electoral expression for their discontents, the mixture of public anger and cynicism has been grafted onto the system in one of two ways: either through voters who decide that incumbents who deliver favors and services are better than nothing, or through nonvoters who see the act of voting as only contributing to the decline of government. And, last, but perhaps not least, there endures a hard core of permanent nonparticipants who either never saw the system working for them or never cared to find out how to make it work.

When we add cynical voters and angry nonvoters together, it becomes possible to explain one of the mysteries addressed at the beginning of the book: how in 1990 a strong (nearly 70 percent) majority of people polled were fed up with Congress, and a solid majority (nearly 60 percent) excused their own representative from the mess, resulting in a whopping (96 percent) majority of those representatives being returned to Washington. As one headline explained it, "voters see politics as 'master instead of servant.' "[50] Many of those still willing to vote are willing to settle for small favors from their public servants.

The voters are not fully to blame, but they have become part of the system. As data presented later in this chapter indicate, they are probably the least happy part—and that turns out to be a good sign for reform. Unless public anger and cynicism are converted into other political actions besides casting grudging votes or going into withdrawal, the system will not change. Indeed, Election '90 offered ample evidence that, despite the highest recorded levels of public discontent, the system was rolling along just fine. It is worth noting a few of the latest marketing, media, and money trends that have kept the system going in the 1990s.

MARKETING, 1990:
FROM NEW NEGATIVITY TO DOCU-COMMERCIALS

Advertising is designed to work. When images are test-marketed and found no longer to move the consumer, they are replaced. New advertising campaigns are born from the ruins of the old. Thus, we can expect negative advertising to be around only as long as it continues working—in this case by persuading undecided voters that one candidate is, if not better, at least not worse than the other. Whether negative advertising stays or goes, what will remain constant is the nearly complete substitution of advertising images for ideas. Unlike the old days, when ads were used to supplement campaigns or to emphasize ideas, advertising in the current electoral system *is* the idea. This pattern will persist until electoral reforms change it.

It turns out that negative ads still worked in 1990, and so they were back. However, boredom being the mother of commercial invention, the negative ads found some new plot twists, and they were joined by a whole new genre of advertisement: the docu-commercial. The traditional way of portraying the positive side of candidates was a sort of home movie format with family shots, kids, dogs, sleeves rolled up, and heart-to-heart talks. By contrast, the docu-commercial takes the candidate into a real scene where there are challenges, dangers, and often a personal test: a crisis, a natural disaster, an angry crowd, a momentous speech, or a public appearance. The candidate triumphs either by saving the day in the commercial or (even more seductively) in the viewer's mind by standing up to that angry crowd of people demonstrated in previous market research to be disliked by the target audience.

Some of the pioneering docu-commercials were done by New York media consultant Hank Morris for the California gubernatorial campaign of

Diane Feinstein. An ad that helped Feinstein win the Democratic primary showed actual news shots taken years before, when she was a San Francisco city official announcing the shocking assassinations of the mayor and another city official.[51] Although Feinstein ultimately lost the governor's race in a record $40 million spending frenzy, another docu-commercial shored up voting support in a key area of vulnerability: the death penalty. The heavily broadcast ad used news coverage of her speech at the previous Democratic National Convention in which many delegates booed her support for the death penalty. The idea was to reassure pro–death penalty voters and others on the conservative flank that she was not a typical liberal. Used as proof was authentic news coverage showing that she was willing to stand up to the liberals at her own party's convention.[52]

In Michigan, a state legislature campaign ad showed the candidate going along with police to make an arrest. The technique used in the ad was similar to popular police TV docu-dramas that reenact crime scenes in realistic ways. In these "real-life simulations," realistic effects are achieved by filming with a shaky camera, using grainy film, cutting black and white with color shots, taking frames out of the footage to create stop-action effects, and running actual news footage into the dramatic script. The irony is that political (as well as commercial) advertisers have resorted to these methods to counter the growing public suspicion of authority figures.[53] The docu-commercial is designed to downplay authority symbolism and commercial staginess by, in effect, staging risky-looking situations in which the product or candidate takes on an adversary of the target audience watching at home. Look for more docu-commercials from candidates in the future.

Still king and destined for continued reign in the 1990s was the negative ad. As with all advertising, however, people quickly tire of the same old hype. As a result, ad formulas continually shift to overcome areas of consumer resistance. Thus, negative ads that took mean-spirited personal potshots at opponents tended to backfire by annoying voters and costing some candidates the election. By contrast, negative ads that linked opponents with unpopular issues, groups, or social problems were in. Some negative advertising even introduced humor to nudge voters away from choosing opponents.

In general, petty negativity is out, as demonstrated in the Michigan governor's race. According to one account, incumbent James Blanchard's campaign peppered opponent John Engler as "an unproductive, obstructionist, career politician who has made back-room deals with politically unsavory elements. . . '. When gasoline prices began to soar after the Iraqi invasion of Kuwait, the governor's media advisor, Robert Squier, produced a TV spot showing . . . Engler's face floating over what appears to be sewage floating from a pipe. 'When big oil needs a favor, they turn to John

Engler,' says the announcer. 'Why? Engler voted four times . . . to let polluters off the hook.' "⁵⁴ Apparently too much for voters with weak stomachs, such unreconstructed negativity backfired and Blanchard lost. Democratic gubernatorial candidate John Silber in Massachusetts suffered the same fate for much the same reason. Silber's vitriolic diatribes against his opponent (whom he called a "back-stabbing son-of-a-bitch") and shots at outgoing governor and 1988 presidential candidate Michael Dukakis left many voters both frightened and angered at Silber. Although Dukakis was very unpopular in the state at the time, the Silber campaign appeared guilty of beating a dead politician.⁵⁵ And then there was Clayton Williams in the Texas governor's race who spent $20 million (much of it, his own personal fortune) to insult his opponent, Democratic candidate Ann Richards. The combination of personal insults (he even refused to shake Richards' hand) and Williams' inability to follow his own stage directions led to a series of gaffes in the final weeks that finally pushed undecided and unhappy voters toward Richards.⁵⁶

In contrast, the new negativity was as abundant as it was successful. The textbook case was the North Carolina Senate race between white conservative incumbent Republican Jesse Helms and black liberal Democratic challenger Harvey Gantt who was ahead in the polls a few weeks before the election. Then, the Helms team began rolling out a battery of slick advertisements linking Gantt to a number of problems feared by white conservatives. At the top of the list were homosexuals, and blacks taking jobs away from whites. In one ad, a white man gets a job rejection letter. As he crumples it up in anger and despair, the voice-over declares: "You needed that job, but they had to give it to a minority because of a racial quota. Is that really fair? Gantt says it is."⁵⁷ A pollster for Gantt feared that Helms' success with such issues could lead to their widespread use in future national elections, driving the Democrats away from even their faint attempts in the 101st Congress to revive something of a party-wide program.⁵⁸ Postelection polls showed the ads not only boosting the enthusiasm of traditional Helms supporters, but also moving undecided voters into the Helms column in the final weeks.⁵⁹ These are the kinds of effects that make other political marketers take note.

Meanwhile, a number of Democratic consultants had been taking notes from 1988 and created get-tough and get-negative stands for their candidates on moral issues important to elusive swing voters. Explaining the Democratic candidates' embrace of the new negativity across the nation, a party pollster in Illinois chalked it up to Republican success with the infamous Willie Horton commercial used against Dukakis in 1988: "Willie Horton did it to them."⁶⁰ Thus, the parties innovate and borrow from each other's successes. As long as the imperative is to sell candidates, not ideas, there is little to keep the two parties from acting much differently than Coke and Pepsi in the battle to win over consumers.

One campaign even succeeded in using humor to turn negativity against the establishment. In the Minnesota Senate race, challenger Paul Wellstone toured the state in an old green bus, accusing incumbent Rudy Boschwitz of epitomizing the greed and selfishness of the 1980s. Referring to the incumbent's fat $7 million campaign fund, the challenger quipped, "It's my bus against his bucks."[61] When the incumbent trotted out the dreaded "L-word" and hurled at Wellstone the tired charge of being a "big spending liberal," the scrappy underdog pointed out that the Republican administrations of the 1980s drove the national debt over $3 trillion. He said: "Rudy Boschwitz lecturing me on fiscal responsibility is like [tight-fisted, tax-troubled millionaire] Leona Helmsley lecturing Mother Teresa on charity."[62]

What can we look for in candidate marketing in the 1990s? Petty, personal negativity is out. Appeals to authority and power are gone, too, even for incumbents. Based on marketing studies of ever more edgy and annoyed voters, the latest commercial mix looks like this: problem- or group-oriented negative ads, some spiced with humor, and most surrounded by defiant, triumphant images created in docu-commercials. This mix will last until voters manage to insulate themselves against the subliminal effects. And herein lies a problem.

Advertising, in general, is designed to overcome rational, conscious resistance on the part of consumers. Varying the ad formulas as in the case of the new negativity makes resistance hard to sustain. But an even deeper dilemma with the new advertising forms has emerged in the 1990s. They resemble ghosts from the traditional electoral ritual described in Part II of the book. That is, American campaigns have always involved negative attacks between candidates, and they always challenge contestants with stressful, grueling campaign character tests. Voters searching for familiar remnants of the past may find themselves trying to pull meaningful cultural clues out of heavily commercialized contests. This is all to no avail, because the difference between "reality" as constructed within healthy political rituals and "realism" as constructed within commercialized, empty rituals is all the difference that once mattered politically. Gone is the chance to see if candidates can handle challenges on their own—much less lead a party or generate broad political support for something that might qualify as an idea. Seeing these ghosts in a commercialized culture, voters may be confused about what's wrong. Compounding the problem, members of a culture are seldom fully aware of how their own rituals work or what happened to make them fall apart. In addition, Americans have grown up in a commmunications environment that continually challenges them with baffling questions like: "Is it live, or is it Memorex?"

Art Buchwald, in a column titled "Voting the Rascals In," nicely captured the state of public confusion. The premise of the column involves a political pundit who decides to do some exit-polling on election day to find out how those pesky voters can condemn incumbents and, at the same time, vote them back in. After informing a selected voter that conventional wisdom would predict a huge backlash by angry citizens throwing the rascals out, the pundit received the following analysis direct from the voter's mouth:

> "We did feel that way, but then we saw the incumbents' TV commercials. We were so impressed with their sincerity and their desire to serve this country to the best of their ability. We were also persuaded that their opponents were thieves, oddballs and soft on crime."
>
> "How did you find that out?" I asked.
>
> "By watching the same incumbents' commercials—hey, who are you?" He suddenly wanted to know.
>
> ". . . I'm one of the people who takes the pulse of the American electorate. . . . Frankly you have surprised and disappointed me. . . . I predicted that you were so fed up with Washington you were going to overthrow the government by force."
>
> " . . . You're lucky that I even came out to vote. I left the house in the middle of 'People's Court' to be here. You pundits think that just because congressmen and senators act like a bunch of jokers, the man in the street is going to exchange them for another bunch of jokers. Voting is like going to the dentist—you try not to think about it and all you want to do is get it over with."[63]

If the irrational marketing of candidates has left voters sounding and behaving in confusing ways, they are not the only players in the system caught up in the overall confusion. Consider, for example, the paradoxical role of the media. At the same time media organizations are reaping huge profits from running political commercials, their news organizations are busily deconstructing those same candidate images while savaging candidates whose image campaigns do not manipulate the media effectively. If that sounds confusing, it is only a reflection of . . .

THE MEDIA IN THE 1990S: MIXED MESSAGES

When we realize that fully half of those big campaign budgets go for advertising, it becomes clear why media organizations are not eager to have the government step in and regulate political advertising in any way. Placing limits on the amount of broadcast advertising or requiring networks to provide a set amount of free air time to all candidates would level the political playing field considerably. It would also cut into corporate profits reaped during the seemingly endless campaign season. Thus, we cannot forget the role of the media in delivering the political messages that cause so much trouble for voters and the larger electoral system.

Then, the news divisions of those same media take over. Often painfully aware that the entire run of campaign news events may be staged to reinforce marketing images contained in commercials, journalists are reluctant to contribute willingly to this propaganda process. News organizations also have discovered through their own marketing research that being manipulated by politicians often makes the media, not the politician, look bad. Add to this the overwhelming public anger at politicians, particularly in their electoral roles, and the nation's news departments have pretty much a green light to deconstruct the commercialization and media manipulation that go on in elections.

The trend noted in Chapter 1 toward increasing news coverage of campaign media strategies continued in 1990 and promises to become a hallmark of election news in the 1990s. The journalistic line between covering campaign media strategies and covering campaign content seems to be harder to locate than ever before. Perhaps journalists, too, have recognized that media strategies *are* the contents of postmodern elections. Thus, it seemed that nearly every campaign story in 1990 made some sort of behind-the-scenes reference to candidate strategy, polling, marketing, media manipulation techniques, commercial advertising, and the like. It would not be surprising to learn that voters exposed to such news coverage quickly get the impression (if they haven't figured it out already) that there is little of substance to campaigns besides images generated to manipulate the media and the public.

Whereas the media covering itself seemed to evolve spontaneously to dominate news coverage of the 1988 campaign, the trend in the 1990s shows signs of ever greater institutionalization—operating as a self-conscious, well-established part of editorial assignments and reporters' campaign beats. For example, a 1990 survey by *Washington Journalism Review* editor Bill Monroe turned up a national trend of news organizations offering critical analyses of campaign commercials to their viewers, listeners, and readers. Among the signs that the media-decoding-the-media is becoming an institutionalized feature of campaign press coverage are the following:[64]

- The Akron, Ohio, *Beacon Journal* regularly reviewed 1990 campaign commercials under the heading of "Ad Watch."
- The *Kansas City Star* ran a series on political ads under the label "Analysis." One front page headline declared "Hard-hitting Ads Trip Up on Facts."
- The *Sacramento Bee* regularly dissected campaign spots in its political news section.
- KRON-TV in San Francisco ran regular features on the political ads that it and other stations broadcast, leading advertisers to deliver along with new ads a lengthy fact sheet (or "spin sheet," as the case may be) to defuse possible criticism by reporters.

As further evidence of reporter skepticism about political advertising, Monroe cited an American Press Institute session between a group of invited journalists and Republican media guru Robert Goodman. The dean of the political marketers proudly presented a new docu-commercial showing a Georgia gubernatorial candidate (in Monroe's words) "preaching to an enthusiastic primary night crowd about the future of the children of Georgia." Goodman offered the ads as something of a breakthrough: a positive appeal by a strong candidate in a real setting. But when the screening was over, the reporters launched into a critique of subliminal images and phony "realism," leaving Goodman blustering, "I'm astounded, frankly, by some of the reactions to these ads. I didn't show them here to be blistered, analyzed and spat upon." This incident encouraged editor Monroe to look to the future with some hope:

> For the first time in most places, a referee in the form of a political reporter is showing up in the campaign arena with the savvy to call fouls and a voice that's being heard. A game with a referee is a different kind of game. And by 1992 editors and news directors all over the country will have an even better idea of how to play it. All of which offers hope that the Willie Horton spots of 1988 may be seen a decade from now as the high-water mark of low TV politics.[65]

Perhaps he is right; indeed, a game with referees is better than one without. Yet the outcomes of such a game will be little changed if one team (in this case, The Incumbents) ends up with the money to buy all the talent (i.e., media consultants and TV ads), while the other team (in this case, The Challengers) is perpetually assigned to play with no talent, no money, and no way to execute a big political play even if it had one in the playbook. In the end, the political victories of the 1990s—until reforms succeed in leveling the playing field—will continue going to the team with the most money.

MONEY IN THE 1990s:
THE WINNER AND STILL CHAMP

To put the continuing lesson about the new electoral system simply: money corrupts voting choices. It does so in two ways: first, by leaving challengers who have no money with no way to get their ideas across; and second, by leaving challengers with money sounding as slick, packaged, docu-realistic and, ultimately, idea-less as the incumbents. Either way the voting choice is painfully tough, and either way the edge goes to the incumbents who have learned how to play the election game (and deliver services to local districts).

In 1990, congressional incumbents received an estimated $275 million in campaign contributions, while challengers raised only $62 million. By one conservative estimate (based on June, not November, tallies), $96 million of the incumbents' political wealth came from PACs, while challengers were able to attract less than $11 million from these interest organizations.[66] Senate incumbents received nearly 4 times as much PAC money as their challengers, and the PAC advantage in the House was nearly 12 to 1. This trend runs all the way down to state and local politics as well, resulting in an electoral system in which, for all practical purposes, there is no opposition in most political contests.

According to one estimate, out of 435 House races, 375 candidates were either unopposed or "facing foes with so little cash they're not considered serious threats."[67] The corresponding figure for the 35 Senate seats open in 1990 was 16 without serious opposition. The trend is even worse at the state level, where as many as 90 percent of the incumbents may face no effective opposition.[68] Here's an even more eye-opening breakdown: of the 406 House incumbents seeking reelection in 1990, 79 ran unopposed, 168 faced challengers who raised less than $25,000, and only 23 House challengers raised at least half of what their incumbent opponents had in the political bank. To put it in somewhat extreme terms, the two richest members of the House had more campaign money between them than all the 331 challengers combined. (The score: Stephen Solarz of New York and Mel Levine of Los Angeles, $3,385,606 versus all 331 House challengers, $3,320,652.)[69] Common Cause provided most of these figures to the media.

These patterns do not require much further discussion. There has been little change in this cornerstone of the current system. Without reforms—and dramatic reforms at that—there is no reason to look for anything different in the 1990s. Even if voters rise up in anger and throw the incumbents out, this system will install a like set of replacement parts. The worst fear is that finance reforms will be conducted as cynically and superficially as the other politics produced by this system. (This possibility should warn citizens not to leave reforms up to the lawmakers on the inside.) Even with a set of honest reforms, it may take years to restore the faith of a generation of Americans who have grown up never knowing an election with choices and never knowing a government that governed. As one of the most sobering journalistic commentaries on the 1990 election results put it, even with a package of sweeping reforms, it will take time to repair the damage done to

> an entire generation of young voters [that] has rarely had the experience of going to the polls to vote with any enthusiasm for a candidate they trust, instead of to choose the lesser of two evils. At the moment, even if such candidates emerged, they probably could not win. If they won, they could not govern. Until that changes, it may be unreasonable to expect more than one-third of voters even to bother going through a process that mainly serves to remind them that they vote their fears, not their hopes.[70]

Meanwhile, Politics Goes On

After the election was over, both parties declared themselves winners, and well they might. In the postmodern sense of it, a winner is someone who does not lose. Given the present system, neither party can lose; therefore, each is sure to win. Searching for the reasons behind their victory, the Democrats pointed to having come up with an issue for a change ("taxing the rich"), and the Republicans pointed to a strong showing for not having had an issue.

As for George Bush, the person who cost the Republicans their only issue by moving his lips and agreeing to new taxes? The president was last seen still wandering in search of the golden sound bite that would set everything right again. After the election results were in and Bush was being hammered on the editorial pages for sacrificing the only remaining shred of party principle, he *again* promised to resist any new taxes. This time, he *really* meant it. So committed was Bush to the new "no new taxes pledge" that he threatened Congress: they would have to raise taxes "over my dead veto."[71] Pundits of all ideological persuasions began to declare Bush and his party in trouble for 1992.[72] A conservative national columnist went so far as to suggest that the Republicans join the Democrats in declaring bankruptcy, claiming that the Democrats' single "soak the rich" idea in 1990 showed more life than the Republicans. "It is too soon to say they [the Democrats] are out of their coma. But there is movement beneath the eyelids."[73] In the end, the president drove these unpleasant images from the news by going to war.

And so the 1990s began with voters searching for escape, pundits looking for vital signs in either party, and the nation's leading newspaper declaring the obvious editorial postmortem on the whole affair: "Voters Needed a Choice."[74] In a system where the parties are struggling for intellectual life, candidates use the same advertising techniques, forward-looking issues turn out to be ghosts from the past, and anything resembling a policy coming out of Washington is hailed as an achievement, perhaps what the voters really need in order to follow the politics of the 1990s is a scorecard.

A POLITICAL SCORECARD FOR THE 1990s

In an age of reduced expectations, the greatest danger is that people will settle for too little. After all, something is better than nothing. As a result of this natural psychological tendency, a party with an issue looks better than a party with none at all—even if that issue is only a weak adaptation from the past. Similarly, a proposal for electoral reform may be welcomed as better than nothing at all—even though weak reforms passed by a self-serving Congress will accomplish next to nothing at all.

As the drumbeat of public anger grows in the 1990s, parties and candidates will come under increasing pressure to do something. And do something they will. More budgets will be passed, and more legislation, too. Even election reforms are sure to come. All will be heralded as signs of political life, party leadership, and solutions to the political malaise of the 1990s. However, a wary public should follow such developments closely, and not settle for illusions of change based on reduced expectations. In order to decide whether significant changes are under way, the reader is invited to keep score in the following categories to judge whether the changes that will come in the 1990s are positive or merely illusory ones.

The Legislative Score: Democrats Versus Republicans

The challenge for the Democrats will be to push beyond weak throwbacks from the past like "tax the rich." This sort of issue may appeal to a few voters in the short run, but it does not promise to move the country anywhere. It contains no vision. In the end, this slogan will quickly lose its standing as an issue in the minds of most voters—if for no other reason than that the Democrats have been (almost) as deeply implicated in favoring the rich as have the Republicans. After all, the Democrats mastered the PAC game, agreed to the budget overruns and tax breaks of the 1980s, were equally responsible for the savings-and-loan collapse, and abandoned the poor at many key legislative junctures during the past decade. The Democratic efforts in the 101st Congress to reconstruct something of a poor people's package with civil rights, minimum wage, and family legislation may be a sign of ideological life as some of the pundits point out. However, the American people are unlikely to support a return to what many see as failed programs of the past.

What can the Democrats do to make a difference? They can begin with developing a party line on national economic priorities and applying it first of all to the budget. Some degree of party unity in budget priorities for the future would mean a de facto reduction of PAC and interest group influence on the party. A resulting opening up of party politics to middle-class and grass-roots interests just might generate the kind of public dialogue a party needs to figure out what its vision of the future really is. The main point of Part II of the book is that healthy rituals, including elections, require a trial-and-error flexibility and a give-and-take dialogue between leaders and followers. This is the best one can hope for in national politics: to trust a well-functioning political culture to bring people into meaningful communication about common problems. If there is a period of some turmoil and shaking out, so be it. The worst casualty is likely to be the loss of some incumbent deadwood in Washington. It is hard to imagine a reduction in governing beyond current levels. While we cannot know in advance what a politically workable and popularly supportable Democratic vision will look like, we can recognize the efforts of a party leadership to present new programs and governing ideas to voters for their approval. Such efforts should receive high scores. At the other extreme is the worst-case scenario in which a party leadership unwilling to open up a dialogue about the future forces tired visions from the past on the citizenry. *If future Democratic congresses settle for single campaign issues or warmed-over Great Society visions, give them a low score (and count on the voters to do the same).*

Since the Democrats have the majority in Congress, it may not be fair to hold the Republicans equally accountable for producing a legislative agenda. Yet, if we bring the president into the picture as legislator-in-chief (recommender of an executive legislative agenda and veto-holder over legislation that does not fit that agenda), we can score the Republicans on their political records, too. The instant analysis on the Republicans is that they had two party-unifying issues in the recent past: anticommunism and just say no to taxes. With the sudden end of the cold war, the party was left reeling. With Bush's agreement on new taxes to rescue a deadlocked budget, the party was decked for a mandatory 10-count.

This analysis, though popular on the editorial pages, is too simple. True, the collapse of the Soviet empire took some of the wind out of Republican leadership in foreign policy, but the end of the cold war did not benefit the Democrats either. The war against Iraq may have answered questions about military strength while raising questions about the vision and the policies guiding the new world order that was to replace the cold war. Perhaps such an order *will* emerge if both parties recognize they have an interest in cautious foreign policy with bipartisan agreement on a few concrete goals: saving the world trade talks from collapse, using whatever means are available to nudge the Soviet Union away from either anarchy or dictatorship, resolving the Third World debt crisis, forging international environmental agreements, and making a timely exit (if that is now possible) from the Middle East.

As for the Republican tax crisis, it is as superficial as the Democrats' mirror-image version of the same issue. The Republican antitax stand is a recurring ghost of party politics dating from before the depression of the 1930s when the wealthy, conservative core of Republican ideology believed that the best way to stimulate economic growth was to create a governmental welfare state for the rich. The Reagan supply-side theories of the 1980s added a few whistles and bells to this abiding conservative belief, and the Bush no new taxes pledge carried it forward into the 1990s. Unfortunately, the Bush renewal of the antitax pledge "over my dead veto" promises only to revive a Republican issue that is as outdated and removed from any programmatic context as the Democrats' opposing promise to tax the rich. Yet faced with the possibility of a revolt within his own party on the tax issue (coming from the likes of blue-blooded Pierre DuPont and purple-prosed Pat Buchanan), Bush and the Republicans may well end up restoring taxes as the issue on which they make their domestic stand of the 1990s. *If the Republicans can offer no greater vision than this for the 1990s, score them low (as will the voters).*

Scoring the Election System: Money, Media, and Marketing

Enough has been said about these elements of the system to allow a few scoring tips to suffice here. The main money development to watch in the 1990s is the finance point spread between incumbents and challengers. In the election cycles of the 1990s, does the campaign finance gap close, stay the same, or widen? If meaningful reform legislation is passed, the gap should close. A high score on the money game should be awarded for only two developments:

1. A dramatic closing of the incumbent-challenger gap to no worse, on average, than a 2 to 1 incumbent advantage. (We are not asking for miracles here.)
2. A restructuring of the finance system so that PACs are eased out in favor of public funding of more races, thus giving idea-coalitions a chance to form among newly competitive parties and their candidates. Give anything less than this a low score.

As for the media, we should continue to award high marks for journalistic decoding of campaign ads and behind-the-scenes looks at media manipulation. However, we must pay close attention to media coverage and editorial postures on electoral reform. In particular, editorial weakness on the elimination of PACs should be given low marks (indicating that the media have yielded to the temptation to preserve their own options as special interest organizations). Even more telling will be media reactions to proposals for government regulation of political advertising. For example, requiring that the television networks give free commercial space in longer (say, three- to five-minute) blocks would not only level the playing field for underfinanced candidates, but also require all candidates to fill the air space with something beyond thirty-second subliminal pitches. Even though virtually all other democracies regulate political advertising in these ways, the U.S. media can be expected to claim infringement of free speech (translate: free profits). *If they do, give the media a low score.*

In the area of candidate marketing, we should expect more of the same, until reforms (like the above) change the rules of the game. Although it may be tempting to score the decline of mean-spirited personal negative attacks as an improvement, we must remember that problem-oriented negative ads and docu-commercials reflect the same underlying problems with the system. *As long as our most meaningful glimpses of candidates come through commercial images and news events staged to reinforce those images, give low scores to campaign communication.*

The Voter Scorecard: Voting May Not Be the Answer

Although voter withdrawal is a distressing symptom of electoral failure, an upturn in voting rates is not necessarily a sign of improvement in the system. In fact, a number of unhelpful factors could produce short-term increases in turnout. For example, highly emotional marketing of the sort reported earlier in the North Carolina Senate race could bring more voters out on the basis of racial antagonisms or moral fears that have little connection to broader, policy-related programs for national renewal.

Even more important, however, is the possibility that the current plight of electoral democracy may be something that citizens cannot simply vote their way out of. If people wait for incumbent politicians to reform the system that brought them such security in office, we may have a long wait ahead. Similarly, entrusting interest organizations like Common Cause to wage the reform battle singlehandedly risks reducing electoral reform to just another issue in the swirl of interest group politics in Washington. Citizens must begin organizing at the grass-roots level both to raise the volume of public opinion about the importance of reform and to push parties and candidates into offering electoral reform as one of their top priorities. *If voters continue to withdraw or wait for half-hearted reforms to be handed down from the powers that be, give them low marks for citizenship. If grass-roots groups begin to raise their voices in support of tough and specific reform programs, while pushing those programs onto the platforms of candidates and parties, raise the score.*

The Electoral Reform Scorecard: Rating the National Debate

Now we come to the bottom line of electoral politics. Will the effect of money, media, and marketing be checked in the 1990s, or will they run on until the possibility of governing society and economy completely collapses under their disorganizing influences? The balance may well be decided by how the public participates in the reform process of the 1990s. Will a cynical public with low expectations settle for half-hearted reforms handed down by the powers that be? Or will citizens organize and raise a loud grass-roots voice in support of fundamental changes?

Part of the answer to these questions depends on how the national debate about electoral reform goes in the coming years. The risk is that Congress and the president will agree on a speedy and superficial reform of campaign financing—perhaps before the 1992 elections. With the wave of a symbolic wand, politicians might move to put the issue behind them before serious national debate has taken place. This risk is all the greater if the mass media continue to report on reform efforts as just another issue on the crowded Washington agenda (as opposed to elevating political reform to a more prominent place on the news and editorial pages). If the media continue to allow politicians to drive the news (and the prominence of reform), the national debate about political change in the 1990s will look just like the other public dialogues of the times: lacking in political leadership, passed along with mixed signals from the media, and intellectually fragmented, resulting in a collection of poorly understood legislative proposals unrelated to broader programs or goals. *If this pattern materializes, score the chances for meaningful change zero.*

If, on the other hand, grass-roots voices begin to emerge, the media exercise their power to "set the agenda" in this area, and a few political leaders hear the call, the cause of electoral reform may be elevated above the buzzing confusion of special interest politics in Washington. Then the proposals of interest organizations like Common Cause may be given a critical public hearing. And then, we may have, as a nation, a chance to think before we act on important legislation affecting voter registration, campaign financing, broadcasting, and political advertising. *If a sweeping package of reforms goes forward under the light of media coverage and through the heat of public debate, score a victory for the possibility of governing in America once again.* Just what might such a package of reforms look like? The next chapter offers some suggestions to get the debate going.

CHAPTER 8

Reversing the Decline by Reforming the System

Since the publication of Yale historian Paul Kennedy's book *Rise and Fall of the Great Powers,* there has been considerable discussion in intellectual circles about whether the United States is on the brink of decline as a superpower.[1] To some, the warning signs are as ominous as they are characteristic of the final days of empires past: fierce foreign competition, budget and revenue problems crippling the chances for social and economic renewal, military commitments that consume an alarming chunk of the nation's productivity, and, appropriate to our argument, a national leadership clinging to glorious images of the past rather than facing the growing problems of the future while there is still time to solve them.

Countering this gloomy picture is a competing thesis that tells a story of triumph, not decline—the impending victory of capitalism and liberal democracy over world communism and the single-party state. The domestic price paid by the United States for this victory was small enough, argue the advocates of this thesis, particularly when we consider the new political and economic business that might come our way from restructuring the communist world. One version of this argument even stated that, far from fearing a decline of power, the impending victory will be so complete that we should instead fear the absence of ideological conflict that gives meaning to life and history itself.[2]

The debate about the decline of America as a superpower has missed (or at least failed to address in much detail) the most fundamental feature of the domestic scene: the governing crisis. Whether or not the U.S. world presence is declining, there is a palpable inability at home to grapple with pressing problems that would send the leaders of most other leading nations scurrying for solutions. The irony in the American case is that the frustrations of domestic politics may motivate leaders to support dramatic interventions in the world scene. The latest example is the costly military intervention in the Persian Gulf. While foreign affairs may beckon to leaders starved for action on the home front, the postponement of action on domestic renewal is building up social and economic strains that could bring the whole system down. In other words, continued neglect of priorities at home may well settle the debate about America's decline as a world power—both decisively and unhappily.

Yet reforming the system to restore party discipline or bring new parties to power while renewing voter loyalty and interest could jeopardize political careers—careers that have prospered under the same system that has served the national interest so poorly. How can we expect politicians to change the rules of a game they are winning on a personal and career level? The short answer is that we cannot expect such selfless behavior from the power brokers in Washington. As a result, the national leadership has little choice but to market itself heavily while trying to wax optimistic about the national future. To do otherwise would require politicians to offer solutions for any problems they might point to on the horizon.

And so, Ronald Reagan invited us to walk with him down the garden path to "Morning in America." When Michael Dukakis was quizzed in 1988 about the possibility of a national decline, he flatly dismissed the idea by saying, "I've read too many stories about how America is supposed to be in decline, about how our children will have to settle for a second-rate economy and a second-class future. I don't buy that."[3] As for George Bush, the president who led us into the 1990s, when he looked across the national political scene, he was apparently blinded by seeing "A Thousand Points of Light." And what candidate in 1992 would challenge the meaning of "the new world order," much less address the disorder at home?

Politicians probably won't address national problems, particularly those of earthshaking scope, when they have nothing they can say to the people in response to them. Jimmy Carter was the last leader to discuss the prospects of national decline without offering a sensible plan of action, and he paid heavily in terms of popularity as a result. It should come as no surprise that when people are given a choice between hearing pessimistic pronouncements with no programs attached and optimistic pronouncements with no programs attached, they tend to prefer the latter.

The worrisome thing about the refusal of politicians to discuss large national issues with the public is that people lose hope that government will do anything to address their collective problems. This understandably raises questions about the very purpose and direction of government itself, which in turn explains why elections often seem to be little more than elaborate referendums on how well the economy is doing. Meanwhile, public confidence in the leadership of national institutions, both governmental and business, has declined steadily since the mid-1960s.[4] Yet, confidence in the institutions themselves remains high—higher than in a comparison group of nations that includes France, Germany, Britain, and

Spain.[5] Nearly 80 percent of the public today place little trust in business and political leadership, but equal or greater numbers of Americans retain confidence in their basic institutions. The bad news, it would seem, is that people feel they have little meaningful choice or subsequent control over their leaders. The good news is that there is still enough faith in basic institutions to mobilize something of a national renaissance should the right leadership be given the chance to audition for the part.

As these striking figures indicate, we are at a national crossroads. To put it bluntly, the people are mad as hell, and they're not going to take it anymore. Or are they? That is *the* political question for the 1990s. On the one hand, it is hard to imagine public cynicism, anger, and discontent growing deeper. On the other hand, most people just don't know what to do about the problem. This chapter looks briefly at a people who have reached the boiling point and then offers a set of simple suggestions about how to turn that cynical anger into constructive action.

PEOPLE AT THE BOILING POINT

It is instructive to begin with a profile of public opinion over the thirty-year period in which the new electoral system has emerged, as described in Chapter 2. The most telling and dramatic change in the polls has come in response to the question of whether the government is run for the benefit of a few big interests. The percentage of those who agree went up dramatically during the 1960–1990 period.[6] The exact figures are as follows:

1960	25%
1970	50%
1980	70%
1990	77%

Accompanying these popular suspicions about whose interests the government serves are equally strong feelings about whose interests are going unrepresented. The current decade opened with 65 percent agreement that public officials "don't care much what people like me think."[7] All in all, 79 percent of Americans looked toward their future as they entered the 1990s with the common concern that their country was in "serious trouble."[8] For many citizens, however, the political choice is an unfortunate one: "if you keep voting, it only encourages them" ("them" meaning the politicians, of course). Yet those who remain in the electorate are caught up in the many contradictions of the system itself. As noted earlier, the decade opened with a majority of the public at once blaming

Congress for many of the nation's troubles, yet continuing to vote for their own incumbent representatives on election day. Even if those incumbents had not figured out how to lavish personal services and images of concern on their own constituents, the absence of much serious competition makes it pointless to vote for the opponents anyway.

To top it all off, the veto system constantly dashes hopeful ideas when they do pop up. As a result, the dwindling supply of eternally hopeful citizens has to be hooked back into the system by new and more creative marketing strategies. Unfortunately, as Jarol Manheim suggests, it is increasingly possible to fool all of the people much, if not all, of the time in this age of sophisticated marketing and media technologies.[9] The inevitable results, of course, are anger and cynicism—cynicism born of recognizing, too late, that one has again been fooled into believing that the *crisis du jour* was real, that the latest "war on (some serious social problem)" was a serious effort, or that the victorious politician was made of something more solid than good coaching and test-market images. Although public discontent and cynicism are thus understandable, they are neither agreeable nor useful attitudes to carry around—unless, of course, cynicism can be channeled into productive criticism and anger can be converted into action. Those are the choices facing a public at the boiling point.

REFORMING THE SYSTEM

What reforms might make a difference in the quality of national elections? Rather than present a laundry list of reform proposals, I will suggest just five simple ideas. Each, if adopted, would go a long way toward removing the limits on national debate and candidate character imposed by big money, political marketing, and media control. These reforms are presented in order from the most sweeping and radical to the most modest and easily imaginable. Thus, the suggestion heading the list is likely to meet with the greatest resistance, but I offer it in the spirit of opening the marketplace of ideas to the widest possible range of considerations.

Reform Proposal No. 1:
A (Limited) Proportional Representation System

The political parties in America are moribund; they no longer serve the purpose of organizing competing national agendas and pushing their members to support those platforms. With the collapse of the parties and the rise of a political star or personality system, the marketplace of ideas has fallen into disorder. One mechanism that might stimulate new life in the national political dialogue is a limited proportional representation rule in deciding races for Congress. (For obvious reasons such a scheme would take root first in the House and later, if at all, in the Senate.)

What would this system look like? First, it would be less European in look than the typical parliamentary process in which the executive and the cabinet are forged from the balance of power in the legislative body itself. We could keep an elected president, while restoring a better representative balance between the people and Congress. The goal of making Congress more accountable to the grass roots would be advanced by a simple proportional representation rule granting House seats to parties whose candidates won at least 10 percent of the vote both locally and nationally. Say, for example, State X has twenty House seats up for election, and the New Ideas party wins 20 percent of the vote in that state and qualifies nationally by winning 12 percent of all the votes cast. In this result, four seats from State X would go to New Ideas. Those representatives would join winning party candidates from other states with qualifying vote margins to form a New Ideas bloc in the House.

Imposing a national qualifying percentage minimizes the chance of elevating isolated state or local movements to national power, while favoring idea-based movements with nationwide appeal. Beginning on a limited scale, the introduction of multiple voice blocs and parties into the power structure will not disrupt the day-to-day workings of government any more than the current party disorientation has already thrown the system into a state of near paralysis.

The point of this shift in the representation process is to give voice to political initiatives that are now eliminated by a winner-take-all system in which the two leading alternatives seldom differ significantly in their ability to join behind competing programs for social renewal. In light of what we know about the press, well-articulated and controversial viewpoints from government officials make the news. Indeed, the newness of this system alone will attract press attention. With the publicity granted to incoming idea groups, existing parties and incumbents would face stiffer competition in the vote marketplace, and voters would be given a chance in subsequent elections to reward parties whose platforms continue to make sense, while punishing those who fail to compete.

Whatever the possible outcomes of this modest experiment in proportional representation, it is unlikely that we will be allowed to witness them. Politicians will join ranks to protect the personal benefits that come their way from the present system. When 96 to 98 percent of the House of Representatives can expect to be reelected, it is unlikely that they will do anything to rock the boat, much less instigate the kind of political debate that would make the electoral process meaningfully competitive.

If the public is interested in opening the party system to more competitive grass-roots ideas, help will not come from Washington. Perhaps the hope lies with states that offer direct popular initiatives and referendums on their ballots. State legislatures could thus become the experimental proving grounds for proportional representation schemes. Successful reforms in a few model states could lead the way for a national constitutional amendment. Even if this initiative gets off the ground, however, it is unlikely to go very far without major campaign finance reforms that would make new ideas parties competitive nationally, particularly at the presidential level. Indeed, with or without a restructuring of the representation system, campaign finance reform is crucial to the reopening of American politics.

Reform Proposal No. 2: Campaign Finance

This is the big one, both because it would make a huge difference in the quality of national dialogue and because it is something that citizens' lobbying groups are already fired up about. When Congress became embroiled in a dangerous ethics war during the closing years of the 1980s, calmer heads negotiated a cease-fire as it quickly became apparent that nearly everyone could be taken down by ethics charges. One marvels at the rich array of creative financing programs the members had worked out: breakfast clubs, free air travel, honoraria, dubious book sales, huge bankrolls of unspent "campaign" contributions, questionable investment opportunities, lobbying services for clients with little or no base in a member's home district, and the list goes on. The representation system itself seemed to be undergoing a transformation from one based in geography and votes to one anchored in high finance and influence.

The extent of special interest representation has become hard to hide, raising the continual specter of public embarrassment because lawmakers find themselves in compromising positions as a matter of routine. Take the case of five U.S. senators who ran interference for a bankrupt savings and loan, delaying its seizure by federal bank regulators. Buying additional time permitted the owners to drain off liquid assets, adding considerably to the astonishing $2 billion cost of the eventual government bailout. The five senators (including the chair of the Senate banking committee) were all respected and powerful legislators. They came from both parties, and a majority were Democrats. Only one actually lived in the state where the savings and loan was headquartered. Connecting them was the more than

$1 million in political contributions from the chairman of the S&L, a man later accused of fraud and violation of national banking statutes. Responding to early questions about interfering in the government's investigation of the bank, the senators all dismissed the episode as a routine constituent service. As indicated earlier, one of them went so far as to say, "I have done this kind of thing many, many times," likening his actions to "helping the little lady who didn't get her Social Security."[10]

The whole system of political finance that gives rise to these routine activities must be reformed if politicians are to develop a healthier sense of the public interest. In the words of Fred Wertheimer, president of Common Cause, the public interest lobby that pushed for investigation of the above case of special senatorial services:

> Washington has become an ethics swamp. Our nation's capital is addicted to special-interest influence money, and members of Congress are benefitting professionally and personally from these funds.
>
> In the last six years, special interests have poured more than $400 million in PAC money, $31 million in honoraria fees, and countless additional millions in illegal soft money and other payments into our system of government. These payments represent investments in government decision making—investments which improperly and unfairly magnify the voices of special interests at the expense of representative government.
>
> We've always experienced individual cases of corruption and impropriety in government. But today we have a system of institutionalized corruption. The rules themselves allow activities to take place legally that are improper and corrupting. . . .
>
> Washington insiders argue that the American people don't really care about Washington's ethics mess. They're wrong. But what's happening is even more dangerous than what they perceive as indifference on the part of the American public.
>
> The American people are moving beyond outrage to a state of deep cynicism. They are reaching a state of "no expectations" about our government leaders. And in a democracy, that's a red flag alert. There cannot be a fundamental erosion of ethical values at the seat of government without grave consequences for the nation.[11]

Reforms in campaign finance must affect all levels of politics from the president and Congress to local offices. Since we are talking about a system of influence, it will do little good to correct one part of the problem without attending to all of it. Electing a president with his or her own ideas for a change will have little consequence if Congress throws up a wall of special interest resistance to putting those ideas into action. The same parallel applies to state and local politics.

The story of recent finance reform efforts follows the familiar plot that our argument would predict: foot dragging, weak measures, lack of party solidarity, and much posturing and moralizing for the benefit of the media. Consider the actions taken by two recent congresses, the 100th (1986–1988) and the 101st (1988–1990). The 100th Congress moved on legislation in the House and Senate that would have limited the amount of PAC money in individual campaigns, created more for the challengers, and set spending limits in ways designed to get around the Supreme Court's *Buckley* v. *Valeo* decision that campaign financing is free speech. However, even these modest steps toward electoral responsibility were halted by a Republican filibuster that ended any hope for final passage. The 101st Congress ended up even more divided: the House favored reduced PAC contributions and voluntary spending limits; the Senate proposed to eliminate PACs at the federal level, while imposing voluntary spending limits; and President Bush threatened to veto any bill that contained spending limits. No legislation made it out of Washington by the end of that Congress either.

Ever optimistic, some members of the 102nd Congress talked about the need to present a reform program to the voters by 1992. Yet any package likely to withstand the three-way pull of two chambers of Congress and the White House is unlikely to contain much substance. Sadly, the media and politicians have begun talking about the acceptability of separate financing arrangements for the House and Senate. This may signal the coming of compromise legislation that would eliminate PACs in the Senate (where they are not as decisive), while perpetuating their reign in the House (where they have their greatest influence). Like other halfway measures, this idea speaks the language of reduced expectations. Even if Washington hands such a reform to voters, it should be recognized and rejected as another defective product of an uncompetitive government.

What kind of finance reform would make a difference?

First, eliminate PAC contributions to political campaigns. Contributions to party organizations might be permitted, but state and national parties should be severely restricted in soft money spending during the several months prior to election day. Let party-building activities take place between, not during, elections.

Next, create a system of public funding for both congressional challengers and incumbents. It would be possible to modify various European models as noted below.

Finally, set spending limits on campaigns, and index those limits according to the office and the size of the district. In order to observe Supreme Court rulings that political finance is a form of free speech, set spending limits on those who voluntarily accept public funding. In conjunction with the other reforms below, it is possible to imagine spending limits set at one-half or even one-third of current spending averages.

How would federal moneys be allocated? Under the most obvious scheme, funds could be given to parties in proportion to their strength in Congress or, at state levels, in the legislature. Party nominees would then be granted shares of the party fund based on the numbers of voters in their districts. This would encourage greater ideological or issue linkages between candidates and party organizations, and it would encourage parties to run better candidates against incumbents in the other party. Fancier schemes could include "incentives" based on some measure of party and candidate performance in the last election. Although no system of financing is perfect or free of corruption, a financial index based on some linkage between party programs and voter support is preferable to the current system in which candidate and party bank accounts are indexed directly to PAC and private investor support.

In this and other electoral reforms, currently successful officeholders are not likely to become advocates of change, preferring, instead, to drag their feet and throw up smokescreens of scary rhetoric. We can expect to hear about the dangers of government intervention in the free market of political ideas. Most voters, however, will recognize this for what it is: so much political self-interest on the part of politicians. Presidential candidates today, for example, are only too happy to take huge sums of government financing currently available after private money has narrowed the field of competition. Why not also keep the effects of PAC and private money to a minimum in the crucial early stages of all federal elections? In addition, to make this system work, the parties would have to be prohibited either from accepting soft money or at least from spending it during the final months of a campaign.

But, the critics will argue, the costs are too great. How can the government afford to back large numbers of political aspirants, many of whom stand no chance of ultimate victory? To put this question in perspective, the costs of financing the entire slate of national candidates, including challengers, in a presidential year would amount to about 1 percent of the annual defense budget—even if current high levels of spending were allowed to continue. Leaving aside the questions of what our national tax priorities ought to be and what dollar value should be placed on democratic competition, there is another, more expedient answer to this criticism. The cost of campaigning could be lowered by over half through one very simple move: eliminate the enormously expensive practice of paid political advertising on television and radio. This could be done in ways that would also end the Madison Avenue–style candidate marketing which is so damaging to the spirit of democracy. This brings us to our third proposal.

Reform Proposal No. 3:
Regulate Political Advertising in the Broadcast Media

Although it is probably unconstitutional to ban broadcast political advertising, various regulatory measures would reduce the quantity of dollars needed to mount an effective political campaign. In the process, quality ideas and flesh-and-blood candidates might be encouraged to fill the void created by the departure of jingles, slogans, subliminal images, and carefully scripted political performances.

Under the present system, the political commercial that reaches the television screen or the rush hour "drive time" radio program does little to stimulate democratic dialogue. To the contrary, the practice of candidate marketing sets in motion a whole antidemocratic syndrome. Rather than promoting dialogues between candidates and voters that might result in new political initiatives, political advertising of the sort that dominates American campaigns short-circuits the very chances for such communications. Skipping the stages of dialogue, reason, feedback, and debate, marketing techniques probe the subliminal mind of isolated segments of the voter market for images and themes that produce quick psychological responses. The resulting interactions between candidates and voters defy the clear understandings on which stable consensus and programs of action depend. Moreover, the practice of scientifically targeting small voter blocs and then aiming the bulk of campaign content at them violates the spirit of broad democratic involvement. Any practice that turns voting and citizen withdrawal into a good thing rather than a cause for alarm should be outlawed as unhealthy to the principles on which the whole system rests. Alas, cultural taboos about free speech permit no such direct solutions.

One solution is to empower the Federal Communications Commission to include elections more centrally within its sphere of public service broadcasting. In particular, networks should be required to donate set amounts of public service air time to candidates and parties during elections, and the time issued (and used by candidates) should be in blocks of five to fifteen minutes. These two reforms would simultaneously cut the costs of campaigning and require candidates to actually say something in the spaces allocated to them. (Further encouragement could be added by requiring candidates to appear "live" in a substantial percentage of the spots.) More importantly, these reforms would help set in motion the right kind of electoral dynamic: free air time would cut the costs of campaigning, making strict spending limits more realistic, and an additional ratcheting down of spending, beyond the costs of air time, would further discourage expensive marketing research.

Many, of course, will rally around the symbol of free speech on this issue. We can anticipate an unholy alliance of broadcasters, who profit enormously from campaign commercial sales, and candidates, who have won office through the assistance of good marketing. These forces will talk about free speech as though their lives had been totally dedicated to advancing that cause. However, the prohibition of political advertising on radio and television (the media where it is subject to greatest abuse) has at least three precedents within the liberal democratic tradition.

First, consider the fact that a number of thriving Western democracies as diverse, for example, as England, Germany, and Sweden, all regulate political advertising on the airwaves. Indeed, most other democracies regulate political advertising in ways that are much more drastic than the present proposal calls for. Their political processes, if not healthier than ours, are at the very least no worse for it.

Second, the United States has regulated various other forms of broadcast advertising deemed harmful to the national health—hard liquor, cigarettes, sexual services, and pornography, just to name a few. The deterioration of political life caused by candidate marketing on television and radio constitutes at least as great a public hazard as these already prohibited commodities.

Finally, the free speech defense crumbles even if it is examined on strict constructionist terms. Almost nobody in public life subscribes to the absolute reading of the First Amendment clause that says "Congress shall pass *no* law . . . ." Since the eminent justice Oliver Wendell Holmes developed the "clear and present danger" doctrine in the early part of this century, most reasonable people have accepted the idea that speech may be restricted if it presents a clear and present danger to the survival of the people or their way of government. Even the Supreme Court decision in *Buckley* v. *Valeo* granted Congress some broad regulatory powers in elections. If a better case is made for the dangers of contemporary electoral speech, perhaps the Court will see fit to expand those powers in future rulings. I would suggest that the effects of candidate marketing, as they are manifest through the commercialization of elections, represent a far greater threat to the principles and practices of our democratic government than any threat that can be conjured by domestic enemies or flag burning.

Reform Proposal No. 4: The Media Coverage of Elections

It would be nice if the press did more than just grumble when political campaigns manipulate news events and restrict journalistic access to candidates. True, the media are running more stories about media manipulation, empty rhetoric, and voter dissatisfaction than ever before, but they have had little or no perceptible impact on candidate behavior. (As for impact on voters, we may well be looking at a kind of media criticism that only adds to voter cynicism.) Of course, reporters cannot force candidates to ride on the press plane and talk candidly about what, if anything, is on their minds. However, new ways of reporting on campaigns could exert considerable indirect pressure on candidates.

There are some promising signs that the press is awakening to a new election journalism. For example, the focus on political advertising noted in Chapter 7 appears to be taking hold throughout the mass media. In another promising move, R. W. Apple, Jr., of the *New York Times* has conducted focus groups with a broad range of citizens during recent elections and converted his reports based on these discussions into something of a dialogue between candidates and voters. By building on this idea of a critical dialogue contained within news reports, several other innovations might be considered.

To begin with, the leading national news organizations could stake their prestige on creating a national agenda reflecting a synthesis of public opinion and the views of bipartisan experts on the major concerns of the day. This agenda could then be used as a reference for analyzing candidate responsiveness to the national interest. In other words, instead of framing the campaign story as an often baseless horserace, journalists could compare candidates on how well they were responding to the items on the national agenda. Of course, it would still be tempting to make a horserace out of an election, as the metaphor seems to have a powerful hold in the culture (going back at least as far as Andrew Jackson's acclaimed entry as the "Tennessee stud" in the presidential horserace of 1824). However, there is no reason why the metaphor needs to be as empty as it has been. Making a horserace out of candidate responses to the national agenda would turn elections into more meaningful contests than the current weekly updates based on popularity polls. As the race progresses, news organizations could update their evaluations by asking the panels of bipartisan experts for continuing inputs. Opinion polls could be figured in as well, but only after vague questions about "popularity" or "who would you vote for?" had been supplemented with questions about the credibility of candidate responses to the agenda items.

Creating national agendas and evaluating candidate credibility might break down candidate ability to control the content of campaign news coverage, while opening up other aspects of the press–politician relationship. By responding pointedly to poor showings against their competition, politicians might actually turn idle promises into more serious issues in the eyes of voters and experts alike. Moreover, if broadcast advertising were regulated, candidates might have to say something substantive just to stay even with each other in precious media exposure.

The pressure on candidates to discuss the national future could also be increased by holding real political debates. As currently conceived, the debates scarcely deserve that name. Candidates do not really engage each other on adversarial terms; instead, they respond to reporters' questions that are usually based on the candidates' own agendas. A debate system in which candidates are permitted to go at each other could provide revealing glimpses of candidate character, along with insights about their ability to function under real pressure. In addition, if they are to continue playing a part in televised debates, journalists could use their national agendas to lead candidates away from the standard campaign script and the predictable posturing. The debates could become opportunities for the media to pressure candidates to address an independently constructed issue agenda (if the press is willing to construct such an agenda, that is).

As with the other reforms, this one, too, will be resisted by media executives who are comfortable with big profits, smooth and relatively standardized news production routines, and the ease of traveling in a pack with other news organizations. I have discussed these and other obstacles to change in the news media elsewhere.[12] The point here is that there are notable weaknesses in the standard reasons offered by media executives when explaining why they can't change their approaches to news coverage.

At issue here is the curious set of norms the press has adopted to define its role. Personal failings and scandals are fair game, not to mention great fun. The press froths at the chance to catch a candidate in a gaffe or indiscretion. Yet breaking from the pack and deciding independently what really matters blurs the neat distinction between news content that emanates from the candidates themselves (scandals and gaffes conform to this rule) and content that is injected into the news from the editorial desk. This old distinction between reporting and editorializing still holds powerful sway and accounts for the ability of campaigns to control media coverage to a remarkable extent.

The irony is that, when reporters do catch politicians in some personal trouble (which falls under the reporting norm), it is easy for the press to come out looking petty, vindictive, and overly antagonistic. As a result, the press has suffered as much as, and perhaps even more than, politicians in terms of declining popular respect and confidence. Journalists often confuse this public disapproval as a warning not to be too critical rather than as a sign of popular frustration about being critical of the wrong things (i.e., candidates' petty personal problems). If journalists shifted their priorities and held candidates accountable for ideas instead of idiosyncrasies, they just might find a resurgence of public support.

As for the problem of editorializing on the news pages, journalists can draw a distinction between an editorial, which is an in-house opinion, and an agenda of national priorities constructed from the opinions of experts and the public. Few of us want to hear personal opinions passed off as news analysis, but an analytical standard constructed from an intelligent definition of public opinion would give people a useful tool for evaluating candidates and locating themselves in the ongoing debate.

As for the objection that no two news organizations would come up with the same national agenda, so much the better. Surely there would be enough overlap to provide some continuity in the news coverage. (The tendency of the press to look over its shoulders to see what the competition is doing would assure it.) Some level of informed disagreement about the shape of the public interest and the degree of party and candidate responsiveness would introduce a necessary critical edge into the proceedings. If many societies thrive with an avowedly partisan press, surely the American people can live with minor media debates about national goals.

Reform Proposal No. 5: Voter Registration

If people are registered, they tend to vote. The United States sits near the bottom of the list of world democracies in terms of the proportion of eligible citizens who are registered to vote. If registration to vote were easier and more uniform across the various states, more people would be introduced into the electoral arena, magnifying the effects of all the reforms discussed here. Few, if any, good reasons exist for cumbersome voter registration procedures. We are beyond the age of machine politics and the corruption of voter lists that may once have justified the ordeal of seeking out a registrar and supplying proof of identity and residence. And there is no longer room for the racial discrimination that led many states to impose one challenge after another to the registration of black voters.

The good news is that various plans have surfaced in Congress to sign up voters at government offices (post office, motor vehicle, etc.), to register by mail, and even to register on election day. The bad news is that feet are dragging on these bills. In 1990, for example, a sensible bill (the National Voter Registration Act) finally passed the House after long and difficult negotiations. However, a barrage of objections killed it in the

Senate. Some senators charged that allowing voters to register by mail would invite fraud. Others claimed that increased registration efforts would be costly without making any difference in the final outcome of elections (because unregistered voters might vote the same way registered voters do). Some even argued that voting rates among registered voters are declining, thus reducing the importance of the whole issue of registration. In an era when the more people who don't vote, the easier the campaign consultant's (and the candidate's) life becomes, any reluctance to simplify voter registration should be viewed skeptically. A brief look at the argument that registered voter turnout is declining too fast to worry about new registration laws illustrates the point.

In years past, it seemed clear that registration was the biggest hurdle to voting. In 1960, for example, 85.4 percent of those who were registered actually voted, suggesting that if the United States reformed its patchwork of archaic and discouraging registration procedures, it might quickly establish a respectable place among the voting ranks of Western democracies. Over the years, however, figures reported by state election officials show that the number of registrants who vote has dropped (to 70.5 percent by 1988). Those figures fueled arguments against reform, enabling opponents to say it was not worth the efforts and monitoring costs of getting the states to comply. This is where the plot thickens.

A nice piece of detective work by political scientist Frances Piven and sociologist Richard Cloward attributes the dropoff in state figures to poor state reporting practices. In some cases it reflects overworked and understaffed registrars, and in others, it represents attempts by states accused of discrimination to inflate their registration figures to hide the true situation.[13] The problem in either case has to do with deadwood, or the continued registration of people who long ago died or moved but whose names were never purged from local rolls. For various reasons, states tend to purge the deadwood from their rolls less often than they used to, while voters themselves are changing residence more often. As a result, more names are on outdated registration lists—names of people who cannot possibly vote in that district. Thus, the apparent decline of voting among registered voters is just that: an appearance created by inaccurate records. For a better estimate, Piven and Cloward cite 1988 census figures indicating that 86.2 percent of registered voters cast ballots in the presidential election of that year. This figure is actually higher than state-reported figures for 1960 and less than a 5 percent decline from census reports of 1968, the first year the census reported such data. Although census data may be inflated by the tendency of people to give the appearance of responsibility by telling census takers they voted even when they didn't, it is clear that state registration data are skewed even more in the opposite direction. A study cited by Piven and Cloward concludes that, conservatively, 15 percent of those reported on state rolls are either dead or gone.

As with most statistical controversies, the truth probably exists somewhere in between. Like most of the reforms on the list, registration has been held up by politicians unwilling to risk their privileged positions in our elected aristocracy. With any luck, this simplest of electoral reforms will not be delayed much longer by aristocratic leanings, state lobbying efforts, or Republican fears of boosting the numbers of registered Democrats. The legislation has been drafted. It simply awaits political passage.

HOPE FOR GOVERNING IDEAS

The five reforms outlined here are suggestive, not exhaustive, responses to our national political decline. They are intended as beginning points for a discussion about what can be done, not hard-and-fast conclusions or detailed working blueprints. Indeed, I can think of nothing more felicitous than for others to take up this discussion and transform these ideas into more numerous and more workable plans.

The point of election reforms is not just to increase voting levels, but to improve the quality of national political rhetoric. Competition in the marketplace of ideas is the best guarantee of a healthy democracy, not to mention the best chance we have to solve problems. If people find meaning in political rhetoric, they will vote more often. More responsive voters in a more competitive electoral environment will sharpen further the quality of political debate and enforce greater commitment by candidates to their political promises. These assumptions have guided the arguments and analyses in this book.

I am not subscribing here to a simpleminded definition of democracy in which leaders try to read the public mind or otherwise pander to the disorganized whims and prejudices of a people. Little is gained by simply telling voters what they want to hear. Indeed, current campaign practices do just that. Marketing techniques search out those areas of fear, greed, prejudice, or patriotism that do not conflict with prior candidate commitments to investors. Campaign rhetoric is then crafted to keep public thinking within those unthinking bounds, reducing the process of political persuasion to Pavlovian and Orwellian terms and, in the bargain, contributing to the poor reputation of political rhetoric these days.

In the words of rhetorician Paul Corcoran, political language in the contemporary era has fallen from grace. No longer does rhetoric bring to mind the refined art of persuasion through critical public dialogue. Far from stimulating dialogue between politicians and public, says Corcoran, contemporary political language is used "not to persuade, but to control, not to stimulate thought, but to prevent it; not to convey information, but to conceal or distort it, not to draw public attention, but to divert or suppress it. In short, contemporary political language may play precisely the reverse role from that classically conceived for political rhetoric."[14]

The classical role of political rhetoric, according to rhetorician Charles Knepper, is to challenge popular thinking through independent leadership: "The goals of Isocrates, Cicero, and Quintilian did not center on the meager goal of being persuasive for the merely pragmatic purpose of maintaining personal power. Rather, the orator was both a thinker and a speaker whose persuasion was built upon accumulated cultural wisdom in solving problems which arose and required public decision and action."[15]

Who today in public life rises above their personal political fortunes to present a perspective intended to generate controversy and challenge public thinking? Such politically risky action would no doubt elicit derision from modern candidates and their handlers. Better to keep away from bold proposals, or principled stands, and instead to aim one's rhetoric below the intellectual belt. Try to get the voters where they aren't thinking.

Those who scoff at the idea of an ennobling, dialogue-producing political rhetoric might point out that the rough-and-tumble of American politics has never been receptive to the intellectual refinements of a Cicero or a Quintilian. This is true up to a point, but it fails to account for a tradition of great oratory dating from Thomas Paine, Henry Clay, Daniel Webster, Abraham Lincoln, William Jennings Bryan, Woodrow Wilson, Theodore and Franklin Roosevelt, down to John Kennedy and Martin Luther King, Jr. The American culture is not averse to challenging rhetoric that inspires and at the same time invites controversy. The contemporary descent into the weakest ranges of the civic culture is nothing to defend or protect. More importantly, even if American political language is simple and homespun, there can be truth and inspiration in simple ideas.

To the extent that we can imagine a more inspiring and useful way of conducting our politics, there is room in the culture for reform and improvement. To the extent that we fail to seize the opportunities for renewal and positive change, society will continue to wither and lose its political creativity. We are not served by those who would elevate the weakest strains of our culture to the standing of archetypes or models. Our political fortunes are better served by striving to become better. As long as we can imagine how to improve our politics, then we can take the steps necessary to bring those imaginings to life. The quality of public life and the scope of government action are limited only by the rhetorical vision that inspires them. Nowhere is that vision more important than in the electoral arena.

THE FINAL ANALYSIS:
IT'S UP TO THE PEOPLE

One can only hope that Americans will convert their anger about a failing government into action. But how can the right reforms get started? There are signs that citizens are stirring around the land. The important question, however, is whether those stirrings will become focused on the right problems and find the right ways to address those problems. For example, there is something of a groundswell around the country to limit terms in office, and even to seek passage of a constitutional term limit amendment at the national level. However, before too much time and energy are consumed in this effort, it would be wise to reflect on whether term limits would solve *any* of the problems outlined in this book. As an angry signal to politicians, term limits may be a start, but as a full-blown substitute for more basic reforms, they are way off the mark.

Similarly, it may be a mixed blessing that a number of third-party initiatives are in the wind these days. There has been talk in recent years of a women's party, a labor party, a consumer party, a "green" party, and perhaps a coalition of such groups in a revitalized rainbow party. Such efforts are doomed to splinter and fail unless they all recognize that their respective issues must be subordinated, first, to the broader issue of campaign reform. Perhaps a reform party with a set of election reform proposals heading its platform would make a difference and win support among discouraged voters. If nothing else, a reform party would provide a focal point (and more importantly an organizational base) for the kind of sustained social movement that will have to emerge in the next decade if Americans are to have any hope of regaining control of their government.

The prospects for a social movement are reasonably good—particularly with a third party as its beacon. Indeed, American history can be viewed as a succession of social movements (the frontier movement, transcendentalism, abolitionism, populism, the progressive movement, the suffrage movement, prohibitionism, labor, civil rights, feminism, the counterculture, born-again Christianity, etc.). In this view, social movements are the noninstitutional, "hidden hand" of change in American life. The time is ripe for another one. The stakes have never been higher: all lesser issues, interests, and groups are affected by the governing crisis. Without a grass-roots movement aimed squarely at regaining popular, idea-based control of the government, democracy may well become an electronic echo in a marketing jingle or a nostalgic image of times gone by. Now is the time for electoral reform while there is still reason to govern.

NOTES

INTRODUCTION

1. Stephen Rose, personal communication. In a forthcoming book Rose, an economist, explains what he calls "the bunker mentality in the Pepsi Generation" as a result of shifts in national wealth and political priorities.

2. The poll data came from *Harper's,* July 1989, p. 17.

3. University of Michigan, National Election Study Data; quoted in Gregory B. Marcus, "Americans Are Increasingly Disgusted," *International Herald Tribune,* October 15, 1990, p. 8.

4. *International Herald Tribune,* September 5, 1989, p. 9.

5. Quoted in Fred Hiat, "Sony's Picture of Columbia," *International Herald Tribune,* October 4, 1989, p. 21 (from *Washington Post* services).

6. "What's Wrong with the Democrats?" *Harper's,* January 1990, pp. 45–55.

7. Thomas Ferguson and Joel Rogers, *Right Turn: The Decline of the Democrats and the Future of American Politics* (New York: Hill and Wang, 1986).

8. Kevin Phillips, "America, 1989: Brain-Dead Politics in a Transition," *Washington Post* feature reprinted in the *International Herald Tribune,* October 4, 1989, p. 8.

9. Results of a *New York Times*/CBS poll reported in the *International Herald Tribune,* November 5, 1990, p. 1.

10. Result of an ABC News/*Washington Post* poll, Associated Press Wire, October 19, 1990.

CHAPTER 1

1. This quote can be found in Kathleen H. Jamieson, *Eloquence in an Electronic Age: The Transformation of Political Speechmaking* (New York: Oxford University Press, 1988), p. 248.

2. The figures cited here will be reintroduced and analyzed in more detail later in this chapter. Full source citations are available in footnotes 20 and 21.

3. For a more extensive discussion of PACs, see Larry J. Sabato, *PAC Power: Inside the World of Political Action Committees* (New York: W. W. Norton, 1985).

4. General estimates for the U.S. and England are from Lewis Lipsitz and David M. Speak, *American Democracy,* 2nd ed. (New York: St. Martin's Press, 1989), p. 259. House and Senate figures are from David B. Magleby and Candice J. Nelson, *The Money Chase: Congressional Campaign Finance Reform* (Washington, D.C.: The Brookings Institution, 1990), p. 36.

5. John Aldrich quoted in Ralph Blumenthal, "To Many, the Best Choice on Nov. 8 Is Just Home," *New York Times,* November 6, 1988, Sec. 1, p. 18.

6. See, for example, R. W. Apple, Jr., "Old Pros Appraise the '88 Campaign," *New York Times,* November 6, 1988, Sec. 1, p. 18.

7. Quoted in Michael Oreskes, "Talking Heads: Weighing Imagery in a Campaign Made for Television," *New York Times,* October 2, 1988, Sec. 4, p. 1.

8. Ibid.

9. ABC correspondent Brit Hume quoted in John Dillin, "News Media Critique Themselves: Many Reporters Unhappy with Campaign '88 Coverage," *Christian Science Monitor,* December 9, 1988, p. 3.

10. Jeremy Gerard, "Convention Coverage: Endangered Species?" *New York Times*, July 23, 1988, Sec. 1, p. 9.

11. Ibid.

12. Michael Oreskes, "TV's Role in '88: The Medium Is the Election," *New York Times*, October 30, 1988, Sec. 1, p. 10.

13. Ibid., p. 1.

14. NBC Nightly News, March 26, 1989. See also Marvin Kalb, "TV, Election Spoiler," *New York Times*, November 28, 1988, Sec. 1, p. 19.

15. Quoted in ibid.

16. On the Democrats, see Philip Weiss, "Party Time in Atlanta," *Columbia Journalism Review* (September/October 1988) 29. On the Republicans, see "Campaign Trail," *New York Times*, October 10, 1988, Sec. 1, p. 10.

17. Lynda Barry, "The Election from Hell," 1988.

18. *New York Times*/CBS News poll reported in *New York Times*, October 25, 1988, Sec. 1, p. 1.

19. Ibid., pp. 1, 10.

20. John Dillin, "Voters on Election '88: Is This It?" *Christian Science Monitor*, November 2, 1988, p. 1.

21. E. S. Dionne, Jr., "The Campaign Has Real Issues in Spite of Itself," *New York Times*, October 30, 1988, Sec. 4, p. 1.

22. Maureen Dowd, "Bush Lays out Foreign Policy Tenets," *New York Times*, August 3, 1988, p. 8.

23. Marjorie Randon Hershey, "The Campaign and the Media," in Gerald M. Pomper, ed., *The Election of 1988* (Chatham, N.J.: Chatham House Publishers, 1989), p. 97.

24. *New York Times*, October 11, 1988, Sec. 1, p. 1. See also R. W. Apple, Jr., "County That's Always Right Dislikes '88 Choices," *New York Times*, November 2, 1988, Sec. 1, p. 12.

25. Michael Oreskes, "Steel City Tires of Politics and Promises," *New York Times*, April 25, 1988, Sec. 1, p. 1.

26. Editorial, *The Nation*, June 25, 1988, p. 1.

27. William Echikson, "Difference between Bush, Dukakis Lost on French," *Christian Science Monitor*, November 2, 1988, p. 10.

28. For an excellent discussion of this subject, see Bruce Gronbeck, "Electric Rhetoric: The Changing Forms of American Political Discourse," Paper presented at the Congress on "Rhetoric and Techniques of Interpretation," Department of Philology, University of Calabria, Italy, September 11–13, 1989.

29. Jeffrey K. Tulis, *The Rhetorical Presidency* (Princeton, N.J.: Princeton University Press, 1987).

30. Roderick P. Hart, *The Sound of Leadership: Presidential Communication in the Modern Age* (Chicago: University of Chicago Press, 1987).

31. Jamieson, *Eloquence in an Electronic Age*.

32. Shanto Iyengar and Donald R. Kinder, *News That Matters: Television and American Public Opinion* (Chicago: University of Chicago Press, 1987).

33. See, for example, Thomas Ferguson and Joel Rogers, *Right Turn: The Decline of the Democrats and the Future of American Politics* (New York: Hill and Wang, 1986), especially Ch. 1.

34. Quoted in Oreskes, "Talking Heads," p. 1.

35. Erik Asard, "Election Campaigns in Sweden and the U.S.: Convergence or Divergence?," *American Studies in Scandinavia* 21, no. 2 (1989): 70–85.

36. Murray Edelman, *Constructing the Political Spectacle* (Chicago: University of Chicago Press, 1988).

37. Murray Edelman, *The Symbolic Uses of Politics* (Urbana: University of Illinois Press, 1964).

38. Ferguson and Rogers, *Right Turn.*

39. Paul Weyrich quoted in Thomas Ferguson and Joel Rogers, "The Reagan Victory: Corporate Coalitions in the 1980 Campaign," in Ferguson and Rogers, eds., *The Hidden Election: Politics and Economics in the 1980 Presidential Campaign* (New York: Pantheon, 1981), p. 4.

40. See, for example, Mark Hertsgaard, *On Bended Knee: The Press and the Reagan Presidency* (New York: Farrar, Straus and Giroux, 1988).

41. "This Week with David Brinkley," ABC, November 6, 1988.

42. Unnamed source, cited in Mark Hertsgaard, "Electoral Journalism: Not Yellow, but Yellow-Bellied," *New York Times,* September 21, 1988, p. A15.

43. Ibid.

44. Jacques Ellul, "Preconceived Ideas about Mediated Information," in Everett M. Rogers and Francis Bolle, eds., *The Media Revolution in America and Western Europe* (Norwood, N.J.: Ablex Publishing Co., 1985), p. 107.

45. Robert Shrum, quoted in R. W. Apple, Jr., "Candidates Focus on Television Ads," *New York Times,* October 19, 1986, p. A16.

46. See, for example, a "Newsweek Poll" conducted by the Gallup Organization on October 11–12, 1990, and reported in *Newsweek* (European edition), October 22, 1990, p. 47. This specific poll found that over 70 percent blamed both Republicans and Democrats in Congress for problems in reaching a budget agreement, while nearly 60 percent approved of the way their representative was handling his or her job.

47. For a review of research on voter ignorance, see Eric R.A.N. Smith, *The Unchanging American Voter* (Berkeley: University of California Press, 1989), Ch. 4.

48. The classic work on this remains Angus Campbell, Philip E. Converse, Warren E. Miller, and Donald E. Stokes, *The American Voter* (New York: John Wiley, 1960). Smith's argument (ibid.) is that little has changed to warrant altering this portrait of our unsophisticated electorate.

49. Nelson W. Polsby and Aaron Wildavsky, *Presidential Elections,* 6th ed. (New York: Scribner's, 1984), pp. 5–6.

50. This tradition follows from the work of V. O. Key (with Milton C. Cummings), *The Responsible Electorate: Rationality in Presidential Voting 1936–1960* (New York: Vintage Books, 1966).

51. See Morris P. Fiorina, *Retrospective Voting in American National Elections* (New Haven, Conn.: Yale University Press, 1981).

52. See Benjamin Page, *Choices and Echoes in Presidential Elections* (Chicago: University of Chicago Press, 1978).

53. For example, an interesting analysis of the 1988 contests showed that while voters were expressing dismay at their choices, they were still actively searching those suspect choices for information (which may explain why political advertising is so often cited as a primary source of information). See Barbara G. Farah and Ethel Klein, "Public Opinion Trends," in Gerald M. Pomper, ed., *The Election of 1988: Reports and Interpretations* (Chatham, N.J.: Chatham House, 1989).

CHAPTER 2

1. Quoted in Richard H. Leach, *American Federalism* (New York: W. W. Norton, 1970), p. 54.

2. Ibid.

3. See Herbert E. Alexander, *Financing Politics: Money, Elections and Political Reform* (Washington, D.C.: Congressional Quarterly Press, 1984).

4. See W. Lance Bennett and William Haltom, "Issues, Voter Choice, and Critical Elections," *Social Science History* 4 (Fall 1980): 792–817.

5. Ibid.

6. These differences will be elaborated throughout the rest of the book. For now, this simple "snapshot" will suffice to convey the basic idea.

7. See, for example, Kathleen Jamieson, *Eloquence in an Electronic Age* (New York: Oxford University Press, 1988); and Mark Hertsgaard, *On Bended Knee: The Press and the Reagan Presidency* (New York: Farrar, Straus and Giroux, 1988).

8. For a history of candidate commercials, see Edwin Diamond and Stephen Bates, *The Spot: The Rise of Political Advertising on Television* (Cambridge: MIT Press, 1984).

9. See Joe McGinniss, *The Selling of the President, 1968* (New York: Trident Press, 1969).

10. See, for example, Nelson W. Polsby, *Consequences of Party Reform* (New York: Oxford University Press, 1983).

11. See, for example, Leon D. Epstein, *Political Parties in the American Mold* (Madison: University of Wisconsin Press, 1986).

12. Based on figures from the Survey Research Center of the University of Michigan compiled through the National Election Surveys conducted since 1952. In 1952, for comparison, the corresponding figures were: Democrats—47 percent; Independents—22 percent; and Republicans—27 percent.

13. For an interesting analysis of these points, see Kevin Phillips, *The Politics of Rich and Poor: Wealth and the American Electorate in the Reagan Aftermath* (New York: Random House, 1990). Phillips' postmortem on the Republican reformation is particularly noteworthy since he was one of the architects of the Nixon southern strategy that started the whole process moving twenty years before.

14. See Michael J. Malbin, "Looking Back at the Future of Campaign Finance Reform: Interest Groups and American Elections," in Malbin, ed., *Money and Politics in the United States* (Chatham, N.J.: Chatham House, 1984). In addition, see Alexander, *Financing Politics,* in Malbin, ed., *Money and Politics.* See also Elizabeth Drew, *Politics and Money* (New York: Collier, 1983).

15. For differing analyses of precisely how the political pie was redivided following the depression, see Thomas Ferguson and Joel Rogers, *Right Turn: The Decline of the Democrats and the Future of American Politics* (New York: Hill and Wang, 1986); and William Domhoff, *The Power Elite and the State: How Policy Is Made in America* (New York: Aldine de Gruyter, 1990), especially Ch. 9.

16. We will return in Chapter 7 to consider some of the larger implications of this Court ruling linking political spending and free speech.

17. For a sampling of these debates, see William J. Crotty, *Political Reform and the American Experiment* (New York: Crowell, 1977); and Larry M. Bartels, *Presidential Primaries and the Dynamics of Public Choice* (Princeton, N.J.: Princeton University Press, 1988).

18. For a highly detailed account of the evolution of PAC politics, see Larry J. Sabato, *PAC Power: Inside the World of Political Action Committees* (New York: W. W. Norton, 1985).

19. Federal Election Commission figures, 1988.

20. For a detailed breakdown of the figures, see Jean Cobb, "Top Brass," *Common Cause Magazine,* May/June 1989, pp. 23–27.

21. The first four quotes are from Representatives Andrew Jacobs of Indiana, Dan Glickman of Kansas, Barbara Mikulski of Maryland, and Richard Ottinger of New York, all reported in Sabato, *PAC Power,* pp. 126–127. The last quote is from a "Democrat from the West" who preferred anonymity in a news story by Tom Kenwor-

thy, "U.S. House Democrats Struggling with Principles vs. PACs," *International Herald Tribune,* October 31, 1989, p. 2 (from the *Washington Post*).

22. Quoted in Sabato, *PAC Power,* p. xii.

23. As with all players, the small donations are as welcome as the large. In a typical year after this statement was made, Senator Dole accepted speaking fees as small as $1,000 and $2,000 from dozens of organizations, including the American Dental Association, the American Pharmaceutical Association, the American Stock Exchange, and the American Academy of Dermatology. Source: *New York Times* data reported in the *Seattle Weekly,* December 27, 1989, p. 19.

24. Walter Dean Burnham, "The Reagan Heritage," in Gerald M. Pomper, ed., *The Election of 1988: Reports and Interpretations* (Chatham, N.J.: Chatham House, 1989), p. 15.

25. See Ferguson and Rogers, *Right Turn.*

26. Ibid., Ch. 1.

27. National Election Study data, Survey Research Center, University of Michigan.

28. See W. Lance Bennett, "Marginalizing the Majority: Conditioning Public Opinion to Accept Managerial Democracy," in Michael Margolis and Gary Mauser, eds., *Manipulating Public Opinion* (New York: Dorsey, 1989).

29. For an example of one such silencing campaign, see W. Lance Bennett, "Toward a Theory of Press-State Relations in the United States," *Journal of Communication* 40, no. 2 (Spring 1990): 103–125.

30. Figures are from Sabato, *PAC Power,* pp. 188–190, and from Federal Election Commission data on 1988.

31. Quoted in Paul E. Johnson, John H. Aldrich, Gary J. Miller, Charles W. Ostrom, and David W. Rhode, *American Government,* 2nd ed. (Boston: Houghton Mifflin, 1990), p. 336.

32. A more detailed analysis of the politics of tax reform is forthcoming in Erik Åsard and W. Lance Bennett, "The Marketplace of Ideas in Sweden and the United States: The Case of Tax Reform." Research in progress.

33. See Phillips, *The Politics of Rich and Poor.*

34. Congressional Budget Office, 1977–1988, national income analysis.

35. Benjamin Ginsberg and Martin Shefter, *Politics by Other Means: The Declining Importance of Elections in America* (New York: Basic Books, 1990).

36. Jarol Manheim, *All of the People, All the Time: Strategic Communication and American Politics* (Armonk, N.Y.: M. E. Sharpe, 1991).

CHAPTER 3

1. Quoted in Charles Snydor, *American Revolutionaries in the Making* (New York: Free Press, 1952), p. 48.

2. Ibid., p. 55.

3. Ibid., p. 57.

4. Alexis de Tocqueville, *Democracy in America,* Vol. I (New York: Alfred A. Knopf, 1945), pp. 259–260.

5. Paul Kleppner, Walter Dean Burnham, Ronald P. Formisano, Samuel P. Hays, Richard Jensen, and William G. Shade, *The Evolution of American Electoral Systems* (Westport, Conn.: Greenwood Press, 1981).

6. William G. Shade, "Political Pluralism and Party Development," in Kleppner et al., *The Evolution of American Electoral Systems,* p. 81.

7. From Paul F. Boller, Jr., *Presidential Campaigns* (New York: Oxford University Press, 1985), p. 107.

8. Quoted in ibid., p. 168.

9. The term *critical election* was coined by V.O. Key. Walter Dean Burnham discusses it extensively in his *Critical Elections and the Mainsprings of American Politics* (New York: W. W. Norton, 1970).

10. Quoted in Boller, *Presidential Campaigns,* p. viii.

11. Walter Dean Burnham, "The Reagan Heritage," in Gerald M. Pomper, *The Election of 1988: Reports and Interpretations* (Chatham, N.J.: Chatham House Publishers, 1989).

12. Quoted in Marjorie Randon Hershey, "The Campaign and the Media," in Pomper, *The Election of 1988,* p. 74.

13. Everett Carl Ladd, "Campaign '88: What Are the 'Issues'?", *Christian Science Monitor,* June 3, 1988, p. 14.

14. The definitive work on this theory of voting is Morris P. Fiorina, *Retrospective Voting in American National Elections* (New Haven, Conn.: Yale University Press, 1981).

15. This *Times Mirror* survey appeared, along with a dramatic graphic, on the front page of the *Christian Science Monitor,* September 29, 1988.

16. Burnham, "The Reagan Heritage," in Pomper et al., *The Election of 1988,* p. 29.

17. Martin Anderson, "George Bush, Environmentalist," *Christian Science Monitor,* January 4, 1989, p. 19.

18. "11 Groups Criticize Bush," *International Herald Tribune,* October 28–29, 1989, p. 5. The Bush quote on the White House effect is from Strobe Talbott, "Why Bush Should Sweat," *Time,* (European edition) November 6, 1989, p. 27.

19. Nicholas von Hoffman, "Goo-goos' Glom onto Issues, Again," *New York Times,* October 12, 1988, p. 27.

20. "Where They Would Lead the Country: Summaries of George Bush's and Michael Dukakis' Positions on Issues Facing the Nation from Position Papers, Campaign Advisers, and Various Issues 'Score Cards,' " *Christian Science Monitor,* November 1, 1988, pp. 14–15.

21. "Campaign '88: Issues Scorecard," *New York Times,* February 4, 1988, pp. 16–17.

22. Robin Toner, "Republicans See Child Care As Aiding Pro-Family Image," *New York Times,* August 9, 1988, p. 9.

23. See the summary of these lengthy positions cited in note 20. Interestingly, the defense statements on Dukakis' issue scorecard were by far the longest of any issue, indicating, perhaps, his handlers' attempt to compensate with verbiage what the candidate lacked in experience in the area.

24. "Candidates Word Wrestle to a Draw," *Christian Science Monitor,* September 27, 1988, p. 3.

25. Ibid., p. 91.

26. These data are reported fully in Hershey, "The Campaign and the Media," pp. 88–91.

27. Ibid., p. 91.

28. *New York Times,* October 20, 1988, p. 11, col. 1.

29. Quoted in Robin Toner, "Dukakis Camp's Insularity Bemoaned," *New York Times,* October 28, 1989, p. 10.

30. Ibid.

31. Quoted in Boller, *Presidential Campaigns,* pp. 109–110.

32. Ibid., p. 12.

33. Ibid., pp. 53–54.

34. Ibid., pp. 55–56.

CHAPTER 4

1. Ben H. Bagdikian, *The Media Monopoly,* 2nd ed. (Boston: Beacon Press, 1987).

2. The classic study here is Leon Sigal, *Reporters and Officials* (Lexington, Mass.: D. C. Heath, 1973). For a fascinating look at the dependence of journalists on officials in foreign policy reporting, see Bernard C. Cohen, *The Press, the Public, and Foreign Policy* (Princeton, N.J.: Princeton University Press, 1963).

3. For a more general review of these pressures, see W. Lance Bennett, *News: The Politics of Illusion,* 2nd ed. (New York: Longman, Inc., 1988), Ch. 4.

4. For a more detailed analysis of the origins and workings of this norm, see W. Lance Bennett, "Toward a Theory of Press–State Relations in the United States," *Journal of Communication* 40, no. 2 (1990): 103–127.

5. Robert M. Entman, *Democracy without Citizens: Media and the Decay of American Politics* (New York: Oxford University Press, 1989).

6. Ibid.

7. See, for example, Edward S. Herman, "Diversity of News: 'Marginalizing' the Opposition," *Journal of Communication* (Summer 1985): 135–146.

8. See, for example, the Gallup poll released by the *Los Angeles Times,* March 9, 1989, and discussed in *Extra,* March/April 1989, p. 15.

9. See Jean Cobb, "Top Brass," *Common Cause Magazine,* May/June 1989, pp. 23–31.

10. Reported in ibid., p. 23.

11. Ibid.

12. For a more elaborate discussion, see Bennett, *News: The Politics of Illusion.*

13. Quoted in Richard L. Berke, "Big Money's Election Year Comeback," *New York Times,* August 7, 1988, p. E5.

14. Herbert Alexander, quoted in *New York Times,* ibid.

15. Ibid.

16. Jean Cobb, Jeff Denny, Vicki Kemper, and Viveca Novak, "All the President's Donors," *Common Cause Magazine,* March/April 1990, p. 22.

17. Ibid., p. 23.

18. Brooks Jackson, "Democrats Outflanked in Previous Elections, Rival GOP in Financing of Presidential Race," *Wall Street Journal,* October 3, 1988, p. A22.

19. Cobb et al., "All the President's Donors," p. 23.

20. Source: Congressional Research Service and Federal Election Commission. Also reported in *Common Cause Magazine,* January/February 1990, p. 45. 1990 figures released by Federal Election Commission in 1991.

21. Quoted in Ross Baker, *The New Fat Cats* (New York: Priority Press, 1989), pp. 10–11.

22. William H. Hudnut III, quoted in David Broder, "How to Clear up Congress? Alumni Say Sweep out the Cash," *International Herald Tribune,* January 7, 1991, p. 5 (from the *Washington Post*).

23. The quote and information cited in this paragraph are from John H. Fund, "Who Drove the S&L Getaway Car?," *Wall Street Journal,* October 31, 1990, p. 10.

24. See Baker, *The New Fat Cats,* Appendix, Table 2.

25. This was for a Senate race in 1986! Reported by Richard L. Berke, "Senate Campaign Reform vs. A Senate Campaign," *New York Times,* May 13, 1990, p. E4.

26. Baker, *The New Fat Cats,* p. 11.

27. Thomas Ferguson and Joel Rogers, *Right Turn: The Decline of the Democrats and the Future of American Politics* (New York: Hill and Wang, 1986).

28. Ibid., p. 15.

29. Ibid., p. 14.
30. See, for example, Seymour Martin Lipset and William Schneider, *The Confidence Gap: Business, Labor and Government in the Public Mind* (New York: Free Press, 1983), p. 17.
31. Ferguson and Rogers, *Right Turn*, p. 24.
32. Ibid., p. 26.
33. Ibid., p. 17.
34. *Extra!*, March/April 1989, p. 15.
35. Elizabeth Noelle–Neumann, *The Spiral of Silence* (Chicago: University of Chicago Press, 1983).
36. Based on an analysis by Common Cause, reported in the *International Herald Tribune*, October 16, 1990, p. 1.
37. Reported in *USA Today* (international edition), November 1, 1990, p. 7A.
38. William Domhoff, *The Power Elite and the State: How Policy Is Made in America* (New York: Aldine de Gruyter, 1990), especially Ch. 9.
39. Benjamin Page addresses these points persuasively in his *Choices and Echoes in Presidential Elections* (Chicago: University of Chicago Press, 1978).
40. *New York Times,* November 3, 1988, p. 14.
41. Frederick C. Thayer, "A Bipartisan Fear of Full Employment," *New York Times,* October 12, 1988, p. 27.
42. Bruce Cummings, "Chinatown: Foreign Policy and Elite Realignment," in Thomas Ferguson and Joel Rogers, eds., *The Hidden Election: Politics and Economics in the 1980 Presidential Campaign* (New York: Random House, 1981).
43. Quoted in Thomas Ferguson and Joel Rogers, "The Reagan Victory: Corporate Coalitions in the 1980 Campaign," in Ferguson and Rogers, eds., *The Hidden Election,* p. 4.
44. Benjamin Ginsberg, "A Post Election Era?", *PS: Political Science & Politics,* March 1989, p. 19. See also Benjamin Ginsberg and Martin Sheffer, *Politics by Other Means: The Declining Importance of Elections in America* (New York: Basic Books, 1990).
45. Mark Petracca, "Political Consultants and Democratic Governance," *PS: Political Science & Politics,* March 1989, p. 11.
46. Ibid., p. 13.
47. Ibid.
48. See Ginsberg, "A Post Election Era?"
49. See Walter de Vries, "American Campaign Consulting: Trends and Concerns," *PS: Political Science & Politics,* March 1989, pp. 21–25.
50. Ibid., p. 24.
51. Petracca, "Political Consultants and Democratic Governance," p. 12.
52. de Vries, "American Campaign Consulting," p. 23.
53. Maureen Dowd, "New Today at the Bush 'Beige' White House: A Glitzy Image Maker," *New York Times Service* article reprinted in *International Herald Tribune,* October 4, 1989, p. 1.
54. Ibid., p. 7.
55. For a discussion of these calculations, see Gerald M. Pomper, "The Presidential Nominations," in Pomper, ed., *The Election of 1988: Reports and Interpretations* (Chatham, N.J.: Chatham House, 1989), pp. 50–52.
56. See ibid.
57. Article by Michael Oreskes, *New York Times,* September 1, 1988, p. 1.
58. See Donald L. Rheem, "House Leader Says Dukakis Made Two Campaign Errors with Blacks," *Christian Science Monitor,* December 9, 1988, p. 6.

59. Quoted in R. W. Apple, Jr. "Willie Brown Sees Dukakis Errors," *New York Times*, October 31, 1988, p. 9.

60. Robin Toner, "Dukakis Works at Warmth but Keeps His Sleeves Down," *New York Times*, August 8, 1988, p. 1.

61. de Vries, "American Campaign Consulting," p. 21.

62. The credit for digging up this gem goes to Marjorie Randon Hershey, "The Campaign and the Media," in Pomper, ed., *The Election of 1988*, p. 83.

63. Hershey, "The Campaign and the Media," p. 87.

64. Maureen Dowd, "Bush's Top Strategists: Smooth Poll-Taker and Hard Driving Manager," *New York Times*, May 30, 1988, p. 11.

65. Ibid.

66. Eric Alternam, "Playing Hardball," *New York Times Magazine*, April 30, 1989, p. 70.

67. Maureen Dowd, "For Bush on the Campaign Trail, the Style Is First Sour, Then Sweet," *New York Times*, October 12, 1988, p. 10.

68. Ibid., p. 1.

69. Hershey, "The Campaign and the Media," p. 81.

70. Barbara G. Farah and Ethel Klein, "Public Opinion Trends," in Pomper, ed., *The Election of 1988*, p. 103.

71. Mark Hertsgaard, "Electoral Journalism: Not Yellow, but Yellow-Bellied," *New York Times*, September 21, 1988, p. A15.

72. Ibid.

73. Hershey, "The Campaign and the Media," p. 98.

74. David S. Broder, "Political Reporters in Presidential Politics," in Charles Peters and James Fallows, eds., *Inside the System*, 3rd ed. (New York: Praeger, 1976), p. 212.

75. Michael Oreskes, "Candidates and Media at Odds Over Message," *New York Times*, October 4, 1988, p. 14.

76. Ibid.

CHAPTER 5

1. *New York Times*, September 21, 1976, p. 1, cols. 1–2. Hereafter, the citation of dates refers to the day on which the speech, event, appearance, and so on, was reported in the *New York Times*. Unless noted otherwise, the date of actual occurrence can be obtained by subtracting one day.

2. The number of people who participate is only one measure of this involvement. An equally important consideration is the degree to which this symbolic flexibility permits candidates to make appeals to a range of groups that cut across various lines of social, economic, and cultural division in the polity.

3. Nationally televised speech, NBC network, March 31, 1976.

4. June 16, 1976, p. 18, col. 1.

5. Joseph Lelyveld, "The Selling of a Candidate," *New York Times Magazine*, March 28, 1976, p. 66.

6. Elections can be viewed as holdovers from ethological leadership struggles common to many societies. These struggles are often performed before the gathered community. The significant signs and symbols in these contests may vary: strength, endurance, virtue, skill, wealth (or the blatant consumption of it), revelation, and so on. In most such rituals, the key element is that the emergence of leadership follows struggle, competition, or the display of a superior attribute. Thus, the direction of public attention to the relevant distinctions between candidate and opponent is a

central feature of leadership competitions like elections. The impact of the performance depends on the clear and effective presentation of these signs and symbols to the audience.

7. May 29, 1976, p. 8, col. 2.

8. May 28, 1976, p. 12, col. 1.

9. Ibid., col. 2.

10. May 18, 1976, p. 20, col. 2.

11. Patrick Anderson, "James E. Carter, Jr.," *New York Times Biographical Service,* December 1975.

12. Ibid.

13. At a time when his nomination was in doubt in 1952, even Eisenhower issued a few well-placed personal attacks. The 1952 Republican convention was controlled by Taft supporters. Eisenhower was the underdog. His nomination hinged on a crucial fight over the rules for seating three contested southern delegations. On the eve of this delegate struggle, Eisenhower briefly abandoned his aloof stance to accuse the Taft forces of chicanery and crookedness. He likened them to "rustlers who stole the Texas birthright instead of steers." (Texas was the largest of the contested southern delegations.) *New York Times,* July 4, 1976, p. 28, col. 3.

14. Udall. Michigan primary, May 14, 1976, p. 16, col. 2.

15. Brown. Maryland primary, May 18, 1976, p. 20, col. 2.

16. Carter. Interview. *Time,* May 10, 1976, pp. 24–27.

17. Ford. Michigan primary. May 17, 1976, p. 22, col. 7.

18. Ibid.

19. For an excellent discussion of the uses of banal language in political life, see Murray Edelman's book, *Political Language: Words That Succeed, Policies That Fail* (New York: Academic Press, 1977).

20. Thomas E. Patterson and Robert D. McClure, *The Unseeing Eye* (New York: G. P. Putnam's Sons, 1976).

21. May 14, 1976, p. 16, col. 1.

22. June 3, 1976, p. 30, col. 1; June 6, 1976, p. 1, col. 1.

23. June 3, 1976, p. 30, col. 1.

24. May 12, 1976, p. 47, col. 2.

25. May 14, 1976, p. 1, col. 2.

26. Of course, this strategy can be carried to extremes. There is a bit of political humor that recounts how Thomas Dewey, the 1948 challenger and front runner, spent so much of the campaign acting like the president that when the election was finally held the people thought it was time for a change. They voted for Truman—the incumbent.

27. Lelyveld, "The Selling of a Candidate."

28. May 13, 1976, p. 35, col. 5. This statement was made on a prior date, but it was reported in an article (William Safire's column) that appeared on this date.

29. The yarmulke clearly was part of the appeal for this elected audience. Even such details like the color (blue) of the yarmulke may reflect some calculation. Carter generally wore blue accents in his campaign attire. One of Carter's media staff revealed "I love running this guy when he's in blue. The blue gets attention. It's optically dramatic." See Lelyveld, "The Selling of a Candidate," p. 68.

30. June 7, 1976, p. 22, col. 1.

31. May 25, 1976, p. 24, col. 7.

32. May 27, 1976, p. 24, col. 1.

33. May 25, 1976, p. 24, col. 7.

34. May 15, 1976, p. 1, col. 2.

35. See Joe McGinniss, *The Selling of the President, 1968* (New York: Trident Press, 1969).

36. For an excellent account of this, see Gary Wills, *Nixon Agonistes* (New York: Signet, 1969).

37. July 2, 1976, p. 9, col. 1.

38. June 1976, p. 12, col. 5.

39. When I refer to the "relationships" that language symbols can occupy in a common context, I refer to particular structural patterns among symbols, the commonly understood features that alert interpreters to process the symbols in particular ways. For example, a collection of symbols may occupy a serial relationship in context. In this case, the interpreter may look for sensible relationships of continuation (how, why, when, how long, what next) between the symbols. Alternatively, various utterances in a symbolization may share common linguistic cues (redundancies, pronoun references, actions in search of objects, etc.). Such cues may constitute a basis for the auditor to call on normative, empirical, or lexical understandings in the process of interpretation. These sorts of structural relations alert the auditor that the context requires that a relationship of a certain sort be established among some subset of symbols in the general composition.

40. See Harvey Sacks, "On the Analyzability of Stories by Children," in J. Gumperz and D. Hymes, eds., *Directors in Sociolinguistics: The Ethnography of Communication* (New York: Holt, Rinehart and Winston), 1972.

41. Underlying this general point is the obvious principle that the choice of symbols in a given context will determine the range of categorical understandings an interpreter can use to understand the symbolization. Subtle shifts in the choice of symbols can produce markedly different category references, in addition to affecting the ambiguity or the clarity of the resulting inference. For example, had the child's utterance been "The baby cried. The woman picked it up," we would be less certain about the nature of the relationship between the two actors. Similarly, had Carter said that Wallace would run until 1988 "if he is so disposed" we would be hard pressed to locate a unique, unambiguous reference for the symbol "disposed." We encountered no such trouble with the symbol "able" in that context.

42. I do not have the exact quote of this statement, as it was overheard on a car radio. However, this paraphrase is faithful to the general theme of the statement.

43. Observers generally conceded that Ford was unable to define "his issues" (e.g., the economy) in terms that appealed to the voters. At the same time, Ford made the mistake of responding defensively to Reagan's charges. In a speech that indicated both his awareness of the situation and his contribution to it, Ford said: "Somewhere between the snows of New Hampshire and the sunny climes of Florida, the focus of this year's Republican campaign for the Presidency began to shift away from the growing strength and prosperity of the American economy to a new and more complex issue—the strength of America's military force." May 11, 1976, p. 1, col. 1.

44. See, for example, Reagan's national speech of March 31, 1976.

45. March 2, 1976, p. 9, col. 6.

46. August 20, 1975, p. 45, col. 1.

47. *Wall Street Journal,* March 30, 1976, p. 24, col. 2.

48. May 27, 1976, p. 24, col. 1.

49. It is interesting that this portion of Carter's welfare rhetoric was similar to that of a conservative candidate like Ronald Reagan who played to fairly homogeneous audiences on the welfare issue. Reagan tended to give virtually the same treatment of the antiwelfare position. This use of categorically specific symbols makes sense if the audience is uniformly disposed toward the issue. However, Carter's audiences were not uniformly disposed on the issue. Nonetheless, Carter proceeded to cite in the same context specific references on both sides of an issue. This practice is rare in politics if only because of its riskiness and because of the rhetorical skill it requires.

50. June 2, 1976, p. 20, col. 6.

51. For example, see the *New York Times* and CBS surveys reported in the *Times* of June 11, 1976, p. 1, col. 7.

52. These quotes are from Reagan's national speech on the NBC network, March 31, 1976, p. 1, col. 7.

53. Ford even defined one of his primary victories (Wisconsin) as a vindication of his support for Secretary of State Kissinger. He called Kissinger "one of the greatest Secretaries of State in the history of the United States." April 8, 1976, p. 2, col. 4.

54. May 13, 1976, p. 1, col. 4.

55. May 17, 1976, p. 8, col. 3.

56. Speech of March 31, 1976.

57. May 10, 1976, p. 20, col. 6.

58. June 4, 1976, p. 12, col. 1.

59. Ibid.

60. June 7, 1976, p. 22, col. 6.

61. However, the California poll showed that Reagan may have lost as much as 5 percent of his support in California as a result of Ford's effective use of the Rhodesia statement. June 8, 1976, p. 23, col. 6.

CHAPTER 6

1. James David Barber, *The Presidential Character,* 2nd ed. (Englewood Cliffs, N.J.: Prentice–Hall, 1977).

2. Benjamin Page, *Choices and Echoes in Presidential Elections* (Chicago: University of Chicago Press, 1978).

3. See, for example a typical day in the 1976 campaign of Mo Udall reported by Richard Reeves in *Old Faces of 1976* (New York: Harper and Row, 1976), pp. 3–4.

4. David Barber, "Characters in the Campaign: The Scientific Question," in James David Barber, ed., *Race for the Presidency: The Media and the Nominating Process* (Englewood Cliffs, N.J.: Prentice–Hall, 1978), p. 160.

5. For an analysis of this remark in the context of the debates, see Lloyd F. Bitzer and Theodore Reuter, *Carter vs. Ford: The Counterfeit Debates of 1976* (Madison: University of Wisconsin Press, 1980).

6. Lou Cannon and Edward Walsh, "War, Peace Dominate Debate," *Washington Post,* October 29, 1980, p. 1.

7. Tom Shales, "The Harassment of Ronald Reagan," *Washington Post,* October 31, 1980, p. C1.

8. Meg Greenfield, "Chronic Political Amnesia," *Washington Post,* September 17, 1980, p. A19.

9. For a more extensive review of standard criticisms of election coverage, see David L. Swanson, "And That's the Way It Was? Television Covers the 1976 Presidential Campaign," *Quarterly Journal of Speech* 63 (1977): 239–248.

10. For various explanations of this dramatic license in American elections, see, among others: Walter R. Fisher, "Reaffirmation and Subversion of the American Dream," *Quarterly Journal of Speech* 59 (1973): 160–167; Edwin Black, "Electing Time," *Quarterly Journal of Speech* 59 (1973): 125–129; and John H. Patton, "A Government as Good as Its People: Jimmy Carter and the Restoration of Transcendence to American Politics," *Quarterly Journal of Speech* 63 (1977): 249–257.

11. On the importance, for social judgment, of the interplay between general norms and public actions, see, among others: Fritz Heider, *The Psychology of Interpersonal Relations* (New York: Wiley, 1958); Erving Goffman, *The Presentation of Self in Everyday Life* (New York: Anchor Books, 1959); Peter L. Berger and Thomas Luckmann, *The Social Construction of Reality* (New York: Anchor Doubleday, 1966); and

Alfred Schutz, *On Phenomenology and Social Relations* (Chicago: University of Chicago Press, 1970).

12. Harold Garfinkel, "Conditions of Successful Degradation Ceremonies," *American Journal of Sociology* 61 (1956): 420–424.

13. See, among others: Erving Goffman, "The Mortification of Self," in Richard Flacks, ed., *Conformity, Resistance, and Self Determination* (Boston: Little, Brown, 1973), pp. 175–188; Erving Goffman, *Asylums* (New York: Anchor Books, 1961); and Sanford M. Dornbusch, "The Military Academy as an Assimilating Institution," *Social Forces* 33 (1955): 316–321.

14. William Foote Whyte, *Street Corner Society* (Chicago: University of Chicago Press, 1943), p. 33. For other degradation rituals involving sex roles and group status, see Hunter S. Thompson, *Hell's Angels* (New York: Random House, 1967).

15. See Elliot Liebow, *Tally's Corner: A Study of Negro Streetcorner Men* (Boston: Little, Brown, 1967).

16. See Roger D. Abrahams, "Playing the Dozens," *Journal of American Folklore* 75 (July–September 1962): 209–220.

17. William Labov, "Rules for Ritual Insults," in David Sudnow, ed., *Studies in Social Interaction* (New York: Macmillan, 1972), p. 125.

18. For an extended analysis of a case from British electoral politics that is similar to Ford's series of blunders, see Charles W. Lomas, "Sir Alex Douglas Home: Case Study in Rhetorical Failure," *Quarterly Journal of Speech* 56 (1970): 296–303.

19. Shales, "The Harassment of Ronald Reagan," p. C1.

20. B. L. Ware and Wil A. Linkugel, "They Spoke in Defense of Themselves: On the Generic Criticism of Apologia," *Quarterly Journal of Speech* 59 (1973): 273–284.

21. Robert P. Abelson, "Modes of Resolution of Belief Dilemmas," *Journal of Conflict Resolution* 3 (1959): 343–352.

22. For discussions of these and other examples of apologia, see Ware and Linkugel, "They Spoke in Defense of Themselves."

23. Bernard Weinraub, "Slip and Gloom Index Rates the Candidates," *New York Times,* November 1, 1988, p. 10.

24. Richard L. Berke, "Gingerly and on Wobbly Footing, Bentsen Opens Cheerleading Show," *New York Times,* July 30, 1988, p. 7.

25. Murray Edelman, *Political Language: Words That Succeed and Policies That Fail* (New York: Academic Press, 1977).

26. Charles Warren, *The Making of the Constitution* (Cambridge, Mass.: Harvard University Press, 1928), p. 1.

27. Catherine L. Albanese, *Sons of the Fathers: The Civil Religion of the American Revolution* (Philadelphia: Temple University Press, 1976).

28. Karl A. Lamb, *As Orange Goes: Twelve California Families and the Future of American Politics* (New York: W. W. Norton, 1974). Both quotes are from p. 178.

29. Ibid., p. 187.

30. Ibid., pp. 185–186.

CHAPTER 7

1. Larry Sabato, "Political Influence, the News Media, and Campaign Consultants," *PS: Political Science and Politics,* March 1989, p. 16.

2. Jeremy Larner, "Politics Catches up to 'The Candidate,' " *New York Times,* October 23, 1988, p. E23.

3. Sabato, "Political Influence," p. 15.

4. Ibid., p. 16.

5. See here the work of Murray Edelman, including *The Symbolic Uses of Politics* (Champagne-Urbana: University of Illinois Press, 1964); *Political Language:*

Words That Succeed and Policies That Fail (New York: Academic Press, 1977); and *Constructing the Political Spectacle* (Chicago: University of Chicago Press, 1988).

6. Poverty data are from the *Budget of the United States Government* (*FY 1991*) (Washington, D.C.: U.S. Government Printing Office, 1990), p. 143.

7. Drug data are from ibid., pp. 111–117.

8. For a discussion of how such a reading of the public mind works, see Bill Moyers' interview with Richard Wirthlin (Reagan opinion pollster and chief marketing analyst), in Moyers' Public Broadcasting Service Series "The Public Mind," Part IV, "Leading Questions," 1989. For a specific discussion of the War on Drugs as an image campaign, see Mark Hertsgaard, *On Bended Knee: The Press and the Reagan Presidency* (New York: Farrar, Straus and Giroux, 1988), pp. 156–161.

9. Jack Honomichl, "Richard Wirthlin, Advertising Man of the Year," *Advertising Age,* January 23, 1989, lead article.

10. On the addictive potential of propaganda, see Jacques Ellul, *Propaganda* (New York: Vintage, 1973).

11. Walter Shapiro, "Feeling Low over Old Highs," *Time,* September 18, 1989, p. 25.

12. *Time,* September 11, 1989, p. 27.

13. From Michael Isikoff, "A 'Sting' Tailor-Made for Bush," *Washington Post* News Service, reprinted in the *International Herald Tribune,* Saturday-Sunday, September 23–24, 1989, p. 4.

14. Maureen Dowd, "U.S. Presidential Road Show," *International Herald Tribune,* September 26, 1989, p. 3 (from the *New York Times*).

15. For these and other symbolic mechanics of the Bush drug program, see Michael Isikoff and David Hoffman, "Bush's Modest Drug Proposal: More of the Same," *International Herald Tribune,* September 7, 1989, p. 6.

16. Michael Isikoff, "Cocaine Use Fell 45% in 2 Years, U.S. Asserts," *International Herald Tribune,* December 20, 1990, p. 1 (*Washington Post* story).

17. See ibid. and the collection of articles in *USA Today,* December 21, 1990.

18. Among other sources of support for this argument, see Paul E. Peterson, Barry G. Rabe, and Kenneth K. Wong, *When Federalism Works* (Washington, D.C.: The Brookings Institute, 1986); Thomas J. Anton, *American Federalism and Public Policy* (Philadelphia: Temple University Press, 1989); and studies of governmental regulation-writing under the New Federalism of the Reagan era released by the Government Accounting Office and the Advisory Council on Intergovernmental Relations, and reported in the *New York Times* on May 21, 1990, p. A14.

19. *Washington Post* editorial reprinted in the *International Herald Tribune,* October 30, 1990, p. 4.

20. Representative Augustus Hawkins (D-Calif.) quoted in Leslie Phillips, "Congress: Where Everyone 'Rules the Roost,' " *USA Today* (international edition), October 27, 1990, p. 4A.

21. Ibid.

22. "Congress Session Good for Gun Lobby," *International Herald Tribune,* November 3–4, 1990, p. 3.

23. For a good analysis of the budgetary politics of the 1980s, see Joseph White and Aaron Wildavsky, *The Deficit and the Public Interest: The Search for Responsible Budgeting in the 1980s* (Berkeley: University of California Press, 1989).

24. See, for example, *New York Times* and *Washington Post* editorials for the week of October 23, 1990. See also Hobart Rowen, "The Deficit Hasn't Been Resolved," *International Herald Tribune,* October 31, 1990, p. 4 (from the *Washington Post*). Also *Wall Street Journal,* October 31, 1990.

25. *Wall Street Journal,* November 6, 1990, p. 1.

26. "Give and Take Process Shows Who Has Clout," *USA Today* (international edition), October 30, 1990, p. 4.

27. Ibid.

28. William Pfaff, "Something People Can Believe In," *International Herald Tribune,* November 10–11, 1990, p. 8.

29. Gallup poll commissioned by *Newsweek* (European edition), reported in the magazine the week of October 22, 1990, p. 47.

30. Reported in *Newsweek* (European edition), November 19, 1990, p. 34.

31. See Eleanor Clift, "Hiding Out in the Capitol," *Newsweek* (European edition), October 8, 1990, p. 42.

32. See, for example, party officials quoted in Richard L. Berke, "Budget Turmoil Leaves G.O.P. Bereft and Besieged," *New York Times,* October 16, 1990, p. 1.

33. *Time* (European edition), November 19, 1990, p. 38.

34. *USA Today* (international edition), October 31, 1990, p. 4A.

35. Quoted in Andrew Rosenthal, "Bush, a Washington Insider, Is Stumping as an Outsider," *New York Times,* October 17, 1990, p. 1.

36. See, for example, Edwin M. Yoder, Jr., "Hogwash from the New Mr. Outside," *International Herald Tribune,* October 28–29, 1990, p. 8 (from the *Washington Post*).

37. Quoted in Michael Duffy, "The Perfect Spy," *Time* (European edition), November 5, 1990, p. 27.

38. Ibid.

39. See Maureen Dowd, "The 'Impossible' Happens to Bush: He Is Isolated, Associates Say," *International Herald Tribune,* October 30, 1990, p. 1 (from the *New York Times*). See also Andrew Rosenthal, "Campaigning for the G.O.P. Bush Discovers He's an Issue," *New York Times,* October 24, 1990, p. 1.

40. "Face the Nation," CBS, October 14, 1990.

41. "Meet the Press," NBC, October 28, 1990.

42. David S. Broder, "Republican Troops Are in Disarray," *International Herald Tribune,* October 31, 1990, p. 4 (from the *Washington Post*).

43. Alan Murray and Jackie Calmes, "How the Democrats, with Great Cunning, Won the U.S. Budget War," *Wall Street Journal,* November 6, 1990, p. 1.

44. See, for example, ibid., and Dowd, "The 'Impossible' Happens to Bush."

45. Geoff Garin quoted in Paul Taylor and Helen Dewar, "In U.S. Races, Tide Shift Against Republicans," *International Herald Tribune,* October 29, 1990, p. 3 (from the *Washington Post*).

46. See, for example, David Mayhew, *Congress: The Electoral Connection* (New Haven, Conn.: Yale University Press, 1974); Richard F. Fenno, *Home Style: House Members in Their Districts* (Boston: Little, Brown, 1978); and Gary Jacobson, *The Politics of Congressional Elections,* 2nd ed. (Boston: Little, Brown, 1987).

47. Cited in *Newsweek* (European edition), October 8, 1990, p. 42.

48. See, for example, David Maraniss, " 'None of the Above' Is Popular for Texas Governor," *International Herald Tribune,* November 3–4, 1990, p. 3 (from the *Washington Post*).

49. Julie Morris, "Many Say 'None of the Above,' " *USA Today* (international edition), November 2, 1990, p. 3A.

50. Story by Judy Keen, *USA Today* (international edition), November 1, 1990, p. 7A.

51. Randall Rothenberg, "Political Ads Turning to Images of Realism," *New York Times,* October 15, 1990, p. A1.

52. Ibid.

53. Ibid., p. A12.

54. From Joe Davidson, "Michigan Governor's Race Defies Logic," *Wall Street Journal*, October 31, 1990, p. 2.

55. Fox Butterfield, "Weld Reaffirms Pledge to Shrink Government," *New York Times*, November 8, 1990, p. A14.

56. See *Time* (European edition), November 19, 1990, p. 40.

57. See Leslie Phillips, "Helms Again Tests Hold on N.C.," *USA Today* (international edition), November 3, 1990, p. 3A.

58. Peter Appleboome, "Divisive Victory for Helms Could Set Political Trend for Campaign Tactics," *New York Times*, November 8, 1990, p. A15.

59. Ibid.

60. Thomas B. Edsall, "Tough Talk: Label Is Democrat but Message Is Republican," *International Herald Tribune*, October 23, 1990, p. 3.

61. Chuck Raasch, "Minn. Senator Gets Run for His Money," *USA Today* (international edition), November 3, 1990, p. 3A.

62. Ibid.

63. Art Buchwald, "Voting the Rascals In," *International Herald Tribune*, November 13, 1990, p. 22.

64. Bill Monroe, "Covering the Real Campaign: TV Spots," *Washington Journalism Review* (October 1990): 6.

65. Ibid.

66. See, for example, Jeffrey H. Birnbaum, "Incumbents Favored to Win in Today's Elections in U.S.," *Wall Street Journal*, November 6, 1990, p. 2. Note: estimates of PAC contributions vary depending on the time span covered. This was an annual estimate. Figures for the 1988–1990 election cycle will be higher.

67. Judy Keen, "Voters See Politics as 'Master Instead of Servant,' " *USA Today* (international edition), November 1, 1990, p. 7A.

68. Ibid.

69. Nancy Gibbs, "Keep the Bums In," *Time* (European edition), November 19, 1990, p. 40.

70. Ibid., p. 39.

71. "Looking for Lessons," *Newsweek* (European edition), November 19, 1990, p. 34.

72. See, for example, George F. Will, "Bush and Republicans: From Bad to Worse," *International Herald Tribune*, November 9, 1990, p. 4 (from the *Washington Post*).

73. Charles Krauthammer, "The Republican Party Ought to Declare Bankruptcy," *International Herald Tribune*, November 13–14, 1990, p. 8.

74. *New York Times* editorial reprinted in the *International Herald Tribune*, November 8, 1990, p. 6.

CHAPTER 8

1. Paul Kennedy, *Rise and Fall of the Great Powers* (New York: Random House, 1987).

2. Francis Fukuyama, "The End of History?," *The National Interest*, Summer 1989, pp. 3–18.

3. E. J. Dionne, Jr., "Economics and Patriotism," *New York Times*, April 30, 1988, p. 8.

4. See, for example, Seymour Martin Lipset and William Schneider, *The Confidence Gap: Business, Labor and Government in the Public Mind* (New York: Free Press, 1983).

5. Lawrence Parisot, "Attitudes about the Media: A Five Country Comparison," *Public Opinion*, January/February 1988, p. 18.

6. Data on 1960, 1970, and 1980 are from Lipset and Schneider, *The Confidence Gap*. The 1990 figure is from a *New York Times*/CBS News poll reported in the *International Herald Tribune,* November 5, 1990, p. 1.

7. *Washington Post*/ABC News poll, reported in David S. Broder and Thomas B. Edsall, "More Than Ever, America Sees Its Ruination in Politicians," a *Washington Post* analysis reprinted in the *International Herald Tribune,* September 17, 1990, p. 3.

8. *Washington Post*/ABC News poll, reported on the Associated Press News Wire, October 17, 1990.

9. Jarol Manheim, *All of the People, All the Time: Strategic Communication and American Politics* (Armonk, N.Y.: M. E. Sharpe, 1991).

10. Quoted in Richard L. Berke, "Defining 'Constituent Service,' " *International Herald Tribune,* November 7, 1989, p. 3 (from the *New York Times*).

11. Fred Wertheimer, "Window of Opportunity: The Climate Is Ripe for Ethics Reforms," *Common Cause Magazine,* July/August 1989, p. 45.

12. See my *News: The Politics of Illusion,* 2nd ed. (New York: Longman, 1988).

13. Frances Fox Piven and Richard Cloward, "Government Statistics and Conflicting Explanations of Nonvoting," *PS: Political Science & Politics,* September 1989, pp. 580–587.

14. Paul Corcoran, *Political Language and Rhetoric* (Austin: University of Texas Press, 1979), p. xv.

15. Charles W. Knepper, "Political Rhetoric and Public Competence: A Crisis for Democracy?," *Rhetorical Society Quarterly* 16, no. 3 (Summer 1986): 126.

SELECTED BIBLIOGRAPHY

Alexander, Herbert E. *Financing Politics: Money, Elections and Political Reform.* 3rd ed. Washington, D.C.: Congressional Quarterly Press, 1984.
The standard reference on campaign finance reform and what it hath wrought.

Asher, Herbert B. *Presidential Elections and American Politics.* 4th ed. Chicago: Dorsey Press, 1988.
Good detailed analyses of recent elections and voting trends.

Bennett, W. Lance. *News: The Politics of Illusion.* 2nd ed. New York: Longman, 1988.
A critical look at the political content of news reporting. Contrasting analysis of how reporting on politics as usual differs from election journalism.

Burnham, Walter Dean. *Critical Elections and the Mainsprings of American Politics.* New York: W. W. Norton, 1970.
A classic explanation of party systems and the history of voter alignments in American politics.

Campbell, Angus, Philip E. Converse, Warren E. Miller, and Donald E. Stokes. *The American Voter.* New York: John Wiley, 1960.
The standard reference on how a poorly informed and nonideological electorate makes individual voting decisions.

Diamond, Edwin, and Stephen Bates. *The Spot: The Rise of Political Advertising on Television.* Cambridge, Mass.: MIT Press, 1984.
An entertaining look at the evolution of advertising in politics.

Domhoff, William. *The Power Elite and the State: How Policy Is Made in America.* New York: Aldine de Gruyter, 1990.
No conspiracy theory here. Even more disturbing is the possibility that behind the push and pull of elite influence there lies no vision at all.

Edelman, Murray. *Constructing the Political Spectacle.* Chicago: University of Chicago Press, 1988.
A view of politics as spectator sport with grand clashes between media-conscious leaders and constructed enemies at the center of the arena.

Ferguson, Thomas, and Joel Rogers. *Right Turn: The Decline of the Democrats and the Future of American Politics.* New York: Hill and Wang, 1986.
A provocative analysis of the Democratic party being pushed to the right due to competition with the Republicans for financing with ideological strings attached.

Ginsberg, Benjamin. *The Captive Public: How Mass Opinion Promotes State Power.* New York: Basic Books, 1986.
An insightful look at how opinion polling and mass communications have tamed and standardized public opinion.

Ginsberg, Benjamin, and Martin Shefter. *Politics by Other Means: The Declining Importance of Elections in America.* New York: Basic Books, 1990.
An analysis of the decay of parties and the decline of popular participation in elections.

Hart, Roderick P. *The Sound of Leadership: Presidential Communication in the Modern Age.* Chicago: University of Chicago Press, 1987.
A systematic analysis of the styles of presidential rhetoric.

Hertsgaard, Mark. *On Bended Knee: The Press and the Reagan Presidency.* New York: Farrar, Straus and Giroux, 1988.

A detailed account of the media management techniques used by the communications professionals behind the "great communicator."

Jamieson, Kathleen Hall. *Eloquence in an Electronic Age: The Transformation of Political Speechmaking.* New York: Oxford University Press, 1988.

A look at what made Reagan "the great communicator," contrasted with rhetorical practices of the past.

Key, V. O. (with Milton C. Cummings). *The Responsible Electorate: Rationality in Presidential Voting, 1936–1960,* New York: Vintage Books, 1966.

The classic work in the "voters are not fools" school (i.e., most people most of the time make the best sense they can out of the choices given them).

Kleppner, Paul, Walter Dean Burnham, Ronald P. Formisano, Samuel P. Hays, Richard Jensen, and William G. Shade. *The Evolution of American Electoral Systems.* Westport, Conn.: Greenwood Press, 1981.

A breathtaking sweep of elections, parties, and society in America from the rise of the Federalists and Jeffersonian Democrats to the decline of parties in the recent era.

Manheim, Jarol. *All of the People, All the Time: Strategic Communication and American Politics.* Armonk, N.Y.: M. E. Sharpe, 1991.

A broad overview at how "spin doctors," handlers, public relations specialists, pollsters, and their political clients apply the arts and sciences of strategic communication.

Mauser, Gary A. *Political Marketing: An Approach to Campaign Strategy.* New York: Praeger, 1983.

An early explanation of how marketing works.

Mayhew, David. *Congress: The Electoral Connection.* New Haven, Conn.: Yale University Press, 1974.

The first compelling analysis of why running for office may loom larger than governing in the lives of members of Congress.

Page, Benjamin. *Choices and Echoes in Presidential Elections.* Chicago: University of Chicago Press, 1978.

A look at the interplay of issues and candidate images in elections, and an analysis of why images become so important when issue-choices are narrowed.

Phillips, Kevin. *The Politics of Rich and Poor: Wealth and the American Electorate in the Reagan Aftermath.* New York: Random House, 1990.

A convincing case that substantial amounts of wealth floated to the top during the Reagan years. The people should be mad as hell. But are they?

Polsby, Nelson, and Aaron Wildavsky. *Presidential Elections.* 6th ed. New York: Scribner's, 1984.

The full view of elections from financing and party nominations to the media and voting.

Pomper, Gerald M., ed. *The Election of 1988: Reports and Interpretations.* Chatham, N.J.: Chatham House Publishers, 1989.

A collection of well-written essays examining the presidential and congressional elections with an eye to public opinion, media coverage, and historical trends. Look for a companion volume on *The Election of 1992.*

Sabato, Larry J. *PAC Power: Inside the World of Political Action Committees.* New York: W. W. Norton, 1985.

A detailed history and analysis of the world of political action committees and the power they wield.

Tulis, Jeffrey K. *The Rhetorical Presidency.* Princeton, N.J.: Princeton University Press, 1987.

A rich, readable look at the importance of rhetoric in the nation's top leadership post.

Wayne, Stephen J. *The Road to the White House: The Politics of Presidential Elections.* 3rd ed. New York: St. Martin's Press, 1988.

A nuts and bolts treatment of the electoral system, campaign finance, party conventions, the media, voting trends, and reforms.

INDEX